The New York Times

CHEERFUL SUNDAY CROSSWORDS

Published in the United States by St. Martin's Griffin,
an imprint of St. Martin's Publishing Group

THE NEW YORK TIMES CHEERFUL SUNDAY CROSSWORDS.
Copyright © 2023 by The New York Times Company. All rights reserved.
Printed in the United States of America. For information, address
St. Martin's Publishing Group, 120 Broadway, New York, NY 10271.

www.stmartins.com

All of the puzzles that appear in this work were originally published
in *The New York Times* from January 4, 2004, to December 26, 2004;
September 6, 2015, to November 22, 2015; or from August 1, 2021, to April 3, 2022.
Copyright 2004, 2015, 2021, 2022 by The New York Times Company.
All rights reserved. Reprinted by permission.

ISBN 978-1-250-87580-8

Our books may be purchased in bulk for promotional, educational, or business use.
Please contact your local bookseller or the Macmillan Corporate and Premium
Sales Department at 1-800-221-7945, extension 5442, or by email at
MacmillanSpecialMarkets@macmillan.com.

First Edition: 2023

10 9 8 7 6 5 4 3 2 1

The New York Times

CHEERFUL SUNDAY CROSSWORDS
100 Sunday Puzzles

Edited by Will Shortz

ST. MARTIN'S GRIFFIN
NEW YORK

1 OFF BRAND

ACROSS

1 A is one
8 Ozone-harming compounds, for short
12 Actor Guy
18 "How awesome!"
19 Play with, as a cat might a toy mouse
20 Naysayers
21 *Five guys?*
23 It might have desks and drawers
24 Shade of purple
25 Those: Sp.
26 *Green giant?*
28 Ambulance driver, for short
30 Finished first
32 "___-ching!"
33 Just
34 Like basalt and obsidian
37 Something sent on a Listserv
40 Police broadcast, for short
41 "Special Agent ___" (animated Disney show about a bear)
42 Main character in Larry McMurtry's "Lonesome Dove"
43 Apt name for a Christmas caroler?
44 ___ Clarendon, first openly transgender W.N.B.A. player
48 *Jolly rancher?*
51 Hole
52 Diagnosis characterized by repetitive behavior, in brief
53 Focus of a marathon runner's training
54 Grand opening?
55 Sides (with)
58 ___ school
59 Dessert with some assembly required
61 Grammy recipient Lisa

63 What pro bono lawyers waive
65 *General mills?*
69 The British 20-pence and 50-pence coins, geometrically
71 Member of a South Asian diaspora
72 Photo finish
75 Every last drop
76 Bank, often
78 Exams offered four times a year, for short
81 Grown-up pup
82 "I promise I won't laugh," often
83 Certain guiding principle
84 *Texas instruments?*
87 Meadow grass with brushlike spikes
90 Fermented Baltic drink
91 "Ugh, gross"
92 Stag's date?
93 Doc treating sinus infections
94 X, in linear functions
95 Dolphins' div.
97 Like many a company softball game
99 "That stinks!"
100 Subj. devoting extra time to idioms
102 ___ milk
103 *Band aid?*
107 Truce
109 Litter box emanation
113 Efflux
114 *Old navy?*
117 Like many a grillmaster
118 Supermodel Kate
119 Headache helper
120 Took a little look
121 [Hey, over here!]
122 Rough patch

DOWN

1 Standing on
2 Texter's "Hilarious!"
3 Soy something
4 Ones working block by block?
5 Hoodwink
6 Drift apart
7 Certain Ivy Leaguers
8 Pac-12 school, informally
9 Qualification shorthand
10 "Ple-e-e-ease?"
11 Help when writing a letter
12 Its national drink is the pisco sour
13 State of disorder
14 Some vacation rentals
15 Lube up again
16 Old pal
17 Actress ___ Creed-Miles
19 South American capital
20 Figures
22 Statements of will?
27 "The power of global trade" sloganeer
29 ___ Millions
31 Into crystals and auras, say
34 Its calendar began in A.D. 622
35 Inflated feeling of infallibility
36 Letters on a stamp
38 ___ B or ___ C of the Spice Girls
39 Actor Alan of "Crimes and Misdemeanors"
40 Binghamton Rumble Ponies or Birmingham Barons
41 "My b!"

43 Sign
44 Feudal lord
45 Plots of western films?
46 Brain freeze cause, maybe
47 Does a summer job?
49 Warrant
50 Magic can be seen here
51 Relating to land, old-style
56 They can help you see or taste
57 Like the odds of finding a needle in a haystack
60 Airline based near Tel Aviv
62 Deserving of a timeout, say
64 Big spread
66 "No need to elaborate"
67 Like the Hmong language
68 ___ Ng, author of "Little Fires Everywhere"
69 12/24, e.g.
70 ___ Perlman, role for Timothée Chalamet in "Call Me by Your Name"
73 Means of divination
74 "What ___?"
77 Indicate availability, in a way
79 "Weekend, here I come!"
80 Side dish at a barbecue
85 Upsilon preceder
86 Producer of the world's most widely read consumer catalog
88 Genre for One Direction

by Matthew Stock

89 "... finished!"
90 Ties
94 Android alternative
95 Exclamation after a sigh
96 Teeny-tiny
97 Sporty wheels
98 Eccentric
99 Explorer Richard who made the first flight over the South Pole
101 Attempt to control the narrative, in a way
103 Lava, e.g.
104 Took to court
105 Omar of "Love & Basketball"
106 Rolls around while exercising?
108 Quick talk
110 What nyctophobia is the fear of
111 Slobbery cartoon character
112 "___ over" (words after letting off steam)
115 Often-contracted word
116 Tech sch. in Troy, N.Y.

2 JIGSAW PUZZLE

Note: When this puzzle is done, insert the five shaded jigsaw pieces into the box at the bottom to get a three-word phrase, reading across, for what jigsaw puzzles provide.

ACROSS

1 Part of a pie or the earth
6 Style that makes waves
10 Doe in a court case
14 Flubs
19 Keister
20 China holder?
21 Axe target
22 Some Madison Avenue workers
23 End of many a sports broadcast
24 Freestyles, perhaps
25 Barflies
26 Botch
27 "First, you're going to want to dump out the box and ___"
31 Francis of old game shows
34 Bounded
35 Capital on a 126-mile-long canal that's used as a skating rink in the winter
39 English breakfast, e.g.
40 "What's most useful next is to ___"
45 College app component
46 Role for "Ronny" Howard
48 Joshes
49 State flower of Utah
50 One of the B's in BB&B
51 Field work of note in 1979
54 Rifle, in frontier lingo
57 "To connect things up you'll have to ___"

63 Ones getting the crumbs?
66 Bonnie with five Top 40 hits in the 1990s
67 Euphoric feeling
71 Love to bits
72 More like a dive bar or certain bread
74 Beehives, but not hornets' nests
75 Daredevil's hashtag
76 Very in
78 One of the B's in BB&B
79 Good name for an investor?
82 High-end Italian auto, informally
83 "As you go, make sure you exercise your ___"
88 At peace
89 Little bouquets
90 "ka-POW!"
93 "With patience and perseverance you're sure to ___"
97 Course goal
100 Songs that can be trilling?
102 Castigates
103 Fairy-tale figure
105 Confer, as credibility
106 Gets wild and crazy
108 Legendary
109 Leave skid marks, maybe
111 N.F.L. standout
113 Homes for high fliers
114 Instruction to drivers leaving cars at a garage
115 "C'mon, slowpoke!"

116 Ends, as a mission
117 Mary Poppins, for one
118 Pick up on

DOWN

1 O-line anchor
2 Feel regret
3 Trojans' sch.
4 Distinctive part of a cookie cutter
5 "Tap tap tap . . ." activity
6 Get into a lot
7 Jacob's brother, in the Bible
8 Moved like waves or muscles
9 A certain degree
10 St. ___ University (Philadelphia school)
11 Rescue dog, for one
12 Response to the Little Red Hen
13 Language related to Manx
14 Egg, e.g.
15 Keats, for one
16 Sounds in a yoga studio
17 Government economic org., at any rate?
18 ___-Cat
28 Big suit
29 Derby, e.g.
30 Menial laborer, metaphorically
31 Loads
32 Take back, for short
33 Retreat
36 "Was it ___ I saw?" (classic palindrome)
37 Mists, e.g.
38 Feeling it after a marathon, say

41 Approves
42 Perspective
43 Achievement for Whoopi Goldberg, in brief
44 Like cioccolato or torta
47 Titus and Tiberius
50 Bosom buddies
52 Staple of skin care
53 Sought office
55 UPS competitor
56 Steady, maybe
58 Wrath
59 Exercise program since the 1990s
60 Sharp, on a TV, informally
61 Peak sacred to the goddess Rhea
62 Noshed on
63 "You'll ___ for this!"
64 Words with a ring to them?
65 Letter between foxtrot and hotel in the NATO alphabet
68 How people often scroll through social media
69 "That's gotta hurt!"
70 "The Puzzle Palace" org.
72 More straight-faced
73 Creamy Italian dish
76 Word that becomes its own opposite by putting a "T" at the front
77 Singer whom M.L.K. Jr. called the "queen of American folk music"
80 Play again, as a TV special

by Christina Iverson and Jeff Chen

81 Companion in Brittany
84 Brain diagnostics, for short
85 Used as a rendezvous point
86 Devote
87 Name suffix meaning "mountain"
90 Fir tree
91 "Is it still a date?"
92 Roman goddess of wisdom
94 Prefix with color or state
95 Sugar ending
96 W.W. II fighters
97 Apps made with jalapeños and cheese
98 "You agree?" (*nudge, nudge*)
99 Gathers some intel
101 Actor Brody
104 Singer Willie
106 Annoying
107 Grannies
110 Blood line
112 Temporal ___

3 THINK TWICE

ACROSS

1 Confound
6 Sarcastic internet laughter
10 Most Times Square signage
13 Performance check
17 Dark hair and a warm smile, for two
19 Samoan capital
20 To's opposite
21 Full-length
23 Something that bugs criminals?
25 Blabberer
27 Duplicitous
28 Musicianship
30 ___ dress
31 Pasture
32 Signed off on
33 Ukr. or Lith., formerly
34 Places for development
36 Corn kernel, e.g.
38 Actress Merrill
40 Genre for BTS or Blackpink
43 Added to the staff?
45 Alerts
48 ___ of lies
49 Aquafina : PepsiCo :: ___ : Coca-Cola
52 #$%& and @%¢!
55 Practice whose name means, literally, "union"
57 Words before "before"
58 "Deck the Halls" contraction
59 Symbol on the Connecticut state quarter
60 Stop along the highway
61 Quite
64 Finished brushing one's teeth, say
66 Racial justice movement since 2013, in brief
67 "Really, though?"

68 Word in many font names
69 Betray . . . or a hint to four answers in this puzzle
73 ___ the Cat (fictional feline of children's books)
74 Thin incision
75 Some $200 Monopoly properties, in brief
76 Set of 50 on the Argo, in myth
77 Coaxed (out of)
79 Insurance giant bailed out in 2008
80 Word before cap or pop
81 Awesomest bud
82 Spirit in Arabian myth
83 Arizona county or its seat
85 Pushing up daisies
90 Neighbor of Mozambique
92 Nonwriting credentials for Conan Doyle and Chekhov, informally
93 Seller's need
95 Artificial habitat
97 Abolitionist Lucretia
98 The avant-garde "artists" Congo and Pierre Brassau
100 Hedy of the 2017 documentary "Bombshell"
103 Kind of chip
105 Question of perplexion
108 "The Raven" writer's inits.
109 Like
110 Big believer in the freedom of assembly?
112 Press ___
113 What the beleaguered are behind

115 Classic folk story that teaches a lesson of sharing
118 Be up for some biking?
120 Fast runners
121 Advanced math degree?
122 Ninny
123 Sternutation
124 Real cutup
125 Landscaper's supply
126 In the past
127 "As You Like It" forest

DOWN

1 Novelist Margaret
2 Absorb the beauty of, as a scene
3 Lacked the gumption to
4 Gladly, old-style
5 Jazzy James and Jones
6 First law enforcement org. in the U.S. to hire a female officer (1910)
7 Nail polish brand
8 List of performers
9 Star man?
10 Half of a '55 union merger
11 "That's enough arguing out of you!"
12 Lip-puckering
13 Things that may be rubbed after din-din
14 Playwright Will who was a 2005 Pulitzer finalist
15 Crew implement
16 One getting special instruction
18 Ink holders in pens and squid
22 "Just like ___!"
24 Like morning people vis-à-vis night owls, around dawn
26 Response to "How bad was it?"

29 Extends, in a way
35 Lead-in to call
37 Cause for an onslaught of yearly txts
39 "If the pessimists are right . . ."
41 Stroke
42 East: Ger.
44 Wednesday, but not Friday
46 Accelerator particles
47 Overwhelm
48 Some tax breaks
50 Boos and cheers
51 Light
53 Latin list ender
54 Some Hershey candies
56 Bought in
61 Time-consuming assignment to grade
62 Xanax alternative
63 Monthly publication of the National Puzzlers' League, with "The"
64 More convinced
65 "The Magic School Bus" was its first fully animated series
66 Sound at the end of December, appropriately?
67 Beach with a girl who "swings so cool"
70 Part of many a corsage
71 Bite site
72 Job to do
78 High-quality cannabis, in slang
80 "Success!"
81 Decorate
82 "I. Can't. Even."
84 Spain's Duchess of ___
86 Classic novel with the line "You must be the best judge of your own happiness"

by Aimee Lucido and Ella Dershowitz

87 Environmental opening
88 When repeated, a reproof
89 Overturned
91 Most chiffonlike
94 Figure out
96 Not thinking
97 The Supremes' record label
99 Bad temper
100 Makeup target
101 Where a "Married at First Sight" contestant meets his or her mate
102 Language in which "kia ora" is a greeting
104 Up on
106 Confused responses
107 Fight site
111 Long runs?
113 "A man's character is his ___": Heraclitus
114 "Suds"
116 Prefix with classical
117 Prof's degree
119 Post on Insta

4 RESETTLING LETTERINGS

ACROSS

1 What a drawbridge may bridge
5 In that case
9 Control tower installation
14 Pass
19 "That one's ___" ("My bad")
20 Amelia Bedelia, e.g.
21 "Go me!"
22 Member of a noble family
23 2004 film about a group of MALIGNERS
25 It might be put on for stage PAGEANTRIES
27 Annual film festival where "Saw" and "Get Out" premiered
28 "___ La La" (1964 hit)
29 Senator, e.g., for short
30 Avoids a bogey, perhaps
31 Being
33 Be hopping mad
34 Cool one
37 W.W. II hero, informally
39 Muletas are waved at them
40 Canon camera
41 Branch of Islam
42 You might be MARVELING AT this as it whizzes by
46 Sort of SCHEMATIC for Christian education
48 Like some casts
49 City nicknamed "The Old Pueblo"
51 French city near the Belgian border
52 Prefix with colonial
53 Tight-fitting
55 Toni Morrison title heroine
56 Annual British acting award
58 Series of questions, maybe
60 Counterpart of elles
62 Opposite of never
64 Many relationships are INSTIGATED on one
68 Healthy eaters may give this A WIDE BERTH
72 Disrupt an online meeting, in a way
74 Mauna ___
75 Grp. that hasn't yet found what it's looking for
76 Wonder Woman and others
79 Valuable load for a mule
81 Influence
84 Pioneering gangsta rap group
85 Burdened
86 Just
88 Preferring one's own company, perhaps
90 They can be NOISELESS while stalking prey
93 Explorers of the UNTRAVERSED
95 Burden
96 Old cable TV inits.
97 Fill in
98 Word repeated in "I ___, I ___, it's off to work I go"
99 Lick, say
100 "___ merci!" (French cry)
101 "On it, captain!"
103 "No need to make me a plate"
106 Five-letter word that replaces a four-letter word?
107 1980s gaming inits.
108 Not even
111 Writing done GRAPHICALLY
115 The Trojans lacked the FORESIGHT to turn this down
116 It's multilayered
117 You should always bring it to a competition
118 Children's author Blyton
119 Be taken aback
120 One way to cook a 116-Across
121 Unenthusiastic
122 They know the drill: Abbr.
123 Word after hard or before short

DOWN

1 "My Two ___" (2015 Claudia Harrington children's book)
2 Top
3 Appliance brand since 1934
4 Pea shooters?
5 "Sign me up!"
6 Complete travesty
7 Feature of many British accents
8 Binges too much, for short
9 As if orchestrated
10 Indexed data structures
11 Directly
12 Fourth person to walk on the moon
13 Do a double take?
14 Boot
15 Almost
16 What makes Shrek shriek?
17 One side in a debate
18 It may be blown
24 They may be blown
26 House Republican V.I.P. Stefanik
28 Star in Canis Major
32 Just so
34 Hot dog topper
35 Airline passenger request
36 Lion ___
38 "Dear ___ Hansen" (2017 Tony-winning musical)
41 Responds to br-r-r-isk weather?
42 Like zebras and lions
43 Voice with an Echo
44 Rub it in
45 "It is what it is" and others
46 Mike Krzyzewski, to Duke basketball fans
47 Rise
50 Hot dog topper
54 A little too silky, maybe
56 Justin Trudeau, by birth
57 Don't believe it!
59 Aftmost masts on ships
61 Gives fuel to
63 Gets a move on, quaintly
65 Who can hear you scream in space
66 Ending with poly-
67 Title meaning "commander"
69 "___ Meenie" (2010 hit)
70 Battling
71 Rings up
73 Showing the effects of an all-nighter, say
76 Give one's blessing to
77 It has more coastline than California, surprisingly
78 Score after seven points, maybe
80 Certain radio format
82 Apropos of
83 "Like that'll ever happen!"

by Stephen McCarthy

86 "Appetizers" or "Desserts," at a diner
87 International cosmetics company ___ Rocher
89 Content people?
91 Larsson who wrote "The Girl With the Dragon Tattoo"
92 Pooh-pooh
94 Common April activity, nowadays
97 Vietnamese sandwich
100 Group trying to sack a QB
102 Make over, as a ship
104 A crowd, they say
105 It has 104-Down legs
106 Obscure, with "out"
109 They may be set by industry grps.
110 Girl in "The Old Curiosity Shop"
111 sin/tan
112 Major Japanese carrier
113 "Kill Bill" co-star
114 You can chew on it
115 Some appliances

5 UH? OH …

ACROSS

1 Sliver
4 Politician with the campaign slogan 30-Across
9 Word with poetry or proportions
13 Something you might click to open
16 Elicits a "Whoa" from, say
18 Trimmed (down)
19 Wrestling star John
20 Tailor
22 Beams of one's dreams?
25 Food served in an omakase meal
26 Having very little mental energy left
27 Moonfish
28 Swimmers in kelp forests
30 See 4-Across
33 Visit a museum to see a Rembrandt exhibit?
35 One prone to looking down
36 His tomb is in Red Square
37 Diamondbacks, on scoreboards
38 Face cards?
41 Destination for oenophiles
43 Sicily's Parco dell'___
45 Bug spray ingredient
49 Bird of prey that's gently petted?
53 Popular pops
55 Kind of attack
56 Longtime hockey star Kovalchuk
57 To read: Sp.
59 Gross
60 Error, in totspeak
62 Buys in
65 Look down on
67 Actor Justin sitting poolside?

71 Adds insult to injury
73 Santa-tracking org.
74 River across the New York/New Jersey border
77 Some rideshare info
78 Exploit
81 Award-winning film set in Tehran
83 Bishop's headgear
84 Hang up the cleats, so to speak
86 Make fun of small orange fruits?
90 Something rectangular that might have more than four sides
91 Two-player card game
92 TV character who said "Time to hit the hay . . . oh, I forgot, I ate it!"
93 Old auto with its founder's monogram
94 Storage spot
97 Opposite of "avant"
99 Reason to reschedule
102 Mashed potatoes, on a Thanksgiving plate?
107 Instrument heard in Spanish folk music
111 Vinyl collection
112 Food brand whose sales boomed after the premiere of "Stranger Things"
114 "When We Were Young" singer
115 Sharp
116 Fourth-quarter meltdown at an N.B.A. game in Oklahoma City?
120 Made out
121 Take home
122 Lather gatherer
123 Remained in bed, e.g.
124 Something to shoot for
125 ". . . sting like ___"

126 Clubs
127 ___ Bleus, nickname for France's soccer team

DOWN

1 Boardwalk treat
2 Plugged in, so to speak
3 Actor Leary
4 Missions, for short
5 ___ State, nickname for Massachusetts
6 Basis for an insurance investigation
7 "Build ___ Buttercup" (1969 hit by the Foundations)
8 Spot for a perfume sample in a magazine, maybe
9 Green prefix
10 Staff
11 Lead-in to com or net, but not org
12 Wrinkly-skinned fruit
13 Largest object in the Kuiper belt
14 And the following, in footnotes
15 His birthday is celebrated as "Children's Day" in India
17 Worries anxiously
20 Mounted on
21 Angry reaction
23 Main port of Yemen
24 They're banned in many classrooms nowadays
29 Thing seen in the foreground of "Washington Crossing the Delaware"
31 N.Y. neighbor
32 Calculators of old
34 Partner of starts
36 Speaking part?
38 "In that case . . ."

39 Paul of "Little Miss Sunshine"
40 Didn't hear the alarm, say
42 Where fruit bat soup is eaten as a delicacy
44 Orange follower
46 Widespread
47 Nonstop flight?
48 Maori for "image"
50 Redeems at a casino
51 Sooners, by another name
52 Have a home-cooked meal
53 Like some obligations
54 Dict. listing
58 Setting for Mets home games: Abbr.
61 Gradually diminish
63 Residential suffix with Angel
64 High-priced violin, informally
66 All-knowing sort
68 It's represented by a dot in the top-left corner, in Braille
69 Mideast palace parts
70 Son of Gloucester in "King Lear"
71 & 72 A pop
75 ___ Alonso, Mets slugger with the most home runs by a rookie in M.L.B. history (53)
76 ". . . ish"
79 People people, for short
80 Exit
82 "What's ___, Doc?" (old Bugs Bunny short)
85 Grapefruit descriptor
87 Kelly of "Live"
88 Remark after losing
89 Nutritional figs.
95 "___ be an honor!"
96 Snapple competitor

by Dory Mintz

98 "Socialism: Utopian and Scientific" writer, 1880
100 Leaning right: Abbr.
101 Four-time U.S. Open champ
102 Four-time Australian Open champ
103 It has its highlights
104 Maker of the MDX, NSX and TLX
105 Bloc party?
106 Fix up again
107 Brown hue
108 Home of many Sherpas
109 ___ Hughes, name of main roles in "Westworld" and "Downton Abbey"
110 Decade after the aughts
113 Blossom
117 Taipei-to-Seoul dir.
118 Frequently
119 ___ Palmas

GO UP IN SMOKE

ACROSS

1 Impersonate
6 Bump on a log
11 Get into one's birthday suit
16 Fruit drinks
20 Home of the isle of Tortuga
21 "___ often costs too much": Emerson
22 Word before rock or football
23 Song word repeated after "Que"
24 Charming sort?
26 Olympics projectiles
27 People in charge: Abbr.
28 ___ Lingus
29 Lucy's last name on "I Love Lucy"
31 Like gasoline nowadays
33 30-year host of late-night TV
37 Legal field concerned with long-term care
39 Commotion
40 Televangelist Joel
42 Prima ballerina
46 Some team competitions
49 The "e" in Genoa?
50 With 97-Across, emerge reborn . . . or what the ends of five Across answers in this puzzle do?
52 "Gangsta Lovin'" rapper, 2002
53 Yoga class instruction
55 Food packaging reassurance
56 Good "Wheel of Fortune" buy for REVERSE ENGINEER
57 Sold (for)
59 Toward the back
60 Where dominoes were invented
62 Rule
64 Jazz guitarist Montgomery
66 Some U.N. officers, for short
67 Super Bowl LV champ
68 Took a swing, say
70 Basketball box score column
74 Addiction treatment locale
76 Lead-off selections?
77 Something to file
78 French article
79 Sweet pea
81 Volkswagen model inits.
82 Give wrong information
83 Boring tool
85 Emmy-winning journalist Finch
87 Website with a Seller Handbook
91 "How ___ . . ."
92 Encrypted URL component
94 Red-handed, say
96 Make haste
97 See 50-Across
99 Brand that stylizes its name with a lowercase second letter
100 What a button on an armrest may control
104 Serenade
105 "___ Pal," early episode of "The Jetsons"
108 Shrinks
109 1980 event in Washington
111 Be completely candid
114 Gryffindor, Slytherin, Hufflepuff or Ravenclaw
117 It may be taken in by a traveler
119 Half of sei
120 Treat thought to be stamped with symbols of the Knights Templar
121 "We ___ please"
123 Within arm's reach
128 Something commonly left in an operating room
129 Going by
130 Where the Volta River flows
131 Tea go-with
132 Pull down
133 Those opposite the center and guards, in N.F.L. lingo
134 More teed off
135 Scattered

DOWN

1 Sounds at a sauna
2 Limit
3 20-20, e.g.
4 Hit TV show created by Donald Glover
5 Something close to a colonel's heart?
6 "Today" competitor, for short
7 –
8 Those against
9 Come back again (again . . . again . . .)
10 Harp-shaped constellation
11 Got ready to ride, with "up"
12 Vacuum tube type
13 "Hi" follower
14 Rack up, as charges
15 No-hassle
16 Countless
17 –
18 Slips
19 Holder of merit badges on a scout uniform
25 Jon of "Two and a Half Men"
30 –
32 Gone-but-not-forgotten
33 L.L. Bean competitor
34 Plant family that jasmine and lilac are part of
35 Safe space
36 Announcement maker of yore
38 In early 2001, one of its executives notoriously said "From an accounting standpoint, this will be our easiest year ever"
41 ___ Minella (Muppet)
43 Pot grower's remark?
44 What snakes grow as they age
45 Corrects, as text
47 They used to be a "thing"
48 Floor coverings that feel good on the feet
51 Politician's concern
54 Detective Lupin
55 Present-day saint?
58 Surprise ending
59 Sparkling wine variety
61 Scolded, as in a library
63 Big name in nail polish
65 –
69 Drive
70 Sets aside
71 Popped in for just a moment, perhaps
72 The Ikea logo shares the colors of its flag
73 Lead-in to "of mind" or "of war"
75 Advocate for the better treatment of elves, in Harry Potter
80 Determination from Santa

by Grant Thackray

84 Big tournament news
86 Bare
88 –
89 Spots for window boxes
90 Verbal cringe
93 The St. Lawrence River's misnamed ___ Islands
95 Far from friendly
98 Fatigued over time
99 Set of rules popularized by "How I Met Your Mother"
101 Doctor's orders, maybe
102 Best ___
103 Shaving brand
106 "Let me get this out . . ."
107 Lead-in to -scope
110 Small lab bottle
112 Loud, as a stadium
113 Former second lady Cheney
114 It often has its kinks
115 Sight from a Seattle ferry
116 Bike ride setting
118 Rides
122 Millennium start
124 See 126-Down
125 Take a ___
126 With 124-Down, feature of van Gogh
127 Get hitched to

WHAT A CHARACTER!

ACROSS

1 They come with bouquets
6 Away
11 "___ put our heads together . . ."
15 Singer/drummer Collins
19 Cell component
20 Pal, in Peru
21 Put one's nose where it doesn't belong
22 Tilt-a-Whirl, e.g.
23 One arm held up with bent elbow and wrist, in a children's song
24 Move obliquely
25 Phenomenon such as the tendency to see human forms in inanimate objects
27 Any of the groupings of circled letters in this puzzle
30 Gin product
31 Incredible bargains
32 "Sorry, Charlie!"
33 Fits together
34 Savory Chinese snacks
37 Jump over
41 Smoking and swearing, e.g.
44 They await your return, in brief
45 Have a good cry
46 Syracuse Mets and Worcester Red Sox, for two
50 "Music's most maligned genre," per critic Tom Connick
51 Word with level or lion
52 "Everything happened so fast!"
54 Farm female
55 "___ Gone Wrong" (2021 film)
57 Brunch beverage
59 One of the brothers on "Malcolm in the Middle"

60 Room in Clue
61 Cause of undue anxiety
63 It may be smoked
64 Hogwash
65 Munch, in modern slang
66 "___ 17" (W.W. II film)
67 One of two in a jack-o'-lantern?
70 Where charity begins, in a phrase
73 Table part
74 Title for Tussaud: Abbr.
76 "Midsommar" director Aster
77 Digs up
78 Carpenter's wedge
80 Does gentle stretching post-exercise, with "down"
82 Amp knob
84 Die like the Wicked Witch of the West
85 Give zero stars
86 Ne'er-do-wells
88 E.R. inserts
89 By birth
90 Plant said to repel bugs
93 ___ Ryerson, insurance salesman in "Groundhog Day"
94 French pronoun
95 Quarter ___ (when the big hand is at three)
97 No-longer-current source for current events
99 Hot, mulled punch traditionally drunk around Christmas
101 Bacteria destroyer
104 French port on the English Channel
106 Like the Minotaur legend
110 University of Oregon site

112 How to see the image formed by this puzzle's circled letters
115 What's formed by the circled letters in this puzzle
117 "We're live!" studio sign
118 Ancient land in Asia Minor
119 Domino, e.g.
120 Martínez with a statue outside the Seattle Mariners' stadium
121 Makes less powerful, in video game slang
122 Domino, e.g.
123 "To . . ." things
124 Dino's tail?
125 Muse of love poetry
126 Arises (from)

DOWN

1 Eastern cicada killers, e.g.
2 Suggestions
3 ". . . said ___ ever"
4 School
5 Resolves out of court
6 Org. that flew a helicopter on Mars in 2021
7 Fail to mention
8 Information, old-style
9 Rounded quarters
10 Without stopping
11 How Alaska ranks first among the states
12 It's often left on the table
13 What "vey" of "Oy, vey!" translates to
14 ___ Games, company behind Fortnite
15 Rey, to Luke Skywalker
16 Sword handles
17 "Einstein," sarcastically

18 Puts pressure (on)
21 What can make men swear from menswear?
26 "___ pass Go . . ."
28 Leading medal winner at the Tokyo Olympics
29 Forman who directed "One Flew Over the Cuckoo's Nest"
35 Farm refrain
36 Weight of a paper clip, roughly
38 Ancient: Prefix
39 Soul-seller of legend
40 Half-baked?
41 Duck and goose, at times
42 "See ya"
43 Group dance popularized in the U.S. by Desi Arnaz
45 77-Down is on the most collected one in U.S. history
47 Epiphany
48 Voice actor Blanc
49 Show with over 1,000 handwritten cue cards each week, for short
51 City hazard
52 "My word!"
53 Pol in the "I am once again asking . . ." meme
56 City whose police cars are adorned with a witch logo
58 Card game with a PG-rated name
60 Boring
62 Purse
65 High degree
68 Not at all popular
69 Messes up
70 x, y and z
71 Chaotic skirmish
72 Fragrant compound
74 Saturn has more than 80 of them
75 Golf course machine

by Alex Rosen

77 He performed 636 consecutive sold-out shows in Vegas from 1969 to '76
78 Burn prevention meas.
79 The future Henry V, to Falstaff
80 Fight tooth and nail
81 One who consumes a ritual meal to absolve the souls of the dead
83 Bits on book jackets
87 Roc-A-___ Records
91 Part of U.C.L.A.
92 Fashion designer Geoffrey
94 It may run from an emotional situation
95 [Mwah!]
96 Departed by plane
98 Green vehicle
99 Frank
100 Duke's org.
101 Pasta topper
102 Like the dog days of summer
103 Acrobatic
105 Make restitution
107 Faint color
108 "Take me ___"
109 Approaches
111 Where the lacrimal glands can be found
112 Pasta topper
113 Pump some weights
114 Not exactly
116 Vaccine-approving agcy.

ACROSS

1 Like the Rock vis-à-vis any of the Stones
8 Small doodles, perhaps
15 ___ pants
20 Surpass
21 Candy bar with an exclamation point in its name
22 To love, in Italian
23 Meticulous magical beings?
25 The land down under
26 Sharpen
27 Screams
28 Calendar column: Abbr.
29 Frenzied states
30 High-ranking figures, collectively
32 Like some cross-Caribbean flights?
34 Three-time Pro Bowl wide receiver in the New York Jets Ring of Honor
37 Biblical father of Eliphaz
40 CNN political correspondent Bash
41 Bushy-tailed rodents
43 Postseason tournament pick
46 ___ Reader (digest magazine founded in 1984)
50 Journals of a certain stunt performer?
52 Commuting arrangement
54 Body shop fig.
55 Owing
56 Buddy of Buddy, maybe
58 What might whet an appetite
59 Taken down and put up elsewhere
63 Relative of cerulean
66 Scale for some judges
68 Possible reason for refusing to wear a tank top?
71 Worries about something
73 2018 crime biopic
74 "Potatoes done perfect" sloganeer
77 Shape of a doughnut
78 Shape of a canine ID tag, often
80 Fossil suffix
82 "Most miserable hour that ___ time saw": Lady Capulet
83 "Checkmate"
85 Means of learning about Chiang Kai-shek?
91 Massachusetts' College of Our Lady of the ___
92 Some post-pollution efforts
94 Become ticked off
95 Ready
96 Wielder of the hammer Mjölnir
98 Tools used by horologists
99 Inept dancers at Oktoberfest?
105 Express line count
107 Mentor of 50 Cent
108 Valedictorian's pride, in brief
109 Mag space seller
111 Smurf with a white beard
115 Dish at a traditional Bedouin wedding
116 New look provider . . . or a homophonic hint to this puzzle's theme
119 Small hill
120 Poorly lit
121 Series of steps
122 Early R&B group for Missy Elliott
123 Stockpiles
124 Felt on the head?

DOWN

1 "2 Broke Girls" co-star Behrs
2 Bounce off the wall
3 Musk of SpaceX
4 Incendiary explosive
5 Big news to share in the biz world?
6 Company acquired by Allstate in 2011
7 Longtime first name in TV talk
8 Unpartitioned apartment
9 Clicking sounds?
10 Letter two after tau
11 ___ E (skin care brand)
12 Guacamole ingredient
13 Major exporter of nutmeg
14 ___ admin
15 "LOLOL"
16 Big name in microwaves
17 Straight sides of sectors
18 Put up
19 Soccer superstar nicknamed "La Pulga" ("The Flea")
24 Water (down)
29 The National Zoo's Xiao Qi Ji, e.g.
31 Agitate
32 Hungarian herding breed
33 Figure on Italy's 2,000-lira note before euros were introduced
34 Common viper
35 Free
36 People can't lie under it
38 Actor who delivered the line "Nobody puts Baby in a corner"
39 Word with power or brakes
42 GQ V.I.P.s
44 Best
45 "___: Vegas" (TV reboot of 2021)
46 Revolted
47 Treat for Mr. Owl
48 Seward Peninsula city
49 Verve
51 "There was no choice"
53 Person with star power?
57 Triangular piece in a party bowlful
60 Rentals that might come with dolly carts
61 "Wrong!"
62 Nickname for someone whose full name is a calendar month
64 Spur
65 Letter two before tau
67 Obie-winning playwright Will
69 Defamed, in a way
70 "Indeed"
71 Reason to see an ophthalmologist
72 Pea jacket material
75 Caterpillar competitor
76 Thomas Jefferson or John Tyler, by birth
79 Org. that bestows the Community Assist Award
81 Liberal arts sch. major
84 Certain curtain
86 On the ___ (no longer friendly)
87 Overseas speed meas.

by Peter Gordon

88 Go from here to there . . . like *that*
89 Quark's place
90 "It's my hunch . . ."
93 Pithy saying
95 Dish whose yellow color comes from saffron
97 "Rude Boy" singer, to fans

99 Divisions of bushels
100 Like the Mideast exclave of Madha
101 Long rides?
102 Used a prayer rug, say
103 Literally, "works"
104 Pieces of work

106 Traditional rivals of the N.C.A.A.'s 'Hoos
109 Church part
110 There are three of them in a Morse "O"
112 Passing through D.C.?

113 USD : dollar :: MXN : ___
114 Part of 79-Down: Abbr.
116 Frequent C.D.C. collaborator
117 "___ Way" (Kitty Kelley biography of Sinatra)
118 Opponent

ACROSS

1 Ones with big heads around the office?
6 With 27-Down, island nation near Indonesia
10 What OPEC and NATO are both in?
14 E, in Morse code
17 Inauguration Day activity
19 Five-times-a-day Islamic prayer
20 Word with earth or muscle
21 Function whose output is 45° when applied to 1
22 German : Freundin :: Spanish : ___
23 Google search info
24 Some whiskeys
25 Piece of work
26 Premium membership designation
28 End ___
30 Small row
32 Sashimi selection
33 Holds
36 Language of the 18th-century poet Mir Taqi Mir
38 (0,0), in math
41 Put on an unhappy face
42 It lets you see the sites
46 Rice dish
47 Mess up
48 Hebrew name meaning "ascent"
49 Walks (on)
53 Talk, talk, talk
55 "How ___!"
57 Contents of some banks
59 Hyphenated beverage brand

60 Holders of multiple passports
65 Transcript fig.
66 Give a hoot?
67 Values highly
68 Trouble
69 Soothe
71 [Ignore that edit]
72 Honey ___ (Special K flavor)
74 First openly lesbian anchor to host a major prime-time news program
77 Pond fish
78 Not looking good at all
80 Follow closely
81 Goth relative
82 "What in the . . . !"
85 $$$ for old age
87 ___ soap
88 Brutes
92 Ones fighting for change
97 Reindeer in "Frozen"
99 Start of a rendezvous request
100 2019 jukebox musical featuring the song "Proud Mary"
101 Sun-kissed, say
102 Funny business?
104 Zip
106 "___ a Crime" (2016 Trevor Noah memoir)
108 Hempseed product
111 Property claim
113 One might be good or evil
117 Michael ___ of "Ugly Betty"
118 End of an era?
119 Bringing up the rear
121 Tops

122 Kind of syrup that's an alternative to honey
123 Homeland of many Paiute and Shoshone
124 Grate expectations?
125 "Spy Kids" actress Hatcher
126 "So true!"
127 One of two poles

DOWN

1 "May God bless and keep the ___ . . . far away from us!" ("Fiddler on the Roof" line)
2 Bad way to go
3 Winans with 15 Grammys
4 Panko-breaded chicken dish
5 Sp. title
6 Fence line?
7 A long time
8 Drops in water
9 Purchase for Wile E. Coyote
10 Sleeveless undergarment, informally
11 Settled (on)
12 Event with a crowning moment
13 Store
14 Pull out all the stops
15 Not sharp, perhaps
16 Thompson of "Sorry to Bother You"
18 Summer ___
19 Soda cracker, by another name
20 Choice words?
26 Pull in
27 See 6-Across
29 Microsoft's answer to the iPad

31 "I'm so sorry for you!"
33 Trendy
34 Alex and ___ (jewelry chain)
35 Mo. metropolis
37 Early development sites
39 Extended-wear manicure options
40 Added bonus, metaphorically
43 Aerie baby
44 Celia known as the "Queen of Salsa"
45 Words of admission
50 Stop ___ (sign)
51 Muralist Rivera
52 Goof (around)
54 Kind of data distribution with two peaks
56 Finish with
58 Tometi who co-founded Black Lives Matter
60 Newsroom sights
61 "So are we!"
62 Used Grubhub or Postmates, say
63 ___ Ing-wen, first female president of Taiwan
64 Alleged
66 Traditional attire for some martial artists
70 Ornate tea vessel
73 Overdone
75 "Howdy!"
76 Put in a seat, perhaps
79 Lakeside city that's at one end of I-79
83 Result of pulling the goalie
84 Jane of "9 to 5"
86 "Don't misbehave!"

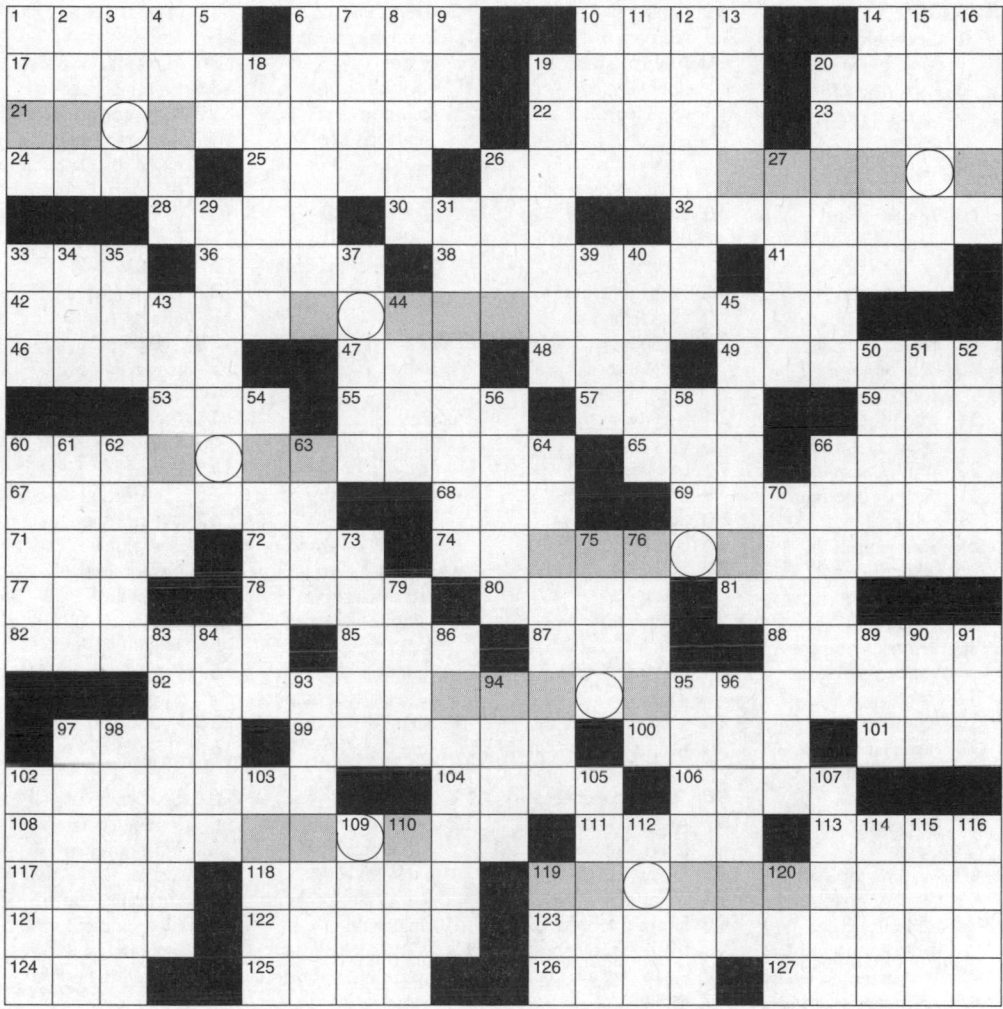

by Priyanka Sethy and Matthew Stock

89 Q followers
90 Letter that rhymes with three other letters
91 Phishing target, for short
93 Encroach
94 Human rights lawyer Clooney
95 Like the Dalai Lama
96 Part of the joke
97 Gawps
98 Go away
102 Take a dive, perhaps
103 W.W. II threat
105 Ringing in the new day?
107 Katie of ESPN
109 Brown or blacken
110 "Duh!," in modern slang
112 [Nodding]
114 Japanese soup ingredient
115 Children's author Blyton
116 Bird with a reduplicative name
119 JFK alternative
120 Dallas and Houston are in it, in brief

ACROSS

1 Goes wherever the wind blows?
6 Person who likes all your FB posts, perhaps
9 Key with five sharps: Abbr.
13 Western film, in old slang
18 Harriet's partner on 1950s–'60s TV
19 China's Chou En-___
20 Paul Simon's "___ Rock"
21 Tree that Athena gifted to Athens
22 Inaptly named bear of a tongue twister
25 Spanish rice
26 Letter-shaped construction piece
27 Endeavor
28 Winter weather hazard
31 Little black ___
32 Art of verse
33 Jurisdiction of a Catholic church official
37 Get closer and closer
40 Mapmaker's subj.
41 Literary traveler to Lilliput and Brobdingnag
42 Transfixed
43 Former telecom giant that merged into Verizon
45 Ostentatious display
48 Kicked back
49 Singer Lisa
51 Pre-euro currency
52 National tree of the U.S.
53 Paradise lost
54 Scatterbrains
56 Grandma, to Brits
57 Frenzy
59 Rattlesnake's warning
60 Ambrose Bierce defined it as "A minor form of despair, disguised as a virtue"
62 Totally over it all
63 Final creature encountered in "Dr. Seuss's ABC"
68 Far-right state
70 Buckskin, e.g.
71 Something stretched out in a yoga class
74 Has over
75 Go after
78 Like varnished wood
79 "Pretty please?"
80 Sci-fi travelers
81 Pan-fries
84 Violated a code of silence
85 Sportscaster Jim with the classic opening "Hello, friends"
86 Opportunities to win a vacation on "Wheel of Fortune"
90 Stocking stuffer
91 Actress Ana of "Love, Victor"
92 "Alas . . ."
93 Bistro sign word
95 Francis' tenure, e.g.
96 Lively, on a score
97 Collect little by little
99 Makes
101 "Which Disney Princess Are You?" and the like
104 Big Ten powerhouse, for short
107 Eye shade
110 Basic skateboard trick
111 Quick nap . . . or a playful description of the 64-Down here
113 Conflagration
114 Diamond who went platinum
115 Scottish denial
116 Popeye creator Segar
117 Footnote abbr.
118 Icelandic work that influenced Tolkien
119 Key for getting out, not in
120 Like May through August, unlike the other months of the year

DOWN

1 What "piano" can mean
2 Côte d' ___
3 Nickname for Isabelle or Isidore
4 Fashion designer Lange
5 Actress Amanda of 2012's "Les Misérables"
6 What B. B. King was king of
7 Rattles
8 Opposite of flatness
9 Members of bevies and broods
10 Tie the knot
11 Mine: Fr.
12 Many a collaboration between Louis Armstrong and Ella Fitzgerald
13 "C'est magnifique!"
14 Spanish composer Isaac
15 "How to ___ a ___" (popular Google search)
16 One of the Gabor sisters
17 Radiation unit
23 Member in the genus Troglodytes, so named for its tendency to enter dark crevices
24 "Jeepers!"
25 Generational divide
29 Former queen of Jordan
30 Nintendo princess
31 Order of roses
34 Kilt-wearing Greek infantryman
35 Fixed, as tiling
36 Northern California town once home to the palindromic ___ Bakery
37 Chain that sells chains
38 "Jeepers!"
39 Levels
40 Old fogy
41 Quiet valley
43 Partner of glamour
44 Comedian Fields
46 ___ garden
47 When repeated, one of the Gabor sisters
50 Mercedes-___
54 Stupor
55 Multitude
57 Pac-Man navigates through one
58 Wood-shaping tool
60 They're taken out in alleys
61 Six-Day War leader Weizman
62 No-nonsense TV judge
63 Unsightly spot
64 Sleep indicators
65 Counterfeit
66 Spike the Beanie Baby, e.g.
67 Having some pep
68 Alternative to Advil or Aleve
69 Birthplace of the Franciscan order
71 Kind of ray
72 Bit of tomfoolery
73 Nervous state
74 Seven: Prefix
75 Football sideline reporter Kolber
76 Brand of pretzels and chips
77 Electric ___

by Trenton Charlson

79 Kvetches
81 Pointy-eared dog
82 Big name in car parts
83 Break away
85 Reason to hang up
87 Victoria Falls river
88 Uniform adornment
89 Center of L.A., once
94 Sufficient, informally
95 Aphids, to ladybugs
97 Beyond cold
98 Woman's name meaning "night" in Hebrew and Arabic
99 Pound and others
100 Worshiper of the rain god Tlaloc
102 Took off
103 One of the Nereids of Greek myth
104 Eleven, en français
105 Parts of snowmobiles
106 Exploits
107 "The White Lotus" airer
108 View from Lake Como
109 Country music's __ Brown Band
112 In a bad way

CLUE: THE MOVIE

ACROSS

1 Syllables when you forget the words
4 The universe has an estimated 10^{82} of them
9 "A mouse!"
12 Beyoncé chart-topper "Single ___ (Put a Ring on It)"
18 Simile center
19 ___ Lawrence College
20 Magazine co-founded in 1945 by Hélène Gordon Lazareff
22 Similar-sounding phrase, such as "I scream" for "ice cream"
23 *Field of Dreams*
26 *Guys and Dolls*
27 Lucrative and undemanding
28 Ingredient in a McDonald's McFlurry
29 Seasonal winds
31 Fictional brand of rocket-powered roller skates
32 "Cross my heart!"
35 Fam girl
36 Sounds of doubt
38 *Star Trek*
40 Woodworker's tool
42 Some tourist spots in San Francisco
43 Tax pro, for short
45 Ancient work that describes the sacred tree Yggdrasil
46 Trendy home gym purchase
50 *Top Gun*
55 Baseball family name much seen in crosswords
56 Jerkface
59 Tightly affixed

60 Parrot's sound
61 Insurance department
63 "___ for me, thanks"
64 Big no-nos
66 *Letters From Iwo Jima*
67 *The Imitation Game*
69 *The Fifth Element*
73 Perfectly comfortable
75 1930s migrant to California
76 Spirits
77 Sesh on Reddit
80 Speed reader?
81 Gave, as gossip
83 Trimmed parts of green beans
84 *A Man for All Seasons*
87 Matricidal figure of Greek myth
89 Golden rule word
90 Spanish "Listen!"
91 Dostoyevsky's Prince Myshkin, so the book title declares
93 Cause for switching positions
97 *Scent of a Woman*
104 "___ you decent?"
105 ___ Toy Barn ("Toy Story 2" locale)
106 Small things that you pluck
107 Breakout band for Harry Styles and Zayn Malik, familiarly
108 Overlie
111 Mad magazine cartoonist Drucker
112 Get the juices flowing?
113 *Wayne's World*
114 *Space Jam*
118 Gene variant
119 Denominator in the velocity formula
120 Beam for train tracks
121 Fragrant ring

122 Candy with the slogan "Not sorry"
123 Skosh
124 Main artery
125 Panic button, of a sort

DOWN

1 Pet that should come with a lint roller?
2 Given that
3 Exasperated parent's retort
4 Flue-like
5 Confucian philosophy
6 Singer Rita
7 "Floating terror" of the sea
8 Many social media users
9 Donkey with a pinned-on tail
10 Two in a million?
11 "The Kiss" painter
12 Successfully uses a password
13 Melodious
14 Place to develop one's chops
15 Innate
16 Part of a makeup test?
17 Texting tech, briefly
21 "___ es!" ("That's right!": Sp.)
24 "Clueless" protagonist
25 Accept eagerly, with "at"
30 Org. with an annual Codebreaker Challenge
32 Double-crossed and half-baked
33 Embarrassing public episode
34 Restless desire
37 Luxurious
39 Product for one who wonders "Am I expecting?"

40 Increased into something much more valuable
41 Spy novelist Deighton
44 Weave off the shoulder?
46 Get ready for vacation
47 Civil rights activist Baker
48 It may be forgiven
49 Mystic's board
50 4x World Series winner Martinez
51 [more info below]
52 Ice cream containers
53 ___ compensation (subject of modern debate)
54 Spanish marinade
57 Drawer of shorts, e.g.
58 Cutthroat mentality
62 Cardinal's hat, in Britain
65 Tender areas
67 Pop in the fridge
68 Hershey's chocolate-and-toffee bar
70 Diatribe
71 Quaint sign word
72 Noun-making suffix
74 Fumble for words
76 Dodos
77 City that replaced Lagos as Nigeria's capital
78 Cameo
79 Predatory insect living in woodpiles
82 French fabric
85 Caramel or hot fudge, basically
86 Euphemistic exclamation
88 Ike's domain in W.W. II

by Brandon Koppy

91 Reason the physicist stayed in bed?
92 "The Shape of Water" director
94 Natasha ___, Boris's partner against Rocky and Bullwinkle
95 Some water park rides
96 Olympics symbol for Madrid's country
98 Sang along when you forgot the words
99 Ingredient in healing gel
100 Latte art medium
101 Arch support
102 Bill killers
103 Utopian
106 Like a birthday cake, pre-party
109 "___ All That" (1999 film)
110 Frequently, quaintly
112 Lugosi of horror films
113 Fish with an elongated jaw
115 Singer Sumac
116 Describe in a negative way
117 Toke

COMMON CORE

Note: This puzzle has five Diagonal clues, in addition to Across and Down. Diagonals (in mixed order): (1) Breakfast side dish, (2) Compassionate; (3) Nickname for Mars; (4) Starts drinking; (5) Truly magnificent

ACROSS

1 Conveniently forgets to mention, maybe
6 Big name in investing
12 How many writers work
18 Ran out of patience
19 Meghan ___, Grammy's 2015 Best New Artist
21 Get warmed up
22 Word with water or Electric
23 Meaningful work?
25 Rock bottom
26 Special ___
27 Like TV's Niles Crane and Monica Geller
28 Their existence is debatable
30 Conflict in 2017's "Wonder Woman," in brief
32 Source of Supergirl's powers
33 Clothing line
36 Ballet supporter, e.g.
41 N.A.A.C.P. ___ Awards
43 REI competitor
44 Shout of support
45 Gamelan instruments
46 Unflappable
51 Basic point
52 Main squeeze, in modern lingo
53 Texas hold 'em pair nicknamed "ducks"
54 "___ and Fugue in D Minor" (piece used in "Fantasia")
56 Lucifer
58 The "vice of narrow souls," per Balzac
59 Goddess who sprang from her father's head
60 Bibliophile : books :: oenophile : ___
61 "Imperialism, the Highest Stage of Capitalism" author
62 Muck
63 Present without being present
66 Ship for 28-Across
69 Like a space cadet
70 Part of the body named after Dr. Ernst Gräfenberg
71 Accustomed (to)
73 On edibles, say
75 A shore thing
76 Posted one's thoughts
77 Makes a comeback?
78 Souvenir for a Final Four team
79 Ingredient in many balms
81 Hones
82 Lock
83 Company with an iconic yellow Running Man logo
84 "The Lion King" trio
86 Receiver of private instruction
87 Ritzy transports
94 Japanese prime minister before Suga
95 Hosp. diagnostic
96 Where Gal Gadot was born: Abbr.
97 Instigate
98 Once
102 Not worth a ___
105 Pal of Buzz Lightyear
106 You wouldn't want them to have a crush on you
110 Director DeMille
111 Chuck E. Cheeses, in part
112 One way to go
113 Better than
114 Off course
115 One of the Magi, along with Melchior and Balthazar
116 Designated things for bikes and buses

DOWN

1 "Sick burn!"
2 Peace Nobelist Yousafzai
3 Cry of success
4 More orderly
5 Fuel for a camp stove
6 Houston A.L.er
7 Field's yield
8 Macbeth trio
9 Golfer Michelle
10 Sight on an M. C. Escher Möbius strip
11 Balkan region
12 Director Welles
13 Fastidious
14 Feng ___
15 As things might happen
16 Something bottled in Cannes
17 Price abbr.
20 GPS recommendation: Abbr.
21 Look over
24 Get a move on
29 Kenan Thompson is its longest-tenured member, for short
30 Reminiscence about an epic party
31 Ming-Na who starred as Mulan in 1998's "Mulan"
34 Played a Halloween prank on
35 Pickle
37 Olympic gold-medal gymnast Korbut
38 Govt. agency that Jimmy Woo works for on "WandaVision"
39 Santiago of "Scandal"
40 Horse of a different color
41 "Aha!"
42 Sit shiva, e.g.
46 Male deer
47 Completely, after "in"
48 Diez menos dos
49 Most of Greenland
50 Like dim sum
52 One hitting the low notes
53 Name that means "God is my judge"
55 Some Chevy S.U.V.s
57 Present, e.g.
58 She/___
60 Droll
61 Kid ___
64 Denouement
65 One who asks a lot of questions
66 The munchies, e.g.
67 Step two?
68 Nine to five, for example
69 Animal on Ontario's coat of arms
72 "Not this again!"
73 Take out of the game

by Jeff Chen

ACROSS

1 One known as "the Alive, the Eternal"
6 Checkout option
11 Org. featured in 2011's "Contagion"
14 Tiff
18 ___ Rose, Catherine O'Hara's character on "Schitt's Creek"
19 Chevron subsidiary
20 Language in the Tai family
21 Kind of skirt
22 Your ex's new date whom you just can't stand?
25 Tabloid twosome
26 Lose sleep (over)
27 Off
28 "Su-u-ure"
29 Half of a legal warning
30 There are 24 in a cuboctahedron
32 Make a big stink
34 Kegels, e.g.?
39 Getting up there
42 Poet Rainer Maria ___
43 "___ yourself"
44 First winner of the Nebula Award for best science fiction novel (1965)
46 It's just passing
47 Therapists' org.
48 Director Craven
51 First square of a crossword?
55 Walking the dog, for instance
58 One might bend over backward
59 Who actually lives in Lapland, some say
60 Accord maker
61 Author of 29 Federalist Papers

64 Laugh and a half
65 Playwright who wrote "Those who cannot change their minds cannot change anything"
68 "I'll be your waiter tonight," e.g.?
70 Raison d'___
71 Do a certain developer's job
72 Something a mover or a movie might have
73 Threesome
75 The "B" in its name stands for "brush"
77 Oldest independent state in the Arab world
78 Genre for "Booksmart" and "Clueless"
82 Conspiracy theory so wild that it can't be aired?
86 Trident look-alike
87 ___ jam
88 Small bird
89 "I did it!"
90 Southern cooking staple
92 Things you can crack without damaging them
94 Affix with a click
96 Plan to leave at a very specific evening time?
100 Orangish shade
103 Fill with joy
104 Stirs up
106 Doctor Zhivago
107 Where subs are standard
109 Semiaquatic creature
113 Missing
114 Blackjack dealer?
117 Niche mag
118 Stick (out)

119 Product that increases volume
120 "Moonlight" actress Janelle
121 Joie de vivre
122 One doing inside work
123 Chain whose name derives from its founders, the Raffel brothers
124 Orchard products

DOWN

1 Book before Obadiah
2 Converted apartment, perhaps
3 "That's ___"
4 Question after an argument has died down
5 Solo traveling in space
6 Crafts
7 Frequent subjects of Taylor Swift songs
8 Measures, in music
9 Word that can precede or follow pack
10 Actor Menzies who won an Emmy for "The Crown"
11 Fills (in)
12 One hell of a writer?
13 One way for packages to arrive, in brief
14 Protect
15 "Quiet!," rudely
16 Lager alternatives
17 Subdued
19 "It takes a licking and keeps on ticking" brand
23 Herb used in smudging rites
24 Theater award
29 Stars
31 Approached

32 Actress Moreno
33 ___ Kong
34 Melee
35 Abdominal procedure, for short
36 Skin-care brand
37 Dry biscuit used as baby food
38 Op. ___ (footnote abbr.)
40 Any slice of pizza, geometrically
41 Greek goddess associated with witchcraft
44 Archaeologist's workplace
45 Workers' advocate, informally
49 Young partner?
50 Back way, often
52 Winona of "Stranger Things"
53 Work, work, work
54 Texas border city
56 "C'est la vie"
57 "Ay" follower
61 "Now We Are Six" author
62 Crush, as a test
63 German denials
65 Members of a certain den
66 Enter without permission
67 A wood frog's ability to freeze itself in winter and an octopus's ability to change color, for two
69 Vaccine holder
74 In with
76 Props for majorettes
78 Bird with an annual 18,000-mile round-trip migration
79 Instrument that's a homophone of 69-Down

by Katie Hale

80 Crucifix inscription inits.
81 ___ New York (Brooklyn neighborhood)
83 2020 Democratic also-ran
84 It's nada to Nadal
85 Actor/comedian Barinholtz
91 Dieted
93 Summer shoe style
95 Bed of straw
96 Who's talking on the phone?
97 Personality that's hard to read
98 Pass over, in a way
99 Mathematician John Forbes ___ Jr.
101 Visually evaluate
102 Out of practice
104 Boo-oo-oo, say
105 Boo-boo
107 Smear
108 Site for some creative entrepreneurs
110 What Vulcan's forge lay underneath, in myth
111 Sport
112 "___ chic!"
114 Party people, for short?
115 Repeated word in the U.S. postal creed
116 Rapscallion

14   CHOICE WORDS

ACROSS

1 Action done while saying "Good dog"
4 Mischief-makers
11 It might click for a writer
14 Fall mo.
17 Kind to Mother Nature
18 Harris in the Country Music Hall of Fame
19 Living ___
20 Member of the superfamily Hominoidea
21 Noted Apple release of 1968, to fans
23 Haphazard
25 Some crumbly blocks
26 Inits. for a theatrical hit
27 Send away, in a way
29 Accomplished the task
30 What wiggly lines in comics may represent
32 Cause of boom and bust?
34 Convene for another session
36 Up to it
37 What's frequently used by poets?
38 "To quote yours truly . . ."
41 ___ dish
42 Heath
43 Desperate
45 Traditional British entree
48 Tries for a role
49 S.F. metro

50 "Hey . . . over here!"
51 Derby lengths
53 Equivalent of the Face With Tears of Joy emoji
56 Give a buzz
61 Inconvenience
64 Execute, as a royal of old
67 Classic concert chambers
68 Noted U.S. rock group?
70 Approximately
73 See captain?
74 Studio fixtures
76 "I'm game!"
77 State of equilibrium
80 Code-cracking grp.
81 Match-ending rugby call
82 Bygone sovereign
85 Dance-a-___
87 Build on
90 Military dismissal
96 "You game?"
98 State to be the case
99 ___ Kornfeld, music promoter for Woodstock
100 Daddy-o
102 Great Basin native
103 Stun
104 Heavy weights in Britain
106 "Murder, ___ Wrote"
107 Samuel ___, business partner of Marcus Goldman
109 Gradually wear away
111 Lipton competitor
113 Keypad triplet
115 Critical remark
116 Regardless of the outcome

118 Hectic trip abroad
121 Card in a royal flush
122 Purposes
123 One runs from Me. to Fla.
124 Seminoles' sch.
125 "You betcha!"
126 Northern ___ (curiously named apple variety)
127 Have
128 Boggy expanse

DOWN

1 Fare that's eaten hands-free
2 Wanted badly
3 Mano a mano
4 Negligent
5 Silicon Valley's ___ Research Center
6 Candy bit that comes in a plastic roll
7 "Battlestar Galactica" robots
8 Clerical vestment
9 F, in music
10 Southern region of Mesopotamia
11 Fabric options
12 Sense of self
13 Fluent speaker of Elvish, say
14 Uttered a sound
15 ε
16 Bugs
19 Relative of a bug
22 Churchill ___ Rooms (London tourist attraction)
23 Long ball
24 City with a Little Havana
28 Nickname for José
31 Farthest down?

33 Anklebone
35 Least messy
39 Sorority member
40 Yang's counterpart
44 "I Wanna Be Sedated" band
46 Horrid
47 Maximum degree
49 The brainy bunch?
52 Profligate sort
54 Measures of electrical resistance
55 One of the fire signs
57 Alveolar trill, as it's commonly known
58 Concept, in Cannes
59 Just in case
60 Glasgow gal
61 Mischief-makers
62 ___ court
63 Stage between larva and imago
64 Consecrates
65 Act investigated by an insurance company
66 ___ ex machina
69 QVC alternative
71 Journalist Fallaci who wrote "Interview With History"
72 Bindis, e.g.
75 Running behind
78 Kinda
79 Berate blisteringly
81 They can be wrinkled or thumbed
83 Field that deals with fields
84 The newest trend, in slang
86 Inits. at Westminster
88 Trigger

by Alex Eaton-Salners

89 Head for the hills?
90 Moved aside (for)
91 Cupidity
92 Changes from commercial to residential, perhaps
93 Words to live by
94 Wash out
95 Popular tick repellent
96 Piercing eye hue
97 Trial
101 ___ of Alexandria (wonder of the ancient world)
105 Clinch
108 Puerto Rico clock setting: Abbr.
110 Ballpark figures, in brief
112 Semiserious "Got it!"
114 Places hangers hang
117 Guff
119 Distributor of CARES Act funds
120 ___ Moines

ACROSS

1 Piles
15 Tablet purchases
19 Setting for Banff National Park
21 Dealer's enemy
22 Disney film with more than a million hand-drawn bubbles
24 Rap's Run-D.M.C., e.g.
25 Ostrich or kangaroo
26 Amtrak service
27 Emulate Ella Fitzgerald
29 Boxer Wolfe who played Artemis in "Wonder Woman"
30 "Yes, indeed"
31 Get-together
33 Rush
35 Clear spirit
36 Seasonal fast-food sandwiches that aren't halal
37 "Star Trek" virtual reality chambers
38 San ___ (European enclave)
39 [stern glare]
40 Italian wine region
41 Certain developer's job
42 Seriously unpleasant
43 Or greater
44 Fall flavoring
45 Some movie theater concession areas
50 Shattered
51 Eateries serving small plates
52 Spoils
53 Up
54 Command center
55 Multiday event, for short
56 2017 CVS Health acquisition
57 Profess
58 Tough bass part?
60 Really grooves with something
61 Quaint locale of first-aid supplies
63 Valorous
64 Bhikkhunis : Buddhist monastery :: ___ : convent
65 The C of C major, e.g.
66 Word with zone or boots
67 Actor Idris
68 Error message?
69 Was completely exhausted
70 Hiking aids
72 Employees who work a lot
73 Bit of reading near a cashier, in brief
76 Grasps at straws?
77 Not at all
78 Big name in pasta sauces
79 N.B.A. coach ___ Unseld Jr.
80 Badly hurt
81 "Capisce?"
82 Rail in a dance studio
83 Images on some Australian silver coins
85 V.I.P. access points
89 Mythos
90 Nutritional plan involving controlled removal of foods
91 Predator frequently appearing in Calvin's daydreams in "Calvin and Hobbes"
92 Special delivery?

DOWN

1 Put on pretensions
2 Island home to Faa'a International Airport
3 It's located in the middle of an alley
4 Drones, e.g.
5 Terse confession
6 Op. ___
7 Bad person to confess bad things to
8 Twisting together
9 Puerto Rico's ___ Telescope, formerly the world's largest single-aperture telescope
10 Impersonate at a Halloween party
11 Immune system component
12 Vegetable in bhindi masala
13 Lens holder
14 Fine crystals used in food preparation
15 Symbol of industry
16 Make a flying jump onto a slope
17 They get left in the dust
18 Treat on a tea trolley tray
20 "___ Mode" (2018 #1 hit for Travis Scott)
23 Labyrinth builder of myth
28 Tarot card said to "radiate" positivity
31 Foretold the future
32 Certain gasket
33 Deterrent to a pickpocket
34 Behaves like a fool, informally
36 Drama linked to the resurgence of the name "Betty" for baby girls
37 Remains tightly secured
38 Acquired family member
39 Actress Meyer of "Beverly Hills 90210"
41 Tested the censor, say
42 Vendors of e-cigs
43 Cruise stop
44 Wet behind the ears
45 Important sales for growing businesses?
46 Argument
47 Totally wipes out
48 Like some very old characters
49 Pallet piece
50 Small drink of whiskey
51 Zap, in a way
54 Items at T.S.A. checkpoints
56 Boeing competitor
58 What the waving of a white flag can indicate
59 Business brass
60 Reduce in rank
62 Style pioneered by Picasso
63 Works at the cutting edge?

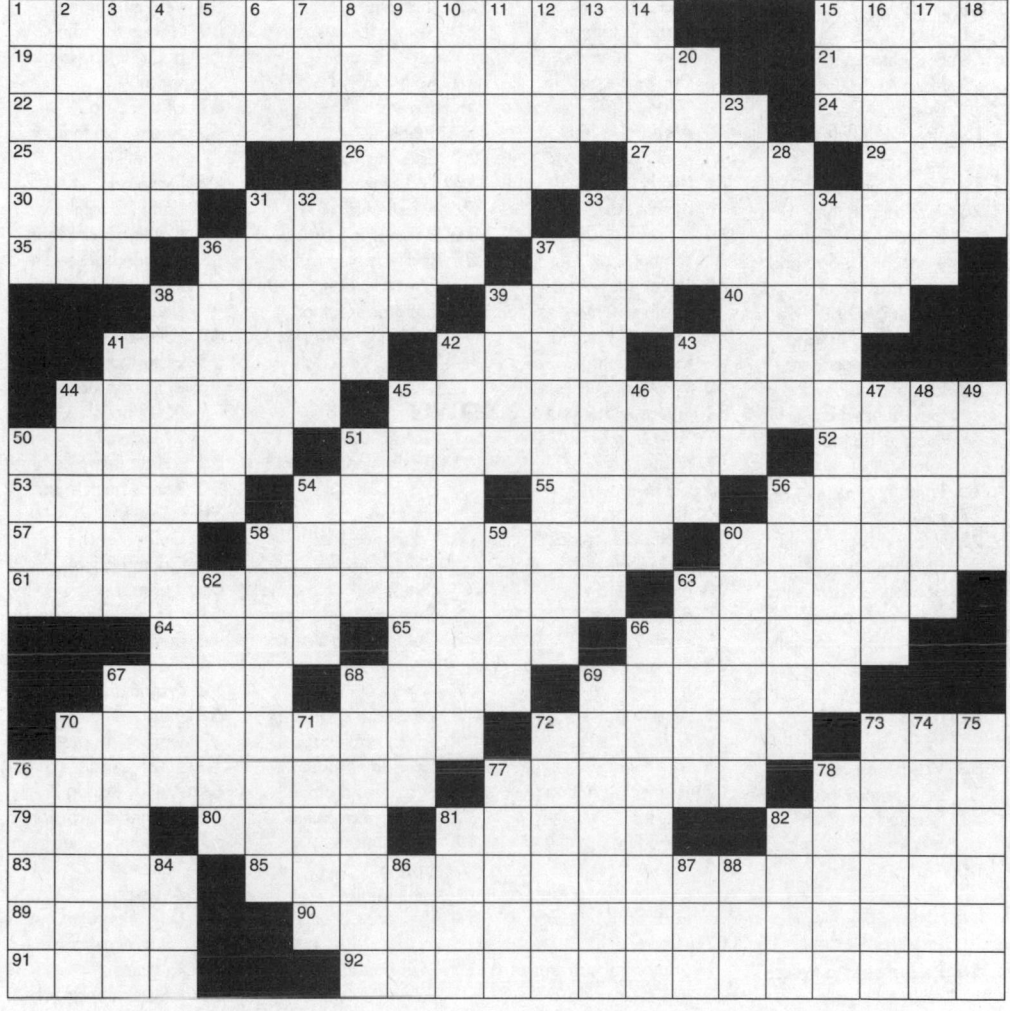

by Sid Sivakumar

66 Hot, in Havana
67 Evidence of a crossword solver's mistake, maybe
68 Dairy-free coffee additive
69 Butcher's offering
70 Quiver
71 Ripply fabric pattern
72 Give a thumbs-down
73 Bespectacled "Peanuts" character
74 Gives a thumbs-up
75 Talk show slate
76 Harped (on)
77 Unfashionable
78 Time off, for short
81 Slightly spoiled, in a way
82 Label signing
84 ___-positive movement
86 Contest
87 Actress Mowry of "Sister, Sister"
88 Authority, metaphorically

ACROSS

1 Miss
5 Fairy tale monster
9 Meat in ragù al cinghiale
13 "Everyone knows the secret now"
19 Lincoln or Ford
20 Purchase in the board game Catan worth one wood and one brick
21 Singer Guthrie
22 Genre for Nirvana and Soundgarden
23 Forgetfulness experienced by soon-to-be moms, informally
26 Final innings, usually
27 Heinie
28 What a baby might start eating at around six months
30 Universal donor's blood type, informally
31 A, in Aachen
32 "Dancing With ___ Hands Tied" (Taylor Swift song)
33 What well-connected people may have
37 Scented plug-in brand
40 "Afternoon, pardner!"
44 "Oh yeah? Give me an example!"
46 Response to a texted joke
47 Worldly wisdom
49 Deg. for a creative type
50 Booting
53 Juice cleanse, essentially
55 Cocktail made from gin, vermouth and Campari
56 Big letters in home security
59 In Latin, it's "stannum"
60 Pound part
61 Church council
62 Succeed in life
64 Portfolio listings
65 Common sense
68 The "gone girl" in "Gone Girl"
70 A negative one might be positive
71 Used colored pencils, say
74 "___ be a real shame . . ."
75 Jovian planets, by another name
78 Changes back to factory defaults, say
80 Way too loud
81 Figure in the iconic "We Can Do It!" poster
85 Quite enough
86 Bit of fiction
89 Suffix with quack and mock
90 National law enforcement, informally
92 Simple flotation device
95 Arranges in random order
96 URL ending
97 TV display option
101 ___ tai
102 Picked up
104 Above
105 Like the bread ideal for bread pudding
107 Theoretical primordial substance
108 Word on an Irish plane
110 Oscar-winning director Lee
111 Obama's birthplace
113 Playing to the crowd
117 Japanese condiment sprinkled on rice
121 Go back to the start, in a way
124 Slogan about willpower . . . or a hint to four pairs of answers in this puzzle
126 Courtroom cry
127 "Something From Nothing: The Art of Rap" director
128 Aptly named bus driver on "The Simpsons"
129 Catering vessels
130 "Whatever you say, sweetheart"
131 Unilever tea brand
132 Bert who played the Cowardly Lion
133 Children's author DiCamillo with two Newbery Medals

DOWN

1 Nordic native
2 Invisible energy field
3 Proofreader's directive
4 Words moaned while eating a cheeseburger, maybe
5 Give one's address
6 Get ready to sleep, cutesily
7 Candidate's focus
8 Ice cream surname
9 British nobleman
10 Like some traditions
11 Et ___ (and others)
12 Sonata movement
13 The uninformed masses, colloquially
14 The Jonas Brothers, e.g.
15 Dish named for a day of the week
16 Toronto's prov.
17 "What a mess!"
18 Your: Fr.
24 Bar ___
25 Queen's "We Will Rock You," e.g.
29 2K, for one
31 Sheep?
34 Award hopeful
35 Passes along to, in a way
36 Like the winner of a handwriting contest
37 Narrow valleys
38 Very affectionate
39 Get on the same page, in corporate-speak
41 URL ending
42 Alternative to fiber or satellite
43 Leave off
45 Early PC software
47 Planting more than one kind of seed in a field, per Deuteronomy
48 Pollution stat
51 Historical subject of Hilary Mantel's 2009 novel "Wolf Hall"
52 Action item
54 Brings back to use
56 Home of Guinea and Guinea-Bissau: Abbr.
57 "Yo ___" (internet meme with rapper Xzibit)
58 Prioritization process
63 It added "essential worker" in March of 2021: Abbr.
64 Author Rand
66 Quaint contraction
67 Title that comes from "Caesar"
68 Assist
69 Day celebrated by "Star Wars" fans
71 Curtains
72 Interior design job
73 Support, as a belief
76 Fellow
77 Like bacon and lobster, in Jewish law
79 Prime-time slot
82 Home of the National Voting Rights Museum
83 Perfect
84 Nail polish brand
86 Like some nachos and questions

by Aimee Lucido and Ella Dershowitz

87 "Real" ones were first issued in the 2010s
88 Muppet who hosts the "Not-Too-Late Show"
91 Fifth-century invader
93 Poisonous shrub
94 Suffix with Euclid
95 Metric for online traffic, in brief

98 Get ready for action
99 The "C" of D.R.C.
100 World of Warcraft, e.g., for short
103 One who's at home on the job?
105 Branch of Islam
106 Thai taxi with a repetitive name

109 Send, as payment
112 Mail, e.g.
114 Actress Taylor-Joy of "The Queen's Gambit"
115 Costa ___
116 Mother of Don Juan
117 Cheese on a meze platter

118 Gillette razor
119 Daily Planet reporter
120 Gaelic tongue
121 Sorority letter
122 "Yikes!"
123 Pile of cash
125 TV button: Abbr.

ACROSS

1 Lets extra light in, in a way
8 Get on the stick?
12 Music genre prefix
15 Arm of the Dept. of Homeland Security
19 Deforestation, for example
20 Not home
21 Pool tester
22 Line through two poles
23 *Salma Hayek: 1996, 2002*
26 Bop on the head
27 Driven, say
28 "___ Flux" (onetime sci-fi series)
29 Yellow belly?
30 Pair in gossip
31 *Dev Patel: 2008, 2016*
36 Jerkwad
39 What remains, with "the"
40 Quail : bevy :: ___ : parliament
41 Liechtensteiner's currency
42 Amount of tips earned by a street performer, maybe
45 Equipment used to play the oldest organized sport in North America
47 Choose
50 *Brad Pitt: 2001, 1995*
54 Accompanier of smoke
56 Texter's "I think . . ."
57 Catherine of "Schitt's Creek"
58 Outstanding finds
59 Broadband inits.
61 "You mean I'm wrong?!"
64 Utilize a company policy for new parents, say
66 When tripled, playful onomatopoeia for shooting laser beams
67 "Here, have a taste"
68 *Owen Wilson: 2005, 2006*
71 Baseless rumors
74 The lowest número primo
75 Pickup line?
79 It's at the beginning of this clue
80 Noted fashion monogram
81 Equal
82 "Sunrise" singer Jones
83 Focus of some smartphone updates
84 Before, in poetry
86 *Joaquin Phoenix: 2014, 2013*
89 Problems with phonograph records
92 Contents of college blue books
94 Early online forum that popularized terms like "FAQ" and "spam"
95 Put on again
97 Some dolls sold in a Universal Studios gift shop
98 When "Alexander Hamilton" is sung in "Hamilton"
101 Mathematician Lovelace
102 *Al Pacino and Robert De Niro: 1974, 1995 (twice!)*
108 Brother of 99-Down
109 Ramirez of "Grey's Anatomy"
110 Historic trade ally of the Monacan people
111 Dark yellow shade
115 -elect
116 Modern tech feature for watching two programs on one screen . . . or an alternative title for this puzzle
120 Bug-eyed
121 High-value deposit
122 Shore soarer
123 Absolutely devoured
124 Takes from
125 TV's "___ Lasso"
126 Name on a toy truck
127 Places for rubs and scrubs

DOWN

1 Expert
2 Song title shared by hit singles for Ja Rule and Flo Rida
3 In the ___
4 High points
5 Kind of force created by the moon
6 Ending with "brown." or "auburn."
7 What tahini is made from
8 Tush
9 Thanks (to)
10 Actress Gadot
11 Olive ___
12 In any way
13 Sleazeballs
14 Kind of muscle
15 Chess's ___ Caruana, onetime youngest grandmaster in U.S. history (14 years, 11 months)
16 Flowerhorn cichlids and vampire tetras, for example
17 Worker who wants to strike?
18 "Go on, shoot"
24 Sister brand of Saucony and Stride Rite
25 Small valleys
32 Cybersquatters make fake ones
33 What 2 is vis-à-vis 1
34 "Hmm . . ."
35 Badger
36 Barrels of fun
37 Satirist ___ Baron Cohen
38 Entree served with a knife
43 Price jockeying of competing airlines
44 Not paying attention
45 Walgreens competitor
46 ___ Khan of Khan Academy fame
48 Prefix with present
49 Goes to hell
51 "Golly gee!"
52 Stock ticker symbol for a longtime clothing brand
53 Corrects in text
55 Brought on
60 River of old song
62 "Clever ___ are never punished": Voltaire
63 [swoon]
65 Meat Loaf's "Rocky Horror" role
66 Surfaces, e.g.
67 Start of many a limerick
69 Massive adversary
70 Whom you might ask "Where will I be in 10 years?"
71 Forensic pros, in brief
72 Words of eventual understanding
73 "'Fraid not"
76 Supermodel Shayk
77 Went up against
78 Sorority letter

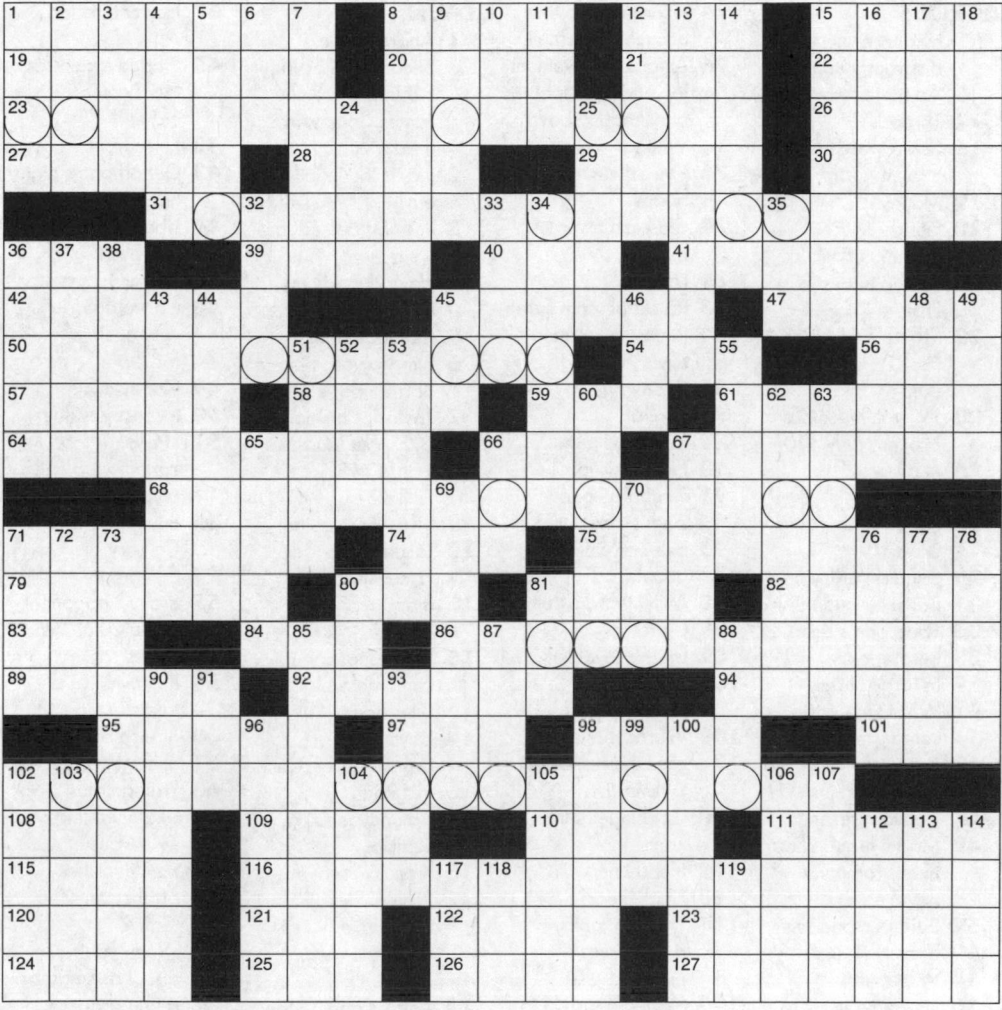

by Adam Wagner

18 GARAGE SALE PITCHES

ACROSS

1 Evidence of disorderly conduct?
5 Animated greetings
11 Threads
15 Some words of Wordsworth
19 Mötley ___
20 Fiend
21 Instrument with a solo in Seal's "Kiss From a Rose"
22 "There's no place like ___" (Alaskan's quip)
23 *TV, volume knob broken, only $10!*
26 A bit
27 "Me too"
28 Food Network host Brown
29 Sandal variety
31 Barbecue side dish
35 Tried one's hand
38 Before, once
39 In large supply
41 What may cover some ground
43 *Baseball mitt, has a small hole, just $1!*
47 Casual greeting
49 Model featured on many romance novel covers
52 Split personalities?
53 Stretch of time
54 Wipe out
56 "Predictably . . ."
58 Much of Italy's north
60 What the universe may or may not be
62 Huey, Dewey and Louie, e.g.
63 ___ colada
65 She can act as a D.J., nowadays
67 Raised
68 *Guitar, never used, $15!*
72 Baseball's Matty or Felipe
74 After-tax investment account, informally
75 Award achievement for Audrey Hepburn and Andrew Lloyd Webber
76 Ones coming on board
79 Classic mower brand
81 Loosen
83 Raiser of team spirit
84 Ready for a refill, say
85 Sucker
86 "Voilà!"
89 Running figure
90 Nautilus's locale
91 *Textbook, a few pages torn out, $2!*
96 Extremely energetic people
98 "Ain't that the truth!"
99 Or rather
102 Least enjoyable parts
105 Super wrong identification?
108 Words that might elicit the response "Prove it!"
110 Goldfinger's first name
112 Blood line
113 Final check?
114 *Two fish tanks, accessories included, $5!*
120 Started a turn, perhaps
121 Like a tautology, by its nature
122 Name for zinc sulfide that is one letter short of a kitchen appliance
123 Demolish
124 Ingots
125 Source
126 Heir to the throne, as a rule
127 Catch a glimpse of

DOWN

1 Andrew who became the acting F.B.I. director after James Comey was fired
2 It gets the lead out
3 A good dessert to split?
4 Having made up one's mind about
5 Outback sight
6 Stingray or Barracuda, e.g.
7 Taylor of fashion
8 U.S. poet laureate with a 1987 Pulitzer
9 "The BFG" author
10 Disperse
11 "Heaven forbid!"
12 Blood-typing letters
13 Word that can come before or after home
14 Lloyd ___, Dukakis's veep pick in 1988
15 Amenity in G.M. vehicles
16 *Prop ax used in "The Shining," a valuable collectors' item, $200!*
17 Actress and gender equality activist Watson
18 Trickle
24 "___ but a scratch": Monty Python
25 As well
30 Set up
32 Back
33 Pin point?
34 "A Clockwork Orange" narrator
36 Actress Madeline of "Blazing Saddles"
37 Horror director Aster
40 Started again, as "99 Bottles of Beer"
42 False front
43 Get off one's high horse?
44 Libertines
45 "Sure is"
46 Target with a pass
48 Concern for veterans, for short
49 Not even close
50 Incense residue
51 *Wallet, in good condition, plenty of card slots, $5!*
55 Person from Calgary or Edmonton
57 Brave's opponent in the 2021 World Series
59 Removes, as a tattoo
60 Stretch of time
61 Special-interest, e.g.
63 Fruit detritus
64 Like a wailing cat
66 TV's Cousin ___
69 Pam's former partner on "The Office"
70 When you're about as smart as a fifth grader
71 Aware of
72 Some beers
73 ♭
77 90° bend
78 Kind of blue akin to cerulean
80 Concerns for a homeowners' association
82 Bonobo, e.g.
83 Banh mi toppings
85 Not a "no no"
87 Hooked

by Jeff Kremer

88 Regular intake
92 Some beers
93 Cattle call
94 Strip
95 Wash. neighbor
97 It's good, in a saying
99 Netflix crime drama starring Pedro Pascal
100 Take a pot shot?
101 Like the smell of rising dough
103 Bare
104 Ice cream container
106 Course standard
107 Tours can be found on it
108 Website with star ratings
109 ___ mia (Italian term of endearment)
111 "___ all be fine"
115 Wash. neighbor
116 Stick on a table?
117 Only's partner
118 Ward workers, for short
119 Term of endearment

COME AGAIN?

ACROSS

1 "Bull" airer
4 Out
10 Win for a 10-Down
15 Yukon automaker
18 Set down
20 With 116-Down, artificial intelligence system that mimics the human brain
21 Who is "too small to make a difference," per a Greta Thunberg book title
22 Propel, as a shell
23 ". . . and to ___ good night!"
24 . . . FLOOR FLOOR FLOOR . . .
27 It's got some miles on it
29 Home to the Burj Khalifa, for short
30 Singular
31 Stark who was crowned Queen of the North on "Game of Thrones"
32 . . . GRIZZLY GRIZZLY GRIZZLY . . .
39 First responder, for short
40 Percussion instrument of African origin
43 What some kings and queens dress in
44 Maker of the classic video game Frogger
45 . . . PROPOSAL PROPOSAL PROPOSAL . . .
49 Kind of milk
50 Rapper with more than 20 Grammys
51 Reps
52 Click ___ (artificial increasers of website hits)
53 Goddess of the dawn
55 Pet lovers' org.
60 James who sang "I Sing the Blues"

61 Grandma, affectionately
65 Roy Lichtenstein's genre
70 Brit's "How shocking!"
71 What many lifeguards have
72 . . . COMMERCIAL COMMERCIAL COMMERCIAL . . .
74 Steve with nine N.B.A. championship rings
75 Chemical suffixes
76 Like the color of honey
77 "Give me a break, would you?!"
78 Philosopher who wrote "A Treatise of Human Nature"
79 Lead-in to ask or suggest
81 Get hitched
83 They're explained by Newton's law of universal gravitation
84 N.F.L. Hall-of-Famer Shannon
89 Inconveniences
94 Company with a Page Program
97 . . . AMBITION AMBITION AMBITION . . .
99 Word-of-mouth
101 Actor Spall of "Prometheus"
102 Literally, "I bow to you"
103 Op. ___ (footnote abbr.)
106 . . . STAIRS STAIRS STAIRS . . .
109 ___ di Pietro, artist better known as Fra Angelico
111 Ta-ta
112 Opposite of down: Abbr.
113 "Let's Stay Together" singer, 1971
115 . . . CAUTION CAUTION CAUTION . . .

122 Slight problem
123 Pablo Neruda work
124 "Please, I can handle this"
125 Many an informant employed by Sherlock Holmes
126 Org. involved in the Scopes Monkey Trial
127 R.S.V.P. option
128 Way up or way down
129 Pocketful in ring-around-the-rosy
130 Syracuse-to-Albany dir.

DOWN

1 Part of a contract
2 Christmas fir
3 Investor behind the scenes
4 Palindromic feminine name
5 One gifted with the "inner eye"
6 Word on a candy heart
7 Before, poetically
8 Piercing spot
9 ___ cavity (where the lungs are located)
10 Likely loser
11 Hawaiian taro dish
12 Family member inaptly found in "ladies only"
13 High school subj.
14 Vehicle company with a market value over $1 trillion
15 Adventurous kids in a 1985 film
16 Napoleon's famed war horse
17 Shout
19 Some diaper changers
25 Rapper dissed by Jay-Z in "Takeover"
26 Young 'uns
28 Popular Toyotas
32 How a zombie might spread the infection

33 Ostrich relatives
34 Peter out
35 "Symphony in Black" artist
36 Something necessary for gain, they say
37 The "grand slam" of showbiz awards, in brief
38 Like some apparel, in song
41 Mimic
42 Opposite of FF
46 Together
47 Kind of jar
48 Org. that hires cryptanalysts
50 Samurai's sword
52 Awful-smelling
54 Give one's take
56 Religion that emphasizes seva, or "selfless service"
57 Astrology or palmistry
58 Sandiego not usually found in San Diego
59 Lew ___, portrayer of Dr. Kildare
61 Badger
62 Brouhaha
63 When doubled, boring result in the Premier League
64 Word commonly following the Oxford comma
66 Messy sort
67 What seven did to nine, in a joke
68 Lament
69 Celebrity gossip site
73 Like New Jerseyans vis-à-vis New Yorkers
80 Destination for Birthright trips: Abbr.
82 Someone's in the kitchen with her, in song
83 Savory Chinese snack
85 Grinder

by Chase Dittrich and Jeff Chen

86 Put ___ on (limit)
87 Dennis the Menace's appropriately named dog
88 Bishops, e.g.
90 Execs: Abbr.
91 Smartphone predecessors, for short
92 Choice words
93 Card-matching game
94 Prefix with binary
95 Male etiquette, as described by Barney Stinson on "How I Met Your Mother"
96 Eyeteeth
98 Clique
100 Exam with a 35-minute timed essay, in brief
104 What 10s represent
105 Notable chameleon feature
107 Grinds away
108 Not friendly
110 ___ Minor
113 Singer India.___
114 Part of the eye
115 Demure
116 See 20-Across
117 Pac-12 athlete
118 Rapscallion
119 ___-yo
120 They're found below the "To" field
121 Tuna, on a sushi menu

JOB SHARING

ACROSS

1 Research subject for which Bohr won a Physics Nobel
5 Grimm account
9 Musical medley
15 Like cranberries
19 Protagonist of Colson Whitehead's "The Underground Railroad"
20 Big-time
21 Tarot deck grouping
22 Trash day reminder, maybe
23 Side hustle for a hairstylist?
25 Rodent-catching feline
26 Maker of Regenerist products
27 Oust
28 French auto pioneer Louis
30 Dan Conner and Danny Tanner, e.g.
32 [Blown kiss]
34 Side hustle for a veterinarian?
36 Manage OK
39 Dangerous crowd
41 Try to lighten up, perhaps?
42 New York Cosmos star of the '70s
43 Metal precioso
44 Polite rejection
46 National gemstone of Mexico
50 Side hustle for a therapist?
56 "A Confederacy of Dunces" author
57 Shed, with "off"
58 Many a Sharon Olds poem
59 Leaf-to-branch angles
62 It may be glossed over
63 Turned
65 Its fleece is hypoallergenic
66 Part of a gig
67 Side hustle for an anesthesiologist?
73 Leon who wrote "Battle Cry"
74 Avid bird-watcher, say
75 URL divider
76 "Mr. Mayor" airer
77 First stroke of the day
78 Holy ones: Abbr.
81 Spanish city north of León
84 Encrusted
87 Side hustle for a carpenter?
90 Netted
93 Give an address
94 Home in the mud
95 Christmas purchase
96 Like Athena
98 Moving ___
100 Record label for Otis Redding and Big Star
101 Side hustle for a marriage counselor?
106 Small sweater?
108 Cold-weather jacket
109 Person with lots to show
111 Kind of license
115 Museum that awards the Turner Prize
116 "Oh yeah? Watch me!"
118 Side hustle for a drill instructor?
120 Tech tutorials site
121 Sub groups?
122 Set of showbiz awards, in brief
123 Hightail it
124 Actress and inventor Lamarr
125 Where the tradition of shaking hands as a greeting originated
126 Clinches, with "up"
127 Show off at the gym

DOWN

1 "Because freedom can't protect itself" org.
2 Animated figure
3 Evil creatures in 7-Down
4 Defiant retort
5 Large orchestral gong
6 Mahershala of "Moonlight"
7 Frodo's film franchise, familiarly
8 Blues great Waters
9 One with a nesting instinct
10 Inflame
11 Shape
12 Something made in a hurry
13 A in French class
14 One getting down, so to speak
15 Cheery "Ciao!"
16 Two-time opponent of Dwight
17 Map lines
18 Guilt-producing meeting, perhaps
24 Maxim
29 Nobel-winning author Gordimer
31 Park supervisor?
33 Refine
35 Economic stat.
36 Male swans
37 Like one Freudian fixation
38 Bouncy toys
40 Thrift-store fashion, informally
45 Blue
46 Order member
47 Hindu, for one
48 Justice beginning in 2006
49 New Testament miracle recipient
51 "Uh-oh" sounds
52 ___ fresca
53 Its etymology may derive from the diminutive of "borough" in Italian
54 "Mission: Impossible" theme composer Schifrin
55 Convention center event
60 Some HDTVs
61 1979 Commodores hit with the lyric "Good times never felt so good"
64 Singer Celine
65 One of two in "Hamilton"
66 Aggressively mainstream, in slang
67 Unit of prevention
68 ___ legend
69 Revise, as text
70 Org. with Divisions I–III
71 Suspense novelist Hoag
72 Pandora native in "Avatar"
78 Side of a block
79 Word after high or weak
80 Classic skit comedy show
82 Sole ingredient in some cookies?
83 Rock with colorful bands
85 Sum total
86 "Buffy the Vampire Slayer" vampire

by Daniel Okulitch and Doug Peterson

88 Like a bad outcome for all
89 Great deal
91 Causing quite a stink
92 Opposite of morn
96 Frank
97 "Hold on . . ."
99 Hotel room restriction
100 Drive to the station, say
101 Come down with
102 Nonsensical
103 Checked a box, maybe
104 Accent ___
105 Wizards' wear
107 Giant bird of Arabian myth
110 Blow a fuse
112 Starbucks size
113 Slurpee relative
114 Party mix ingredient
117 Big game show prize
119 Scatter

ACROSS

1 They might be put on
5 Singer Grande, informally
8 Undercover attire?
11 ___ Creole (Caribbean language)
18 Drive-___
19 Certain urban map
22 Demoralize
23 Little tyke / Flatter, with "up"
25 Things bachelors might have
26 Certain Scandinavian
27 "Gimme ___!" (start of a cheer at three Big Ten schools)
28 Noted Dadaist
30 ___ Helmer, Ibsen heroine
31 Scalpel creations
33 Relative of a tee-hee / Bit of marginalia
39 M.L.K. or R.B.G.: Abbr.
41 Stage name of rapper Yasiin Bey
42 Forest spirit
43 Pep / Onesie feature
47 "Sure, I'm game"
49 UNICEF address suffix
50 H.S. subj.
51 Words before point or rate
52 Ring / Hold, as inhabitants
55 Med school subj.
57 Certain Scandinavian
58 "The One I Love" band
59 ___ Hall ("The Wind in the Willows" residence)
60 Loud but friendly growl
61 Bow
62 Adjusts the spacing between, as typed letters
64 No ___ (apartment policy)
67 Big name in cast-iron cookware
69 Reduce in volume / As new
72 It'll knock you out
74 Ogler
75 Chiwere speakers
76 Christmas ornament, often
78 Modern prefix with medicine
79 Becomes less taut
82 Old "Up, up and away" sloganeer
83 Mannheim madame
84 Fivers
85 Kind of leaf / Scientist born on Christmas Day in 1642
89 With 111-Down, cholesterol reducer
90 Musician Brian
91 Paris's ___ Saint-Louis
92 ___ Finch, "ER" doctor
93 Possible result of getting one's wires crossed / Moolah
96 Singer/actress Shore
98 Big block
101 Two-time U.S. Open tennis champion while still a teen
102 Breakfast dish / Fruitcake tidbit
106 Amasses, with "up"
108 Nuclear medicine units
109 "___, Virginia, there is a Santa Claus"
110 ___ culpa
112 Trig function
113 Some laundromat machines
116 This puzzle's images, in two different ways
121 Physician awarded a Presidential Medal of Freedom by G. W. Bush
122 Party staple
123 Prefix with space
124 Chandelier part, often
125 ___-mo
126 Football units: Abbr.
127 Hurdle for a J.D. wannabe

DOWN

1 Court sport grp.
2 Course preparers
3 Becoming faint
4 Solarium activity
5 National dance co.
6 It was eliminated from the U.S. in 2004
7 Library IDs
8 Kitty
9 Project
10 Outback orders
11 Cabinet dept. since 1965
12 Come to ___
13 Fit
14 Nightmare
15 "Got it"
16 "___ Maria"
17 Super Mario Bros. platform
20 Downfall
21 Dropped the ball
24 Remove, as a ribbon
29 Green shampoo
32 Italian thoroughfare
34 Wishy-washy response
35 Get, slangily
36 Genuine
37 Filmmaker von Trier
38 Little lead
40 Some graffiti
43 First and reverse
44 Not learned
45 Proverb-spouting Panza
46 Lancaster-to-Scranton dir.
48 Citrus hybrid
52 Come to ___
53 Present opening?
54 "Gonna Let It Shine" singer
56 Personal essence
58 Where to go on a trip?
62 Not a mystery
63 One keeping others up at night, perhaps
65 Something else
66 Singer Gomez
68 Went in a different direction
70 "What's ___ you?"
71 Pride and prejudice, e.g.
73 Fix, as a lawn
77 Pirate
80 Set
81 Mushroom
83 Woman in Progressive ads
85 Classic dog name
86 Hip bones
87 What some neighborhoods do
88 More than enough
89 Volts/amp
93 Long-tailed monkey

by Laura Taylor Kinnel

94 Blowout party
95 Piano performance, possibly
97 Some ranges
99 El ___ ("View of Toledo" painter)
100 ___ Cradle (maritime rescue device)
103 Popular adoption agcy.
104 "Sign me up!"
105 High-maintenance
107 Richard famous for large-scale sculptures
111 See 89-Across
113 Agcy. fighting epidemics
114 Bobby of the N.H.L.
115 Part of R.S.V.P.
117 Old-fashioned menorah filler
118 "Kitchy-kitchy-___!"
119 Raises
120 Teetotaler's opposite

ACROSS

1 Appoint
7 People of the Southwest
13 Wishy-washy response
19 Had the opportunity to, casually
20 Entertainment with a private audience?
21 *Malice, more formally*
22 *One wearing chapstick, perhaps*
24 Be up against
25 Poker variety similar to Texas hold 'em
26 Counterpart of "Thx"
27 Saves for later, in a way
29 Ploy
30 Lost
32 *Antarctic coordinate*
35 "A man has cause for ___ only when he sows and no one reaps": Charles Goodyear
38 Bit of tinder
41 First side to vote
42 ___ course
43 New York City transport stopping at Kennedy Airport
46 Beginning stage
47 Prefix with thermal
50 There might be a catch with this
51 *Blouse and broach, perhaps*
54 Wet bar?
55 Form of nepotism, symbolically
57 Herd member
58 Sauce
59 Place, as ceramic tiles
60 Like autumn air
62 Person helping with a delivery
63 Word before film and after clip
65 *It has many beet and beef options*
70 "___ Trois Petits Cochons" (French fable)
71 Sport at the Special Olympics
73 G.I. ___
74 Calling
76 Not be able to stand
77 Ending with invent
78 War and peace, in "War and Peace"
83 Like most dorms nowadays
84 *Tickled*
87 Focus of modern mining
88 "___ be an honor!"
89 They can be graphic
90 Surround, as with light
91 Considerations for N.C.A.A. eligibility
92 ___ Wintour, longtime Vogue editor in chief
93 Spring locales
94 Takes by force
96 *Pop fly*
100 Some family babysitters
102 Match
103 Sarge's boss
105 A-number-one
106 The Venetian way?
110 Alternative to Dropbox
113 Gradually fix something . . . or what to do to understand this puzzle's italicized clues?
116 *Briefly, e.g.*
117 What's used to catch some waves
118 Supreme Egyptian god
119 Bum out
120 Famous cryptid, familiarly
121 Intimates

DOWN

1 Number of sides on a sign reading "ALTO"
2 Space
3 ___ mater (brain cover)
4 Politico-turned-TV host
5 Form thoughts
6 Catch
7 Seeks a favor, say
8 ___ favor
9 Working hard
10 Java activity
11 Product from un ave
12 Boo-boo
13 Texter's qualifier
14 One might be put through the wringer
15 Geek Squad members, e.g.
16 "I can thrill you more than any ___ could ever dare try" ("Thriller" lyric)
17 "The Glass Bead Game" author, 1943
18 Pecan or peach
20 Sch. where a live bear used to take the field during football games
23 Echo, perhaps
28 Pimple lookalikes
31 It usually works in corners
33 "Catch!"
34 Baker's Joy alternative
35 Record speeds, for short
36 Adams of New York City politics
37 *Antelope, say*
38 Parable or allegory
39 Devices with Nunchuks
40 Business news magazine
44 "For shame!"
45 Slugging stat
46 Member of the inn crowd?
47 *Approach for directions*
48 Onetime collaborator with Ice Cube and Dr. Dre
49 Some sports tournaments
52 Big name in women's hair and skin care
53 Boo-boo
54 Word with story or sister
56 Economist/author Emily
58 Screw up
60 Relative of a club, for short
61 Place for boarding
63 You can count on them
64 Member of the modern work force
66 Great Lakes natives
67 Kind of bean
68 Taiwanese electronics giant
69 "I'm about to tell you something shocking"
72 Haddock relative
75 Doesn't put it all on one pony
78 Suvari of "American Beauty"
79 Sounds heard in 93-Across
80 Destructive 2021 hurricane
81 Nouveau-Mexique, e.g.
82 Lip or cheek
84 Put over the moon
85 One hanging around Queen Elizabeth?
86 With it, in old slang
89 "Snowpiercer" airer
92 Sporting a certain natural style

by Christina Iverson

93 Avoids
95 Tortoise's challenge to the hare
96 Nickname for the French Alexandre
97 No longer squeaky (one hopes!)
98 John Wayne, by birth
99 Who ran against George Washington for president
100 "___ chance!"
101 Letters that complete this word: _P_ROPRIA_E
102 Snaps
104 Squeezes (out)
105 Good thing to be in
107 Letters on dreidels
108 Taj Mahal's home
109 Exam that once required fingerprint identification, for short
111 Exercise
112 Animal house
114 Demon of Japanese folklore
115 Folklore villain

ACROSS

1 Game option represented by a flat palm
6 Singer with the 2016 #1 album "A Seat at the Table"
13 Disney queen
17 Not clash
18 Front lines?
19 Said without saying
21 CERISE + LAVENDER = certain baby animals
23 God sometimes depicted with green skin
25 State in which "Parks & Recreation" is set: Abbr.
26 Pull some strings, maybe?
27 Clinches
29 Chip away at
30 Employee on an airline or cruise ship
32 CORAL + GOLD = pet store purchase .
36 Veto
37 ___ stick
38 Quarterback who holds the N.F.L. record for most consecutive games started (297)
39 "You're on!"
41 Train set
42 Tailor, maybe
43 One-named singer with the album "Lovers Rock"
45 Lipstick choice
46 AMBER + GREEN = imported brew
48 Final Fantasy character who shares his name with a U.S. city
49 Sashay, say

50 ___ B. Wells Society for Investigative Reporting
51 A bunch
52 PEAR + CRIMSON = fighting group
54 Bottle flipping in the mid-2010s, e.g.
55 Hospital settings, briefly
56 Poster board?
57 Max's opposite
58 Bo or bonsai
60 LIME + MAGENTA = visualization
64 ["You're *still* talking?"]
68 Subj. of some collegiate bragging
70 Actor Gallagher
71 Go astray
73 "Herc could stop a show / Point him at a monster and you're talking ___" (lyric in Disney's "Hercules")
74 RUST + SCARLET = celestial group
78 Daughter in the comic strip "FoxTrot"
80 Cha chaan teng serving
81 Plot problems
82 Dis-tressed
83 CREAM + PEACH = nonviolent protest
85 Plantings lining the Literary Walk in Central Park
86 Skier's accessory
87 Many an art print, briefly
88 "No injuries here"
89 2019 space film
91 B's in math?
92 Devotee, informally
93 A ways
94 TEAL + OCHER = breakfast option
97 Absolves

100 Fisher of 2018's "Eighth Grade"
102 One towering over the rest of the field?
103 Actress Rooney
104 ___ Giedroyc, co-host of "The Great British Bake Off"
105 Nappy : U.K. :: ___ : U.S.
107 MAUVE + TANGERINE = restaurant handout
112 African antelope
113 Frenzied
114 Goddess who turned Picus into a woodpecker
115 Throws in
116 Unbelievable rumors
117 Takes the edge off

DOWN

1 2024 Olympics host
2 Deal maker
3 Christopher Street Day celebration
4 Still, for a poet
5 Outlet store come-on
6 Miffed
7 Fantasy creature whose name is an anagram of another fantasy creature
8 Rural setting
9 What's the point of leatherwork?
10 Newcomer
11 Artist El ___
12 "The motor industry's Titanic," per a 1994 book
13 Nwodim of "S.N.L."
14 Ne'er-do-wells
15 Keep from sticking, say
16 "Wait for It" singer in "Hamilton"
18 Stave (off)

20 Got ready for guests, in a way
22 Prefix with centric or vision
24 Volleyball teams, e.g.
28 Lost traction while driving over
31 Sinuous dance that emulates a creature
32 3/4 and 7/8, e.g.
33 Done
34 Hound sound
35 Homophone of the sum of this clue number's digits
38 Took off
40 Who says "That I did love thee, Caesar, O, 'tis true"
41 Wood in some incense
42 Bring down
43 Truth ___
44 "Jung at heart" persona?
46 Talent
47 Par for the course
48 ___ to go
49 Chemistry, for one: Abbr.
52 Grinding tooth
53 Come out
56 High on marijuana, in slang
59 Way to go
61 Twangy, as a singer
62 "Us," "It" or "Her"
63 Progressive alternative
65 Ones doing stellar work
66 Total
67 One arranging for flood insurance?
69 Parts of many gaming rigs
72 Payment sent
74 In a bundle, as documents
75 Wasn't straight

by Paolo Pasco

76 Culinary phrase after "pollo" or "scaloppine"
77 Vessels hunted by K-ships
78 Element in many henna designs
79 "I'm in heaven!" sounds
83 Doner kebab bread
84 Latin 101 word
86 For
87 Film director ___ Isaac Chung
90 "That's it"
91 Heavy footwear choice
92 Evening in Italy
95 Car model name made entirely of Roman numerals
96 Novelist Ferrante
97 Of the flock
98 Cross swords
99 Sooty channels
101 Modern checkout device
103 Diagnostic scans, for short
106 Map lines: Abbr.
108 Clean energy grp.
109 Stuff in cigarettes, but not e-cigarettes
110 ". . . is there more?"
111 Rapper known offstage as Mathangi Arulpragasam

ACROSS

1 Disseminated
5 JPEG alternative
8 Quick-witted
14 "Forbidden fruit is the sweetest," e.g.
19 Kind of writing
21 Hurting more
22 Mineral used as a flame retardant
23 Aromatic herbal drink
24 Carmen McRae or Anita O'Day, notably
26 Disorganized
27 Sound in the Serengeti
29 Tying words?
30 Horrible boss, say
31 Neighbor of S. Sudan
32 Endpoint of a Shinto pilgrimage
36 What's going up in Chicago?
38 And so forth
40 Munchkin
41 Spade with a short handle?
42 Morse morsel
43 You can have a blast with this
44 "Yes, indeedy!"
47 ___ volente
49 Makes clearer, in a way
51 1997 pop hit with a nonsensical refrain
52 Fete
56 Anago, on a sushi menu
57 In ___ fertilization
58 & 59 Flag bearers, for short?
62 Clap back
63 Many moons
64 Chaired
66 Many, many, many moons

68 Subj. line heading
69 Birthplace of five U.S. presidents, with "the"
73 German title
74 Like discriminatory employers, often
75 Just roll with it!
76 See 88-Across
77 Eliminates, mob-style
79 Driving stick?
81 ___ out a victory
83 Pack (in)
84 Fracases
85 Start of some conventional wisdom
88 With 76-Across, Mexican business magnate who was once the world's richest person
89 Means of a quick recharge
92 "___ funny!"
93 Fab
94 Akin to
95 Rapper ___ Cudi or DJ ___ Loco
97 Comprehension
99 Domain of Mars
100 Boise-to-Spokane dir.
102 Post-default event
104 "Eureka!"
108 "That's the spot"
110 Kinda
111 Lunkhead
113 Court order
114 Red accessory for cartoondom's Huckleberry Hound
116 Scientific contribution from 98-Down, discovered in a manner suggested by this puzzle's theme

120 Crow's-nests, e.g.
122 One living in the rial world?
123 Lingerie fabric
124 Blights
125 More mirthful
126 Defiant refusal
127 ___ Plaines, Ill.
128 Start of a story, in journalese

DOWN

1 Cause of a jolt
2 Really busy, perhaps
3 It's nothing to joke about
4 Artist known for his lampooning cartooning
5 Startin' place
6 "___ moved on"
7 Calming words
8 Holy city near Baghdad
9 Hardly a lover of hot wings?
10 Radio frequency meas.
11 Ad or show follower
12 ___ P. Morton, Benjamin Harrison's vice president
13 Lost deposits, as a bank?
14 Attorney's org.
15 Sorrow
16 Thank you, in Tokyo
17 Stovetop device
18 Breadths
20 Sled dogs, e.g.
25 Word in some cocktail names
28 Baseball's "Master Melvin"
33 Westernmost sch. in Conference USA

34 Actress ___ Pinkett Smith
35 "Er . . . umm . . ."
37 Nonbinary possessive
39 Game show invitation
45 Modern lead-in to "X"
46 Got out fast
48 Exit
50 Tom Petty hit with the opening line "She's a good girl, loves her mama"
51 Rendezvous
52 Nickname for Virginia
53 Declare
54 Is beaten by
55 You might take a lift to one
56 Married mujeres: Abbr.
57 All-in-one purchase from a smoke shop
60 Unforgettable, unstoppable sort
61 They're not to be trusted
65 Julie who played Catwoman on old TV
67 Puzzle (out)
70 Personal bearing
71 Strong pan
72 Hard thing to do?
78 German title
80 Capital of Bangladesh
82 Mushroom in miso soup
86 Afterword
87 Nicolas who directed "The Man Who Fell to Earth"
88 Lab where the Higgs boson particle was discovered
89 Inventory

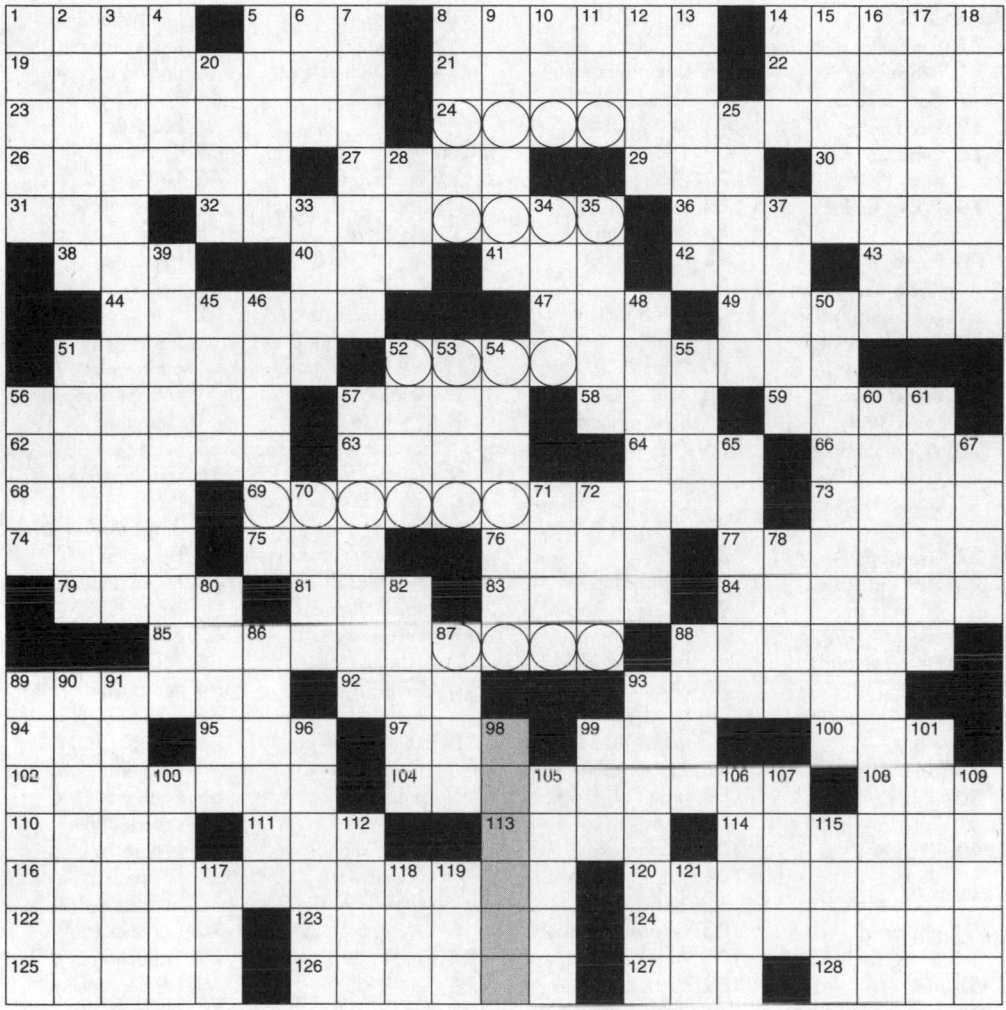

by Timothy Polin

90 "My Cousin Vinny"
   setting
91 Airport route
93 Squealed
96 Opposite of
   a glut
98 Who was famously
   hit over the head
   with inspiration?

99 Tech release of
   2006
101 Didn't act rashly,
   say
103 Pit
105 Words before relax
   or remember
106 Small section of a
   pit

107 Bowl-shaped
   cooking vessels
109 German
   state that includes
   Frankfurt
112 Manage
115 What's got ewe
   covered?
117 Hemlock relative

118 Old ___ (London
   theater)
119 Gag line?
121 Spanish "hey!"

ACROSS

1 Symbol of authority, informally
7 Compañero
12 Delhi issue
16 Reaction to puppy pics
19 Water buffalo, for one
20 French ___ (trick-taking game)
21 Land of blarney
22 Pass during the N.F.L. playoffs
23 THE LADY VANI____ (#2, 1964)
25 Who infamously boasted "They can't collect legal taxes from illegal money"
27 Luxurious
28 Suffix in some pasta names
29 BILLE (#3, 1972)
31 He gave Starbuck's orders
34 NATO members, e.g.
35 Adorable sort
36 x⁰ (#1, 1985)
41 Barnyard baby
42 Keep one's mouth shut?
43 Porky Pig's girlfriend
44 It cost 5¢ in 1965
47 Home of Iowa State
49 Help with a crime
50 Google web browser
53 Laser pointer chaser
54 Like the Balkans in the 1990s
57 Certain peaceful protest
58 Country singer McEntire
59 Captivate
60 VAUDEVILLIAN (#2, 1988)

65 Become more complicated, say
66 Getting together
67 Sheen
71 LOST, E.G. (#1, 1984)
73 Glacier-scaling tool
74 Yard tool
77 Private student
78 Figure it out
79 ___ Lilly (pharmaceutical giant)
80 "Jeez!"
82 Actress Garr
85 Beach shaper
86 Only player to win the U.S. Chess Championship with no losses or draws
88 Darling
91 Harbor helper
92 ___ story (tale of a car company's bankruptcy?)
93 CHAN_E _PPEA_ANCE TO CONCEA___D MISLEA_(#1, 1968)
97 Islamic spirit
99 Brand of insecticide strips
100 Madhouses
101 TITTLE-TATTLE (#16, 2011)
103 Opposite of post-
105 Airline posting
109 Furnace for calcium oxide production
110 ENTICEMENT (#1, 1983)
114 Big club in Las Vegas?
115 The final word
116 Give a lift
117 Know-it-all
118 "___ Como Va" (Santana hit)
119 Female Olympian of note
120 Palindromic battlers

121 Place of worship whose third, fourth and fifth letters are appropriate

DOWN

1 One of eight in a stick of butter: Abbr.
2 Jolly laugh
3 Dec. 24 and 31, e.g.
4 Minor accident
5 Mary ___ Evans a.k.a. George Eliot
6 Opposite of paleo-
7 Memo abbr.
8 When doubled, Hawaiian food fish
9 Pique
10 Terk in Disney's "Tarzan," e.g.
11 Opera with the aria "Ave Maria"
12 Naval engineer
13 Air traveler's accumulation
14 Quint's boat in "Jaws"
15 Enclosure for a bike chain and sprockets
16 180
17 Arthur who invented the crossword puzzle (1913)
18 Overgrown, say
24 Kind of terrier
26 Young chicken, e.g.
30 Actress Tyler
32 Move barefoot across a scorchingly hot beach, maybe
33 Shock's partner
34 Throw ___ (rant and rave)
36 No longer frozen
37 Kind
38 Crop up
39 Chafe
40 Out of gas, informally

41 Internet ending that's also an ending for inter-
44 Part of the brainstem
45 Chatter
46 Greek letter that might follow "z"
48 Affix, in a way
50 Eyelashes
51 Ketchup brand
52 "One ___-dingy" (Ernestine the operator's catchphrase on "Laugh-In")
55 Arch type
56 Landlord's due
57 Petrol unit
58 Surgically remove
60 Unearthed
61 Mi, in a C major scale
62 Number twos
63 Pelvic bones
64 Air carrier
68 Island where Paul Gauguin painted
69 Book that's the source of the phrase "a land flowing with milk and honey"
70 Go back (on)
72 Instruction in an oatmeal recipe
74 "Zebra"
75 Slugger from Louisville
76 Florida city whose name has three pairs of doubled letters
78 Upscale watch brand
80 Annual eight-day celebration
81 Basketball stat: Abbr.
82 Numbskull

by Derrick Niederman

83 Poetic dusk
84 Color of traffic on a GPS
87 Craft carried over a portage
88 Rhythmic part of a heartbeat
89 Same: Prefix
90 Sense of self
93 Protagonist in "The Stepford Wives"
94 FedEx competitor
95 Clears for takeoff?
96 Old Glory
97 1964 Tony Randall title role
98 Like oranges and some gossip
99 Duck or Penguin
102 Frost
103 Davidson of "S.N.L."
104 Richard and Jane in court
106 Commercial prefix with postale
107 Out of office?: Abbr.
108 One-named Irish hitmaker
111 Tops
112 Madrid's country, in the Olympics
113 Song lead-in to "Believer," "Loser" or "Survivor"

ACROSS

1 Web site?
6 Browser window
9 Streaming service acquired by Fox in 2020
13 Civil rights grp. once led by M.L.K.
17 Fictional character who says "I will take the ring, though I do not know the way"
18 Scorpion, for one
20 Wasn't overturned on appeal
21 Artists sketching pectorals?
23 Stays out all night?
24 Glowing or shining
25 Work rotations
26 French "I like"
27 "Right on!"
28 Spot at a casino
30 Either side of a beaming grin, in a phrase
31 Tony winner McDonald
32 Something to make after you wake
33 Vow to remain mum about hotel guests' secrets?
37 Hoops org.
40 Possibility
41 Scoffing sound
42 Driver of film
43 Nonbinary people, informally
47 Declined
49 Over-poetical?
50 Modern-day "carpe diem"
51 Early times in verse
52 Small distance covered by a naval armada?
56 First sitting prez to fly in an airplane
57 Words after walk or cash
58 Hyperbolic wait time
59 Like climates where cacti thrive
60 Pointy part of a charger?
62 Group of followers
64 Willem who played Jesus in "The Last Temptation of Christ"
66 Some pianos and motorcycles
68 2000s Fox teen drama
69 Playwright Simon
70 "Emotion in motion," per Mae West
71 Thomas ___, British general at Bunker Hill
72 Sweetie
73 Boxer lacking a left hook?
77 One of the boxing Alis
78 Gumbo ingredient
80 :-) alternative
81 Below par
82 Something unleashed in a denial-of-service attack
83 Destination for a return flight
84 Himalayan humanoid
86 ___ eyes
88 "I'm a frayed ___" (punch line of a classic joke)
89 What brass band music has?
92 Court
95 Groups of Greeks, informally
97 Watcher of the skies, for short
98 Old ___ (motherland, affectionately)
99 Announced
100 You can count on them
101 Beat in a race
104 Very productive
106 Not even a little off
107 Tree feature in winter?
109 Quaint bathroom sign
110 Galosh
111 Lumberjack's favorite kind of beer?
112 "What are the ___?"
113 Audience for Cocomelon, the most-viewed YouTube channel in the U.S.
114 Omega's place
115 Columns with angles

DOWN

1 Home with a pointy roof
2 Worked on Wall Street
3 Bring to a repair shop, say
4 Creative springboard
5 Cereal once advertised by Woody Woodpecker
6 Subject for Laozi
7 Sounds from a lab
8 "The Art of Fugue" composer
9 One's kin, casually
10 Loosen, in a way
11 Some zeros and ones
12 Bar necessities, at times
13 It has several steps
14 What a dog walker and a strong-willed pooch might vie for?
15 Run easily
16 Makeup of some music libraries
19 Main
20 Huge quantity
21 Lacking color
22 Brief period of work
26 "Easy . . . everything's going to be OK"
29 Bottle marked with a skull and crossbones
31 Cost for a spot
33 Garden shed items
34 Caramel-filled candy
35 "You can leave this to me"
36 Declaration by one who's done playing
38 Benjamin Franklin famously considered it "a rank coward" with "bad moral character"
39 "Te quiero" sentiment
43 Mideast V.I.P.
44 Response to "No offense"
45 The Bee Gees' Barry, Robin and Maurice Gibb?
46 It might gather lint
48 Somersault
52 Adversary
53 To's opposite
54 Old-timey reproach
55 Scottish cap
58 Aromatic trees
61 Really bother
63 Jacqueline or Jacques
64 For sure, for short
65 Something a snowboarder catches
66 Last word of "Ulysses"
67 Goal in musical chairs
69 Nick of "48 Hrs."
70 Beer brand whose name spells an article of apparel backward

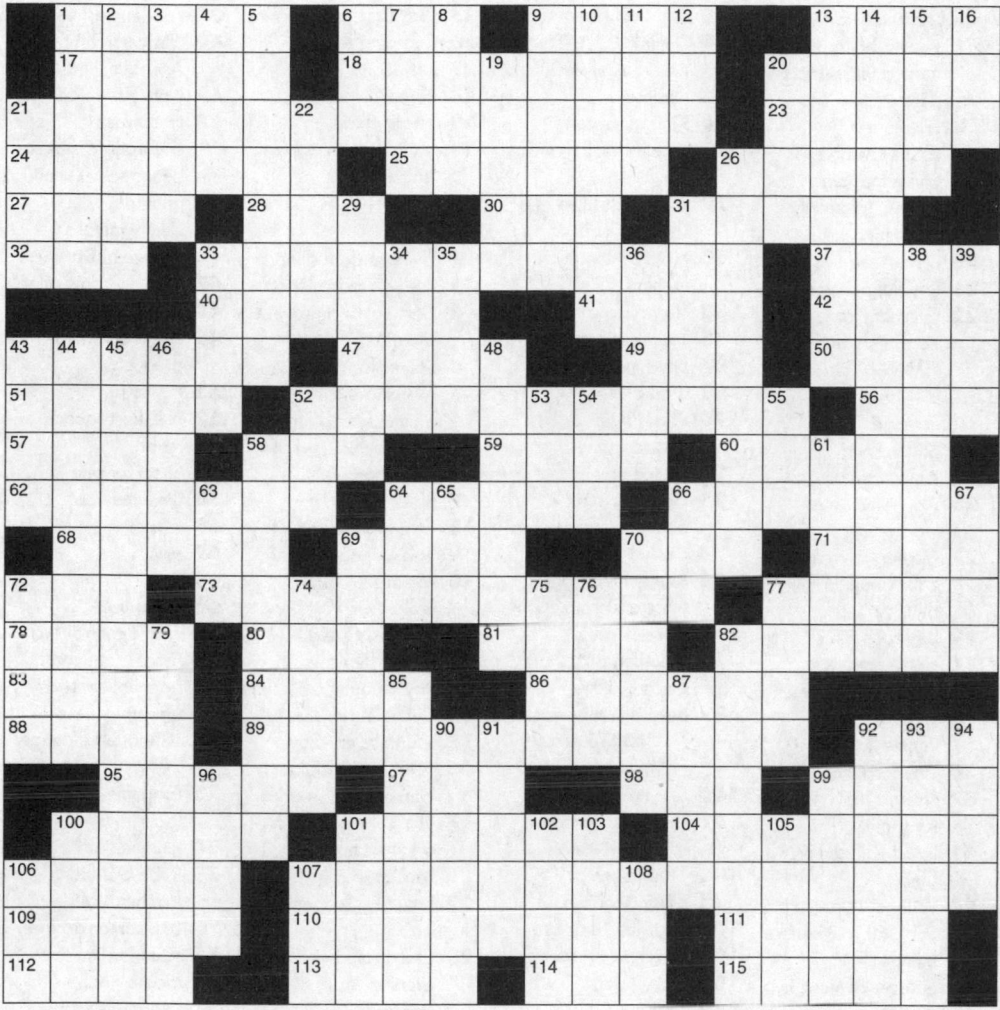

by Nancy Stark and Will Nediger

72 Knock on the head
74 Carolers' repertoire
75 ___ dancer
76 Minotaur's foot
77 Bird known in the U.K. as a diver
79 Draws
82 Red-light district establishment
85 Like some vodkas
87 Fly into a rant
90 Spuds
91 Tall tales
92 Dispensed with
93 N.H.L. team with five championship-winning seasons in the 1980s
94 Praising poetry
96 Ballet sections
99 Play station?
100 Got rid of
101 "Duh," in modern slang
102 Pine
103 Like the Radio City Music Hall sign
105 Harvest
106 Something swollen on a pro athlete?
107 Totally fine
108 Alternative to Webster's, in brief

ACROSS

1 Rock subgenre named for its vocal aesthetic
8 Like some space-saving beds
14 Styles that are picked, informally
18 Amateur
20 Disinclined (to)
21 Royal figure of sci-fi
22 Grammy for Kendrick Lamar's "DAMN." or Cardi B's "Invasion of Privacy"
24 Shuts down
25 American, abroad
26 Apt name for a worrier
27 Moving toward equilibrium, in biology
29 Legerdemain
31 Horse color
34 Prepares for a Ms. Olympia competition, say
36 Tiny foragers
37 "Here's an example . . ."
41 Insect with distinctive pincers
44 Without stop
45 Subj. for some future bilinguals
46 Sources of music in musicals
50 Splinter group
51 Brewing brothers
54 Capital of Japan's Hyogo Prefecture
55 It might be broken in overtime
56 Waits to publish, as an article
59 Second-rate
61 Pronoun pairing
63 Loop trains
64 Hornswoggle
67 De-creased

69 Luxury Hyundai
70 "Still da ___" (Trina title track of 2008)
72 Fluster
74 Kind of squash
77 One using cloves or garlic
79 What gets filled at a shell station?
80 Monthly condition, for short
83 Hairstyle protectors
85 Tabbouleh topping
87 Build, as interest
89 Kind of test
90 Board figure, informally
92 Recipe unit
95 Goddess in a peacock-drawn chariot
96 Marilyn Monroe wore a fuchsia one while singing "Diamonds Are a Girl's Best Friend"
99 Beverage that was a medieval source of nutrition
100 ___ President
101 Literary protagonist raised by wolves
102 "The Sound of Music" household
105 "Horned" creature
107 Turn one's back on
109 Laces (into)
110 Apelike
112 University of Montana city
115 Weasel word?
118 ___ Fielding, co-host of "The Great British Bake Off" beginning in 2017
119 Suffering from a losing streak, in poker slang
122 Secret exits represented five times in this puzzle's grid

125 "Bus Stop" playwright
126 Camping shelter
127 Advocates
128 Romanov ruler
129 Vulnerable
130 Most likely to inspire "thirst"

DOWN

1 Twins, e.g., for short
2 Site with tech tutorials
3 Gets out of a grave situation?
4 Scores for placekickers
5 Mental health org.
6 They're thumped at supermarkets
7 Balls
8 Overly simplistic
9 Bake-off equipment
10 Major-___ (pro ballplayer)
11 OB/GYNs, e.g.
12 Application
13 Royal pain
14 Circus apparatus
15 Laugh or cry, say
16 "Old MacDonald Had a Farm" sounds
17 N.Y.C. retailer with a famed holiday window display
19 Rum ___ Tugger (cat in "Cats")
23 Like a romantic evening stroll, perhaps
28 [someone else's error]
30 Cause chaos
32 —
33 "That's it?"
35 Camping shelter
37 Only person to win an Oscar, Emmy and Tony in the same year (1973)
38 Kitty ___, stunt performer once known as the "fastest woman in the world"

39 Four-limbed animals
40 "Raiders of the Lost Ark" biter
42 Plato's P
43 Halloween decorations that can be made with cotton balls
46 Heavy metal's "Prince of Darkness"
47 "Am ___ only one?"
48 Level
49 Some skin-care products
52 Power up
53 A.L. East squad: Abbr.
57 Slice, for one
58 Give the ___
60 Stopover
62 —
65 —
66 Put on ice
68 Traffic control org.
70 Disco ___ (iconic garment for Lady Gaga)
71 "Chandelier" singer, 2014
73 Longtime record label
74 Annexes
75 Rube Goldberg machines, e.g.
76 Like some vaccines
78 A, in Berlin
80 Incline
81 Expansive work of art, usually
82 Disreputable
84 Annual Austin festival, familiarly
86 "This is too much"
88 One to be dethroned
91 One being coddled, maybe
93 Lacking any adulteration
94 Zing
97 One who may have attachment issues?

by Ross Trudeau

98 Small Nintendo console, once
100 Spring month in France
102 ___ 1, Yuri Gagarin's spacecraft
103 Cries in a tattoo parlor
104 Frothy coffee invented in Greece
105 —
106 Sign of resistance
108 Some bank deposits
110 Foul mood
111 Pelicans' home, informally
113 —
114 Girl in a tartan
116 Miner discoveries
117 Relative of "Hey!"
120 March Madness "trophy"
121 Road goo
123 Maliciously reveal personal info about online
124 "Mais ___!"

ACROSS

1 Goal for many a T.A.
4 There's a Winter one in St. Petersburg and a Summer one in Beijing
10 Confront
16 QVC alternative
19 Grande preceder
20 Many a video game player has one
21 Hebrew name of God
22 Major N.Y.S.E. events
24 Vainglory
25 Good side in 70-Across
27 Reid of "Sharknado"
28 Grade school basics
30 Scoundrel
31 Points all around?
32 Celsius of the Celsius scale
33 Director Nicolas
35 Good cheer
37 People to pick from
38 Major role in 70-Across
41 Smartphone forerunners, in brief
42 "___ kingdom come . . ."
43 Big stretch
44 Bluish-gray shade
46 Mobile ___
48 Time might be shown on the side of one
50 Score of 8, in golf slang
52 Events where one person's trash may be another person's treasure
56 Pull back (in)
59 Capital-B Belief
61 Family name on TV's "Succession"
62 Vote in favor
63 Prefix with futurism
64 Outback offering
65 Locale of the 2002 and 2022 World Cups
67 Long-term damage
68 Some copywriting awards
69 The volcano Emi Koussi is its highest point
70 The better of two major sci-fi film franchises?
72 Climb (up)
73 Gives a bad hand?
74 "But ___ counting?"
75 Gentle hill
76 Grams, by another name
77 Voice heard by 500 million people
78 ___ Majesty
79 Not for moi?
80 Pump choice
82 Spot for a patch, perhaps
83 Begins to like
86 Regular at Citi Field
89 Small spot for a castaway
91 Ian McKellen, e.g.
92 Skin-care brand with an accent over its last letter
94 Mens ___
95 Sends a Telegram, in brief?
97 Not looking good
99 Major role in 70-Across
102 Stop at the liquor store?
103 Comforting phrase
106 Newton of the Black Panther Party
107 "___ Darko" (2001 cult film)
109 Distend
110 Who wrote "April is the cruellest month"
113 Scratch-and-sniff page, e.g.
114 Dramatic accusation
115 Good side in 70-Across
118 Misfortune
119 Cousin of a skimmer
120 ___ One
121 "Do you mind?"
122 Brown of HBO Max's "Gossip Girl" reboot
123 WaPo competitor
124 "There's not much hope"
125 Bumper attachments
126 Sazerac cocktail ingredient

DOWN

1 Records in advance
2 Time for a shootout
3 Memorable quote from 70-Across
4 Apple device
5 Affirms
6 Some college classes
7 "Thanks, but I already ___"
8 Diet Coke doesn't have a single one: Abbr.
9 Wipes out
10 "The Clan of the Cave Bear" heroine
11 What's raised in a ruckus
12 Waste of an election?
13 Confesses
14 Bad thing to be stuck in
15 On-line connection?
16 Arrive at, as a solution
17 Memorable quote from 70-Across
18 "Take your time"
23 Audacious
26 A target for Target, say
29 It might be a shocker
31 "The Simpsons" character
33 Social media star Addison
34 Partner of one
36 French skin-care and cosmetics giant
38 ___ teeth (proverbial rarity)
39 Noble title
40 Follower of black or special
44 Slanders
45 Director Waititi
47 Ones involved in a transaction
49 Nutty confections
51 So-called "Breakfast of Champions"
53 They might end on a high note
54 Sound of a jaguar
55 Let out, in a way
57 Some contents of golf bags
58 Needing to butt out
60 Potato or pea preparer
64 Albert who developed a polio vaccine
66 Leaves in a huff, with "off"
67 Body part that precedes "band"
68 Innocent
69 One of the Prairie provinces: Abbr.
71 "It's a ___!"
72 Show of scorn
74 Question of confusion or disgust

by Stephen McCarthy

79 Sound of a Jaguar
81 Reassuring words
83 "___ Hiring" (business sign)
84 Kind of card
85 The "quail" in Beethoven's "Pastoral" Symphony
87 By plane, say
88 Obvious untruth

90 Q preceder?
93 Aloof
95 "Seems so"
96 Like the inside of a lava cake
98 Devices in atomic clocks
100 Converse, e.g.
101 Rank
102 Common waiting room viewing

104 Jeer
105 Shock treatment, for short
107 Slobber
108 Noises that come from pens
111 "Girls" creator Dunham
112 Carded, informally
113 Tabbouleh go-with
115 "*Enough* already!"

116 Suffix in organic chemistry
117 Quirk

CHANGE OF HEART

Note: The middle letter of the answer to each starred clue can be replaced by a different letter to form two new words across and down. Read the new letters, in order, for a bonus.

ACROSS

1 Bank offerings, in brief
4 Twists
9 Losing roll at dice
13 In itself
19 Piece played with four hands
21 Tart sorbet flavor
22 Kind of bed
23 *Opposite of endearing
24 *Freely expressive
26 Winter eaves dropper
27 Some attacks on castles
29 Día de ___ Muertos (Mexican holiday)
30 Stories that may or may not be true
31 12-year-olds, e.g.
34 Ballerina's bend
35 App whose icon features a camera, in slang
37 Aimee with two Grammys
38 Plank targets
41 Only trisyllabic rainbow color
43 Ferrari of automotive fame
46 *Communicating (with)
49 *Contracting
52 Acceptance principle of improv comedy
53 2-year-old, e.g.
54 What may connect the parts of a school assignment?
55 "Who ___?"
58 Relative of an alpaca
60 "A Christmas Carol" cry
61 Dress in
62 Things people catch and then ride
63 Fifth sign

64 Actress Hepburn
67 Poke
68 Nickname in baseball and gossip columns
69 *Harsh language
71 Up
72 Loses firmness
73 Country with the most archaeological museums in the world (110+)
74 Brand seen at speedways
75 Cut off
76 French menu phrase
77 Sushi chef's eggs
78 Uncle for whom an annual award is supposedly named
80 Not so many
81 When nothing goes right
83 Dutch name starter
85 Frank Robinson or Brooks Robinson of the Baseball Hall of Fame
87 *Watered artificially
89 *Goes well with
94 Turn in a game
95 Canine coat
97 Instant, informally
98 Island with a trisyllabic name
99 Sat around
101 In the thick of
103 Ending remark that's surprising
105 Starting point
108 Suffix with labyrinth
109 Czar known as "the Great"
112 Once called
113 *Noisy disagreement
116 *Ordered

120 Service with a Capitol Corridor route
121 Promote aggressively
122 Without accompaniment
123 Crows
124 Ones in hills or farms
125 Luxury vessel
126 The dark side

DOWN

1 Brains of a tech start-up?
2 Racket
3 Noticeable
4 Roused from a nap
5 Neighbor of Nev.
6 Barely usable pencils
7 ___ sandwich
8 Like some roller coaster drops
9 Task for a crossword constructor
10 Washed quickly
11 Bon ___
12 Instrument used in a medical checkup
13 Out of whack
14 Vessel with a hatch, informally
15 The "teardrop of India"
16 Not exceeding
17 "Dark Lady" hitmaker, 1974
18 ___ Park, N.Y.
20 Christianity's ___ Creed
25 Word with code or card
28 Good witch in Oz
31 "That's enough about your sex life!"
32 Pallid
33 Some have combinations

36 Like J, alphabetically
39 English majors' degs.
40 Having three unequal sides
42 Equal: Prefix
44 Outmoded storage device
45 Witness
47 Some breads
48 Smitten
50 British exclamation
51 One of three for German nouns, or one of four for those in Africa's Zande language
53 Like a tug-of-war rope
55 One may go off in the middle of the night
56 Scientist whose name is associated with a number
57 Wine list section
59 Heavy medieval weapons
60 Robot sound
62 Hot condiment
63 Italian bread that's no longer made
65 Comply with a peace treaty, maybe
66 Some camping excursions
67 "I'm relieved!"
70 H.S. subject
73 "La Tauromaquia" artist
75 Come off as
77 Went ballistic
79 "Easy there!"
80 Small particle
82 Binder inserts with tabs
83 Literally, "revenge"
84 Org. that evaluates toothbrushes
86 Good cheer

by David Steinberg

88 Singer ___ Marie
89 Joins firmly
90 Epoch when palm trees grew in Alaska
91 In an obvious way
92 All-time connector
93 Big ___
96 Plan in detail
100 Puppy "kisses"
102 Rot
104 Ill-suited
105 9-5 automaker, once
106 Muppet who refers to himself in the third person
107 "At Last" singer James
110 Almond ___ (toffee brand)
111 Computer with a Pro model
114 Ship pest
115 H⁺ or I⁻
117 A ticket may be given for a high one: Abbr.
118 Man's name derived from the Bible
119 Man's name derived from the Bible

ACROSS

1 Tobacco plug
5 Manipulate
10 Graduates of Quantico, informally
14 Taller roommate of 15-Down
18 Showgirl in the 1978 hit "Copacabana"
19 Boomer's kid, maybe
20 Declare
21 Snack item with approximately 53 calories
22 Positive thinker's motto?
25 Textbook section
26 FireWire alternative
27 Letter between November and Papa in the NATO alphabet
28 It might be set at sea
29 When a prime-time drama might air
31 Reason-based belief in God
33 Repeated sound that's hard to get rid of
34 Means of becoming a god?
36 "Call the Midwife" network
38 Had something nice
40 Nonsense
41 Place in danger
45 Ernst and Young, e.g.: Abbr.
46 Peroxide ___
47 It's an affront
51 Where Rapunzel let down her hair?
53 Quarrel
54 It matures quickly, in brief
55 Angled to get attention: Abbr.
56 Suffix with serpent or opal

57 Offed
60 Reach quickly, as a conclusion
61 Perhaps
62 Doc. to ensure secrecy
63 It surrounds a pupil
64 United group, e.g.
65 Holy water?
70 Excites
72 "Salus populi suprema lex ___" (motto of Missouri)
73 Charade
74 One of 17 in Monopoly: Abbr.
77 One with pressing work
78 Feed the guests, maybe
79 Dish that's cooked underground
80 Feb. 14
81 673 parts of the Louvre Pyramid
82 "Old man"
83 Answer to "What is Roquefort or Brie?"?
86 Offed
87 Go the wrong way
88 Green-lit
90 Like drunken speech
91 Announcement on National Coming Out Day
93 Inappropriate
95 Early bird?
96 Spilled milk?
100 Front of a semi
102 Ubiquitous advertiser with an acronymic name
106 Seeing as
107 Weight of an empty container
108 What's clothed in summer and naked in winter, per an old riddle

110 China's largest ethnic group
111 What BankAmericard became in 1976
112 The queen with her pets?
116 School where some of "Shakespeare in Love" was filmed
117 Annual Memorial Day race, informally
118 Red Sox' div.
119 Bit of sports equipment that may be electrified
120 Casino tool
121 Philippine money
122 Fleas and flies
123 What's left on a map?

DOWN

1 Obscure
2 Windsor, e.g.
3 A criminal's may be unbelievable
4 "Time ___ . . ."
5 Big name in jelly
6 Like mosaic tiles
7 Lose possession?
8 One of the books of the Torah: Abbr.
9 Where Wagner's "Tannhäuser" was first performed
10 Prima ___
11 Word that becomes more dramatic when you add an "R" in front
12 Caribbean land, at the Olympics
13 Administer an oath to
14 Echoes
15 Shorter roommate of 14-Across
16 Control, metaphorically

17 Completely, in slang
19 Pedal on the right
23 Man of La Mancha
24 Late-night trips to the fridge, e.g.
30 Shirt or blouse
32 Bit of magic
35 Projecting front
37 Temporarily replace
39 Most likely to win at Trivia Night, maybe
41 Long-billed wader
42 Parent company of Facebook
43 Game starter
44 Home for Holmes
48 One who sees what you're saying?
49 Berliner's "old"
50 Sight on winter roads
52 Sign of overuse
53 "All ___!"
54 Prefix that's mega mega?
58 Not merely annoyed
59 Split
60 BuzzFeed staple
64 Wide ties
66 Netflix series set at Green Gables
67 Manipulates
68 Place to go on a ship
69 Them's the breaks!
70 List in "The Idiot's Guide to . . ."
71 Neighbor of Siberia, in Risk
75 Common still-life prop
76 Looked at
78 Architectural columns in the form of sculpted female figures
80 Threshold
82 Gunslinger's command

by Victor Barocas

84 Schools
85 Held tight
87 A narcissist may go on one
88 Shockingly bizarre
89 What the quadriceps muscle connects to
92 N.Y.C. commuting inits.
94 Bugs
96 Where bile is produced
97 Loos who wrote "Gentlemen Prefer Blondes"
98 Casual response to an apology
99 Panasonic subsidiary
101 Orchestra section
103 "If my luck holds out . . ."
104 Pens
105 Beginning
109 Rhinitis treater, in brief
113 Phoenix-to-Albuquerque dir.
114 Bottle labeled "XXX" in the comics
115 "Do the ___" (soft drink slogan)

ACROSS

1 Items used with PINs
9 There's one for the U.S. Census
15 In a tussle
19 Dismiss
20 Takes it one step at a time
21 Pad Thai garnish
22 *Sea captain: robber, thief (2003)*
25 Photographer's tool, for short
26 Unlike this puzzle, we hope
27 Source of suffering
28 They're hoppy at happy hour
32 Quaint lead-in to while
33 All the kings' men?
34 *True fellow is a find (1946)*
40 With room for interpretation
41 Top
42 Game pieces in Mastermind
46 Word after contact or before cover
47 Chill (out)
49 Bit of deception
50 Unfinished attic space
52 *Re: town fire one night (1974)*
56 "Whoopee!"
59 Origin of the words "club" and "gun"
60 It's a lot in London
61 Tip of the tongue?
62 Best-selling crime novelist Gregg
65 Breed featured in 2009's "Hachi: A Dog's Tale"
67 Miff, with "off"
68 One seeking a new agreement, perhaps

70 Ground-breaking tool
73 "Not interested"
75 *Evil Streep had award (2006)*
80 Be a paragon of
81 Guys that rhyme with "girls"
82 Folder attachment
83 The "Y" of Y.S.L.
87 Beams
88 Wallop
89 One of the Roys on "Succession"
91 *M. Ryan, what's her yell? (1989)*
96 They have massive calves
100 "OK!" in Okayama
101 Puts forth
102 Account
103 Protected creature in the Congo Basin
107 Alternatives to tablets
110 *R.E.M.: alarming to the teens (1984)*
115 ___ colada
116 "Louisiana ___," music show that helped launch Elvis's career
117 Fried, filled Filipino fare
118 Part of STEM: Abbr.
119 Angry dog sounds
120 Elf at the North Pole, e.g.

DOWN

1 First courses, informally
2 Drudgery
3 First Black woman to win the Nobel Prize in Literature
4 When doubled, a dance
5 Quick to learn
6 Spawn in the sea

7 "___ thou love life?": Benjamin Franklin
8 Drove (away)
9 ___ Men ("Who Let the Dogs Out" group)
10 One with a password, maybe
11 Document stamp abbr.
12 That: Sp.
13 Blimp, e.g.
14 Humanitarian org. with Halloween fund drives
15 First name in Harry Potter
16 Ranks
17 Would you look at that!
18 Believe in it
20 Onetime dentist's supply
23 Front
24 Company with sound financials?
29 Target with a throw
30 "!!!!!" feeling
31 Crack
33 Held tightly
34 "'Tis an ___ cook that cannot lick his own fingers": "Romeo and Juliet"
35 The third of three X's
36 Opposite of da
37 All ___ (English card game)
38 Release, in a way
39 Soul singer Bridges
42 School for the college-bound
43 Paper slips?
44 Signs in a bookstore, perhaps
45 Encourages
48 Out of the park

49 Each
50 Airborne irritant
51 Chicken . . . or cowed
53 Addicted
54 Broke the finish line ribbon
55 "___ on parle français"
56 Lead-in to day or year
57 Pulmicort targets it
58 Adverb in many legal documents
63 Impose, as a fine
64 ___ Lanka
65 Certain banner fodder
66 Didn't ditch
69 Certain partners' exchanges
70 Brand with an iComfort line
71 Less vibrant
72 Harvard dropouts, maybe?
74 Recurrent space in The Game of Life
76 Depends (on)
77 Break-even situation
78 Aid in putting together a fall collection
79 Drives the getaway car for, say
84 Slangy SoCal dialect
85 Sharp turn
86 Designing
88 Rhea with four Emmys
90 Phone-tracking org.
91 Accompanying
92 Shrubby areas
93 Europe's Three Countries Bridge crosses it
94 Big name in locks

by Sheldon Polonsky

95 Grain variety
96 ___-Nuts
97 World leader who appeared on a Time magazine cover 40 years after his death
98 Sailing through
99 The world's most expensive one, the Gurkha Royal Courtesan, costs over $1.3 million
103 Angry dog's sound
104 Trompe l'___
105 Sticks
106 Some finds in Fortnite
108 Hand over
109 Have the lead (in)
111 Actress Cash of FX's "You're the Worst"
112 Who might bug you?
113 Headwear with a pompom
114 Vaccine molecule

ACROSS

1 "Bon ___!"
8 "See ya later!"
13 It covers more than 30% of the earth's surface
20 Donna ___, member of Bill Clinton's cabinet
21 Klein who wrote the best seller "This Changes Everything: Capitalism vs. the Climate"
22 Desert whose soil has been compared to that of Mars
23 Biting writings
24 Breakfast treat
25 Convinces a customer to pay more
26 "Or so"
27 Much of a delivery person's income
29 Makes a choice
31 Hoppin'
32 Prearranged
33 Suffix with official
34 Nickel found in a pocket, say
35 Actor Barinholtz of "The Mindy Project"
36 Classic Camaro
38 ___ K. Smith, poet who won a Pulitzer for "Life on Mars"
40 Cosmetic that can be applied with a brush
42 Neighbors of exclamation marks
43 "La Dolce ___"
45 Stuffed one's face
47 Bump on a frog
49 Question regarding a mic
51 Hubbub
52 One of the Blues Brothers

55 Above criticism
56 Question from the befuddled
57 Syrian city with a historic citadel
58 What "10" can mean
60 Extra
62 Rolled one's r's, say
63 Linguistic unit
64 Giraffe's closest living relative
65 Deb ___, secretary of the interior starting in 2021
66 Opposite of 'neath
67 Regarding
69 Exams for some future clerks: Abbr.
71 Cold open?
72 Hang out on a line
73 U.K. award bestowed by the king
74 West Coast news inits.
75 Blunder
76 They cast lots
78 "Love covers a multitude of ___": I Peter 4:8
79 Lawn material
82 Something's essential aspect . . . or what's spelled out by letters in this puzzle's eight "cups"
87 Comedian Margaret
90 2011 film for which Octavia Spencer won a Best Supporting Actress Oscar
92 It takes blades to blades
93 Deal
95 Like the consonants "t" and "d"
97 Eject forcefully

98 Records request inits.
99 ___ history
101 Utah's state flower
102 Org. that sets permissible exposure limits
103 Karaoke instruction . . . or what to do starting at 10-Down
109 P.R. consultant on "Ted Lasso"
110 Start playing for pay
111 Into really small pieces
112 Scott who sued for his freedom
113 Afford, casually
114 Add salt to, say

DOWN

1 Home of St. Clare
2 Starfleet weapon
3 Election night calculation . . . or what's traced by the circled letters
4 Name that's 6-Down backward
5 Save it for a rainy day!
6 La Corse, par exemple
7 Brewery employee
8 Comb through
9 Bubs
10 Worker's "on vacation" inits.
11 "Actually, I disagree"
12 Rococo painter of "Allegory of the Planets and Continents"
13 They might be pregnant
14 Organic energy compound, for short
15 "Mi ___ es su ___"

16 Part of a cold compress
17 Become clear . . . or make like the object represented by the circled letters
18 "So then my response was . . ."
19 Hereditary divisions
28 Physicist Newton
30 Loyalty that's pledged
37 Lemonlike fruit
38 Big rigs
39 "Well, fine then"
40 Age beautifully, informally
41 Cuss out
42 Big Brother's creator
44 Pink pad on a paw, in slang
46 The Lord, in the Hebrew Bible
48 Start of a simple request
49 Roly-poly, scientifically
50 ___ torte (Austrian cake)
53 Warm-up act
54 Move shakily
59 Ross Perot founded it in 1995
60 Lack of engagement
61 More wacky
62 "You're just assuming"
68 It's blown in the winds
70 Showed off one's pipes
77 Airport with a Harvey Milk terminal: Abbr.
78 Harry Styles tune about a woman who "lives in daydreams"
79 Lines of notes

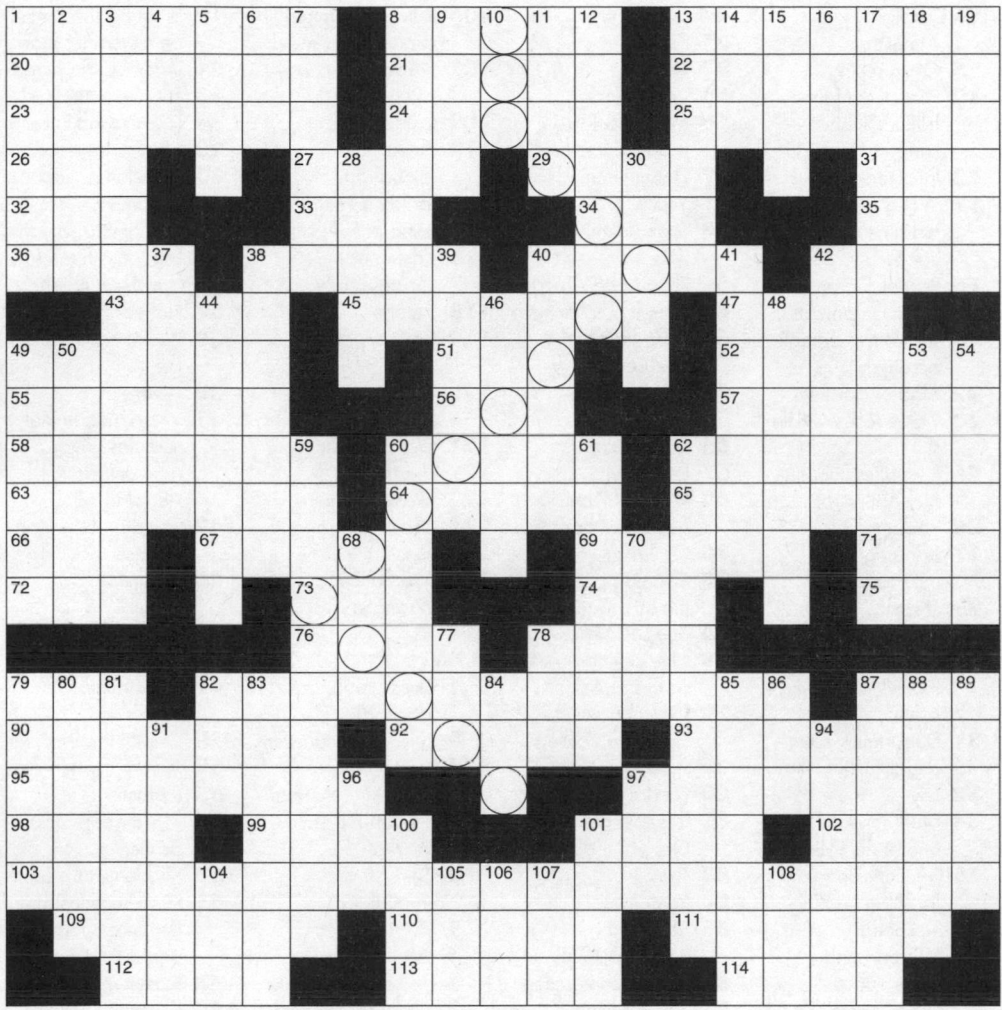

by Matthew Stock and Will Nediger

ACROSS

1 Almost
5 Oven setting
10 Portrayer of the boxer Clubber Lang in "Rocky III"
13 In case
17 When repeated, old-time call to listen
18 Part of a prank
20 Govt. organization with a two-syllable acronym
22 Kind of clarinet
23 Came to know, old-style
24 It empties into the Bay of Bengal
26 Radar spot
27 Bringing in, as income
29 "Keen!"
30 With 12-Down, spend much more than a fair price
31 Department store department
32 Lay __ to
34 Question that's not one of the five W's
35 Big consideration for the expecting
37 Ticket fig.
40 Wisteria and honeysuckle
42 Video game character in a hit 2020 film
43 Educator/writer __ Johnson McDougald, first African American female principal in New York City public schools
45 Belief of roughly 25% of the world's population
46 Director Craven

47 Downstairs
51 Kept in
53 Lets out
55 Vape's lack
56 Martini & Rossi product, familiarly
57 Emmy-winning Ward
58 Took down, in a way
59 Fly around Africa
62 Doughy dinner item
64 Drug agent's seizure
65 Deseret News reader, typically
66 Did nothing
67 Professor __
69 With 74-Across, gesture of approval
70 On fire
73 Chomping at the bit
74 See 69-Across
78 One cutting down, so to speak
79 What babies do faster than college students
80 Feudal land
81 O's, but not P's or Q's
83 Petty
84 Some posers
86 Self-titled rock album of 1958
88 Quaint contraction
91 Smoking spot, for short?
92 Former baseball commissioner Bud
93 Sound, e.g.
94 Moves like muck
96 I.T. help center, often
98 Ending with bear or bull
99 "Uncle!"
101 Rocker Rose
102 Heard in court
104 Promotion

105 Letters that might change your mind?
107 Prepare, in a way, as eggs
109 Irritable
112 En voz __ (aloud: Sp.)
113 Insincere, as a remark
116 Kristen of "Bridesmaids"
118 Jaunty
119 Counterpart of "adios"
120 "Yes" or "No" follower
121 Old Icelandic work
122 Fivers
123 Idiosyncrasy
124 Greek performance venue
125 Alternative to Wranglers

DOWN

1 Blues group, for short?
2 Fully ready to listen
3 Loretta who sang "You Ain't Woman Enough (To Take My Man)"
4 Cold climate cryptids
5 "The __ they are . . ."
6 Messenger __
7 Walk around at a rest stop, say
8 "Bus Stop" playwright
9 Be in store
10 "Who, me?"
11 Invitation letters
12 See 30-Across
13 Subjects of some tests
14 Actress Burstyn
15 What some insects and insults can do
16 Primo

19 Bit of bad weather, on a weather map
21 Indo-__ languages
25 They're numbered in Microsoft Excel
28 More agreeable
33 Theodor __ a.k.a. Dr. Seuss
36 Will Smith/Tommy Lee Jones film franchise, for short
37 Flat-earther?
38 Like many a stuffed toy
39 Aware of
41 Word that, fittingly, contains all four different letters of APPEAL
42 Question following a clever trick
44 Shows scorn toward
46 Take by force
48 Wood strip
49 Peak in the "Odyssey"
50 One of the five W's
52 Arcane matters
53 Panache
54 Leave gobsmacked
58 Scatter
60 Sudden sharp pain
61 Have seconds and thirds and fourths and . . .
63 Flatten
64 Lilies with bell-shaped flowers
68 Rachel Zegler's role in 2021's "West Side Story"
70 Allow entry
71 Forehead mark on Hindu women
72 City SW of York
75 Safe bettor
76 Instruments with endpins
77 Some sources of leafy greens

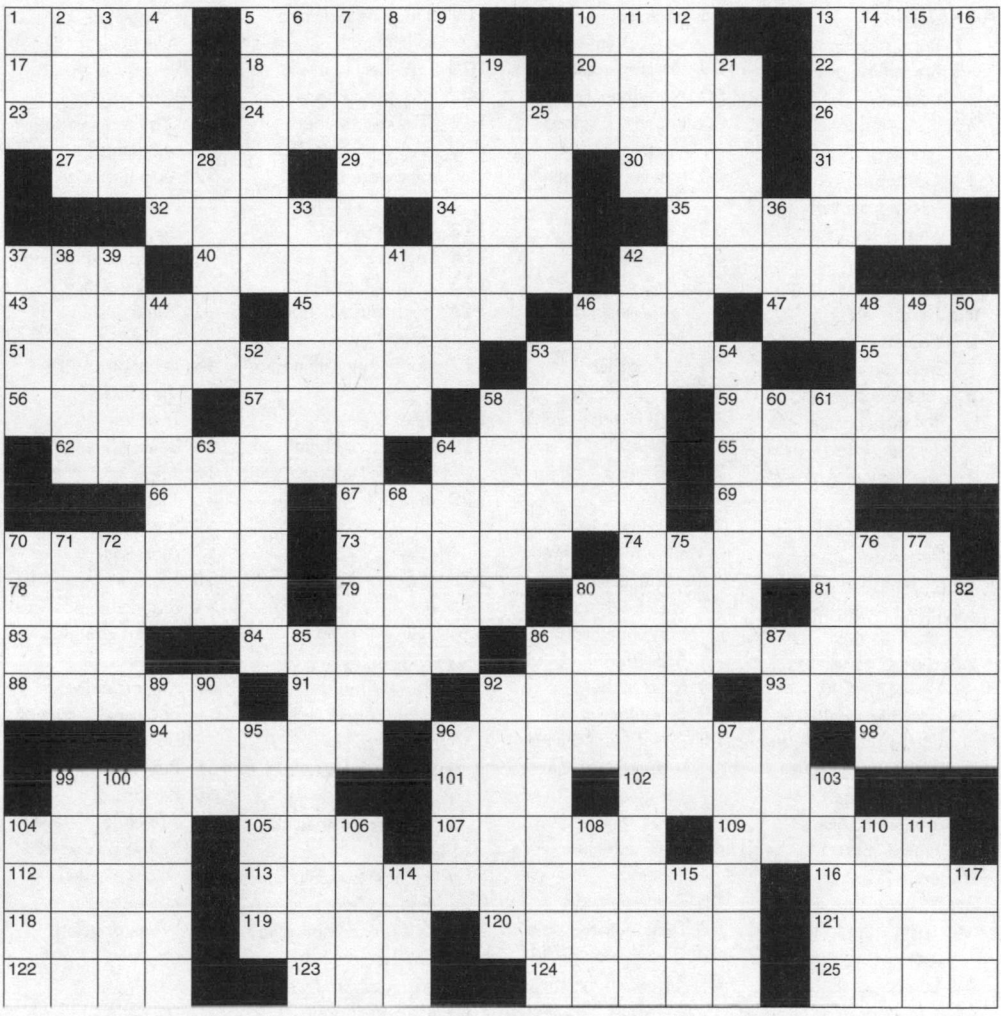

by Christina Iverson and Katie Hale

ACROSS

1 Band of supporters
5 Something absolutely necessary
10 "___ and Janis" (comic strip)
14 Oomph
17 Word from the French for "high wood"
18 Washed out
20 Dock
21 Something a winner may run into
22 "It's tough finding the right person. My first boyfriend was a perfectly nice atheist, but he . . ."
24 Tour de France seasons
25 Side dish at a fish fry
26 Main component of Saturn's rings
27 Lena of "Enemies, a Love Story"
28 "So then I dated a fun couch potato, but he . . ."
31 Non-starters?
33 Toeing the line
34 Fútbol cheer
35 Italian wine region
36 "30 for 30" airer
39 The 1 in {1,2,3}: Abbr.
40 Lab vessel
42 Camphor, e.g.
45 One getting depressed during exams?
47 They're found near traps
48 "Then my friend set me up with a recluse, but he . . ."
52 Comedian Mort
54 Classic Hawaiian folk song
55 Superman and others, for short
56 Book with a notable world premiere?
59 What middlemen do
60 Noisy beachgoer
62 Bun in a bamboo steamer
63 Internet encryption inits.
65 Binary
66 "I dated my rock climbing instructor for a while, but he just . . ."
68 ___-Pacific
69 Not sparkling
71 Blast furnace supply
72 Baloney
73 Bad signs for a bank robber
75 Academic journal with a "Breakthrough of the Year" award
77 U.K. track star-turned-politician Sebastian
78 Mishmashes
79 Swindled
80 "Then I had a fling with a Pittsburgh Penguin, but I knew he . . ."
83 Cuisine featuring som tam
86 Drill command
88 Feel another's pain
89 Cavalryman of old
91 Big ___ (Olympic snowboarding event)
92 Whimper
93 Starters, for short
97 Outback speedster
98 Keep rhythm, as a conductor might
101 Wisconsin town with a clothing namesake
104 "I was in a serious relationship with a hippie, but he . . ."
106 Org. issuing vaccine standards starting in 2021
107 It may be part of a solution
108 Together, in music
109 Fading sea name
110 "Finally, I started seeing a charming magician, and he . . ."
113 Pan, in part
114 Fun-size
115 Kind of thesis
116 Weekend warrior's woe
117 Happening offline, to a texter
118 Relaxation
119 Devotee of Haile Selassie, informally
120 Bit of kitchen waste

DOWN

1 Big name in pricey cigars
2 You can't say it doesn't count
3 Lizzie is one, in the "Cars" movies
4 Crossword solving option
5 Watch maker since 2015
6 It lands on the White House's South Lawn
7 ___ Bator, Mongolia
8 On the ___
9 Fastened, in a way
10 Making change
11 Well past the freshness date, say
12 "My Fair Lady" composer
13 Actor/comedian who was a regular on Johnny Carson's "Tonight Show"
14 Meathead
15 Military uniform feature
16 Bluish-gray shades
19 Scintilla
21 "Shameful!"
23 Alley-___
29 Possessive types?
30 Way to go: Abbr.
32 "You're so wrong about that!"
37 Lead-in to Cat
38 Something that all but three U.S. presidents have had while in office
41 "Time out" in the N.B.A.
43 What makes the short list?
44 Total jerk
45 Boxing highlight
46 Apply to
48 Jokesters
49 Some native Alaskans
50 Tile work
51 Leadership position
53 Bit of a chuckle
56 Rubberneck
57 "A house divided against ___ cannot stand"
58 Rubylike gem
60 Richard of "Chicago"
61 Native people for whom a state is named
62 When doubled, a candy
64 Quick with a clapback
66 So-called "Father of Liberalism"
67 Conflict taking a couple of seconds?
70 Soccer star Messi, to fans
73 Capital of Fiji
74 "How ___ Your Mother"
76 Beloved site for the Irish . . . and French

by Brad Wiegmann

77 Journalist who was the first woman to guest-host "Jeopardy!"
78 Hard stuff that jiggles
80 "We'll be in touch!," often
81 Dr. of 112-Down
82 Counterpart of full, in a way
83 Wise guys?
84 One might be smoke-filled
85 Not surprisingly
87 Big name in hot dogs
90 Face on a penny, familiarly
92 Strong suit
94 Regulate
95 Cupid's love
96 Mideast currency unit
99 Features of some halls
100 Mucky substances
102 Twin sister of He-Man
103 What, in multiple senses, might get tipped
105 Take place?
106 Redding who wrote "Respect"
111 Crispr material
112 See 81-Down

35 I'M STILL STANDING

ACROSS

1 Swears (to)
8 L.A. region
13 Motto meaning "to the stars"
20 Place with carts
21 Square
22 What oil may do in frigid temperatures
23 1990s–2000s Volkswagen seven-seater
24 Things
25 Overseas land measure
26 Not needing a thing
27 "___ homo"
29 Siri uses it
30 Halliwell a.k.a. Ginger Spice
31 Dino friend of Buzz Lightyear
32 "___ it ironic?"
34 Storm
37 What an up arrow might mean
39 Green-light
41 Approximately 5.5 million tons of it was used to build [see circled letters]
43 Bellini opera that takes place in Gaul
46 A=B, B=C, ergo A=C, e.g.
48 Purchase plan
50 Sneaker, in British lingo
51 See 5-Down
55 Committed to memory
56 Western Hemisphere grp.
57 Gunslinger's cry
59 Former Japanese P.M. Shinzo ___
60 Country between Ghana and Benin
61 Word repeatedly said while plucking petals
62 Clipped
63 Opposing vote from a horse?
64 Blue ribbon or gold star
66 Yarn
68 Make secret, in a way
71 A chance to dream
74 It's often played for
75 Website with an "Everything Else" category
76 Some small batteries
78 C sharp equivalent
80 Mexican poet Juana ___ de la Cruz
81 Sass
82 U.F.C. fighting style
83 Radio host John
84 Head, in slang
85 Play group
87 Frequent victim of an April fool
90 Creep
93 Municipal facility: Abbr.
94 Kind of bar
96 Waterfall feature
98 One forced into a force
100 One-act Oscar Wilde play
101 Burial ___
103 Fútbol cry
104 "You no-good dog," e.g.
105 Spoils
106 ___ bean
108 Some December purchases
109 They're stored in pollen grains
111 Villainous "Star Trek" collective
113 Like some chicken cutlets
116 Element named after a German river
120 "Ugh!"
121 Prehistoric Southwest culture
122 Little squirt
123 Sign of success
124 Trendy
125 Vardalos of "My Big Fat Greek Wedding"

DOWN

1 Periods in history
2 Level
3 They wrap things up
4 Prefix with system
5 With 51-Across and 15-Down, group in which [see circled letters] is the only one still largely intact
6 Egyptian desert, e.g.
7 Harmonize
8 ___ generis (unique)
9 Prompt
10 Greek name for this puzzle's enclosed answer
11 Targets
12 Sleeve fillers
13 Not just smart
14 Active sorts
15 See 5-Down
16 Pepper's rank: Abbr.
17 High-arcing shots, in basketball lingo
18 Like a T206 Honus Wagner baseball card
19 Lion in the "Madagascar" movies
28 Most massive dwarf planet in the solar system
30 Pass it on
33 Singers' star turns
35 Contents of some belts, informally
36 Reason for an R rating
38 It comes before one
39 Regarding
40 Harp-shaped constellation
41 Turkish money
42 Provide resources for
44 [Big kiss, dahling!]
45 Pay (up)
47 ___ and the Pacemakers (1960s pop group)
49 They reflected rank in old Rome
52 "Ooh-la-la!"
53 It gives you a lift
54 2003 #1 Outkast hit
58 Tad
60 Mat made of soft rush
62 You might take them out for a spin
65 Artful
66 Mujeres con esposos
67 Outdoor game for kindergartners
69 Time out?
70 "The Office" role played by Jenna Fischer
72 College voter, perhaps
73 Light shades
74 With 101-Across, where this puzzle's enclosed answer is located
75 Disney's ___ of Arendelle
77 Smooth, in a way
79 Number of 101-Acrosses in [see circled letters]
85 Workmates, e.g.
86 Pale ___
87 Tiffs
88 Sleeve filler
89 Brewer Frederick
91 ___-Magnon
92 Like a book with a bookmark in the middle, say
95 Chewy confection
96 Oxford, e.g.

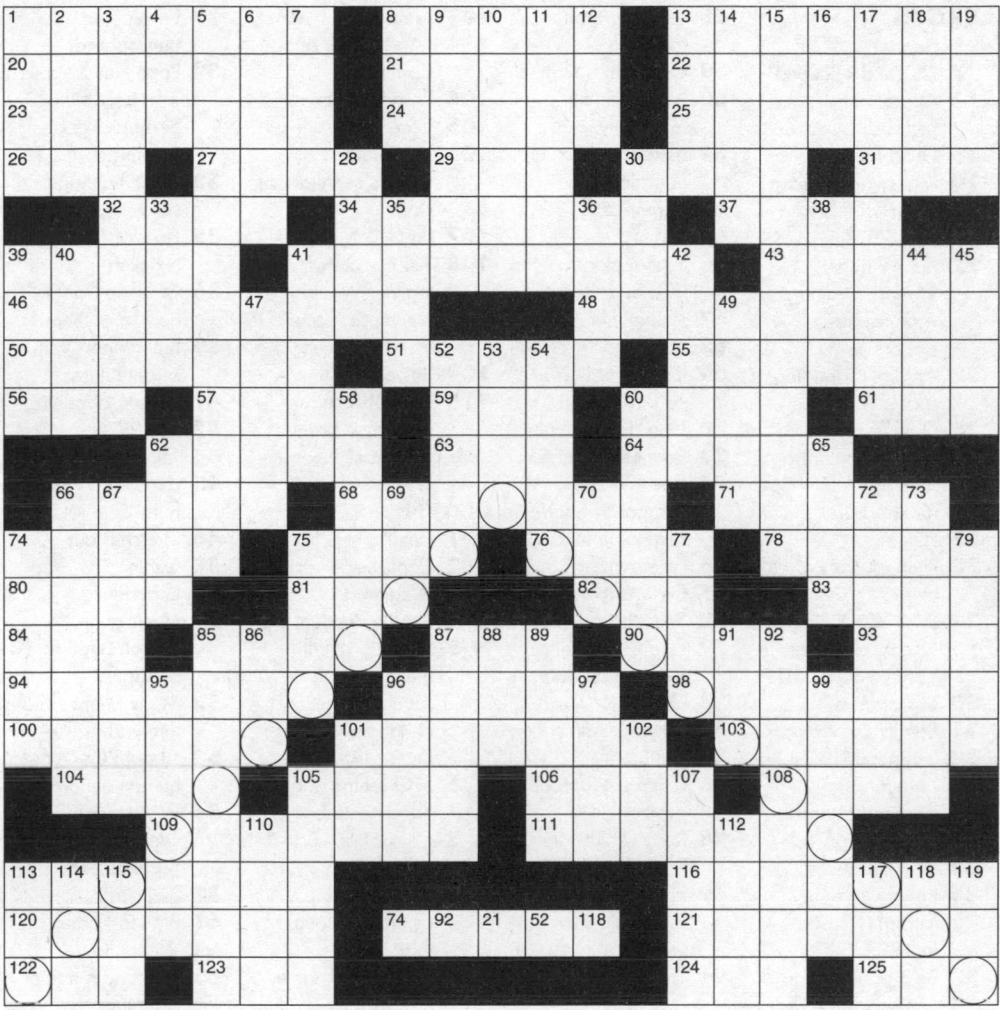

by August Lee-Kovach

ACROSS

1 Hearten
7 ". . . and it flopped"
11 Attack with snowballs, say
15 Graceful bird
19 Crossword header
20 Clearer in hindsight?
22 ___ Winans, 15-time Grammy-winning gospel singer
23 Apollo 11 landing spot
25 Eligible receiver?
26 Quickly maturing security, for short
27 Helps
28 Flying terrors of myth
29 With 42-Down, Oscars category from 1963 to 2019
30 Misfortunes
31 Semicircular recess
32 Items used by barkeepers, barbecuers and blacksmiths
34 Wackadoodle
35 Enhanced tape format released in 1987
37 Beat poet Cassady
38 Spewed forcefully
40 Take off the board
43 À la ___ (spit-roasted)
47 Spree
48 Black-___ albatross
49 Knee-jerk response
50 Remove cargo from
53 Describing the 32-Down's image
55 Milk source
56 Impends
57 Inscribed with some ancient characters

58 Whirling toon, familiarly
59 Order, in a way
60 Nonfiction films, informally
61 Metaphor from an hourglass
64 "Come ___!"
65 This: Sp.
66 Sitcom planet of the '70s and '80s
67 Animal life
68 Pondered
69 It's probably over your head
70 One star, typically
73 Relentless go-getters
74 Carl XVI ___ (king of Sweden beginning in 1973)
76 Little bump
77 Eve's third son
78 Soccer chant
79 ___ 3000, half of the hip-hop duo Outkast
80 Persuade with patter
84 A majority
86 Offensive football positions
88 Ruby of "The Jackie Robinson Story"
89 Edgar Rice Burroughs novel, with "The"
94 Talk Like a Pirate Day outbursts
95 Dormer section
96 Turn aside
97 Actress Amanda
98 Taking a bow at the symphony?
99 Waif
100 "A warehouse of facts, with poet and ___ in joint ownership" ("The Devil's Dictionary" definition for "imagination")

101 Its motto is "Agriculture and Commerce"
104 Opposite of exo-
105 Woe for a speeder
106 ___ Blinken, Biden's secretary of state
107 Bit of "kit chat"
108 1974 spoof with the tagline "Would you buy a used secret from these men?"
109 Bits of machinery
110 Latin phrase meaning "based on forecasts"

DOWN

1 Having legs
2 Cool shade
3 Weakness
4 Sledge, wedge, etc.
5 Sports org. with the Pittsburgh Maulers and Philadelphia Stars
6 SFO setting: Abbr.
7 Sang hosannas to
8 Car part the Brits call a "wing"
9 Heading for commonly sought info
10 Capote nickname
11 ___ light
12 Sweeping works
13 Reveals
14 Don't give up
15 Intellectual movement
16 Tyke
17 Performing well on
18 Candy with two flavors in one box
21 Flexible cutters
24 Kid Cudi or Lil Baby, e.g.
29 Fixed look

31 Enveloping atmospheres
32 Pope Pius XII called it "a holy thing perhaps like nothing else"
33 Odor-fighting spray brand
35 Parts of some brackets
36 "Yankee Doodle" has 16 of them
39 Entertainers with bright futures
41 Partner of poivre
42 See 29-Across
44 Juice regimen
45 Like épées vis-à-vis foils
46 Stretches out
48 Curve
50 Experience
51 Music genre for Erykah Badu and D'Angelo
52 Many people find it intolerable
53 About 98% of the human genome
54 Word meaning "desire" in a classic Sanskrit text
57 ___ avis
61 Big tear-jerker
62 Went under
63 Word with fine or signature
68 Hands, in slang
71 1980s White House nickname
72 Dilute something, in a way
73 Battery parts?
75 Up in the air
77 Maker of the Ring in "The Lord of the Rings"
80 Surgical instrument with thumbholes

by Byron Walden

81 Joy who wrote "Born Free"
82 Forgiving
83 Talent for discernment
85 Mic check noise
87 Cattle ranch identifier
89 "The Crucible" setting
90 Sheepish?
91 "Swell!"
92 "I can do this. Hit me"
93 Some 10-pointers in Greek Scrabble
95 Dish made from durum, say
98 Prefix with futurism
99 Kids of boomers
101 Grads-to-be: Abbr.
102 Not prescription, in brief
103 Scottish negative

ACROSS

1 Trace
5 Cheap
11 Gobble (down)
16 Shepherd's charge
19 1930s film canine
20 Faith, Hope or Charity
21 Land on the Yellow Sea
22 Radio knob: Abbr.
23 Suffix with phosphor
24 Bicycle mechanic?
26 Goddess whom Homer called "rosy-fingered"
27 Music genre
28 Dimwit's brain size
29 Have control of
30 Actress Beulah
32 Obstetrician?
39 Paw
41 Woman, to a waiter
42 Belts a line drive
43 Bits
44 About 10% of New Zealanders
46 "Cats" monogram
47 Econ. indicator
49 Getaway driver?
54 Sailing
55 Hardened
56 Had control of
57 Chinese port also called Xiamen
58 Likelier to win a baby contest
59 Lost traction
61 It's often masked

62 Spade portrayer
63 Dry cleaner?
68 Announcement inside the front door
70 Wrinkled, maybe
71 Site of many tie-ups
72 Slick
73 Took advantage of
74 1990s pact
77 Bond yield: Abbr.
80 Der ___ Fritz (Friedrich the Great)
81 Usher?
85 Came together
86 Tai ___
88 Lodge with a mud roof
89 Defunct women's magazine
90 Early progress
93 Prefix with phobia
94 Minuscule
95 Urologist?
99 Like wine barrels
100 Tre + tre
101 Something that's picked
102 Hitchhike
105 Humans and apes, e.g.
106 Electrical inspector?
112 Security procedure
113 Brian of the original Roxy Music
114 Accident cause
115 One with a flag
116 "___ you not"

117 Colo. Springs-to-Santa Fe direction
118 Rodeo tie
119 Halloween bagful
120 Wall St. initials

DOWN

1 Stray
2 Analogy part
3 Not yet done
4 Prepare for camp, say
5 Tube plug
6 Closer to its prime
7 Loud, as a crowd
8 Corp. shares
9 Peach or plum
10 "I do" preceder
11 Orients a certain way
12 Tree
13 MGM motto start
14 Automotive pioneer's initials
15 Support group?
16 Venus, e.g.
17 Furniture cover
18 Old comic actress ___ Janis
25 Work with feet
31 Western Indian
33 Shindig
34 Not hold back
35 Prepared, as pears
36 Parade stopper
37 ___ Gritty Dirt Band
38 Festoons a tree with bathroom rolls, briefly
39 Stored computer images, for short
40 Goal of a tryout

44 "All in the Family" spinoff
45 U.S./Eur. link
48 I or II, e.g.
50 Tired
51 MoMA display
52 Love figure
53 Swed. neighbor
54 Boring article
58 Blast furnace fuel
59 None-too-subtle encouragement
60 Lawn additive
61 80-Across, in English
62 Pipe type
63 "You're asking me?"
64 Purse filler
65 Kind of arch
66 Mother of Castor and Pollux
67 Sign up for an offering
68 Vidi, translated
69 Teams in the West
73 Practical
74 Some Dodges
75 Trade talk
76 R.D.A. label requirer
77 Warning to a puzzle doer
78 Film ___
79 Part of a low straight
82 Friend's addressee, maybe
83 Q.E.D. part
84 Doesn't do just an outline of
86 Pulpit's locale
87 In

by Patrick Merrell

91 1965 #1 hit "___ of Destruction"
92 Hustling places
93 1983 Super Bowl designation
94 Host holders
95 Dawdlers
96 Prefix with transmission
97 Home to over a billion
98 1962 Jackie Gleason movie
103 Roaster's spot
104 "The NeverEnding Story" writer
107 U.K. foe
108 Monopoly props.
109 It can make molehills out of mountains
110 Bump
111 Shoshonean

ACROSS

1 Satirist Mort
5 Company store exchange
10 La ___, Calif.
15 1960s–'70s Pontiacs
19 Plant with spiny-edged leaves
20 Pass over
21 Civil War side, with "the"
22 Go on and on
23 Part of an M.D.'s sched.
24 Reason to call the exterminator?
26 Fencing piece
27 Extend a college athlete's eligibility
29 90-Down college town
30 Former Michigan/ Indiana tribe
32 Actress Massey
33 Car in a Beach Boys song
34 Ski trail
35 They may be taken in an emergency
37 Combine
38 Pavements
41 Buccaneer's locale
42 Haberdashery robberies?
45 Stuffy-sounding
46 Blood classification system
47 Handled
49 Dealer's foe
50 Zap

51 "___ Lisa Smile" (2003 film)
53 Clean fish?
56 Criticize severely
57 Footwork?
59 Revolting ones
60 Away
63 Popular rejoinders
64 Tolerate
66 F.B.I. operative
67 Hair ointment
70 Singer India.___
71 Problem
75 South American tuber
76 Directive to a masseur at a Jewish spa?
80 It's pushed in Kensington Gardens
81 "Shane" star
83 Card
84 Rig owners
86 "Dee-lish!"
87 Latin name for ancient Troy
89 Limited, as some 1960s military service?
91 Accord
93 Like many beachgoers
95 "Daniel Boone" actor
96 Ammonia derivatives
97 Barbaric
98 Elite
100 Injured
101 Unoriginal argument
103 103-Down appendage

104 Accumulates
107 Have ___ for
108 Swindle at Ben & Jerry's?
111 Very
112 Judges' seat
113 Bridge expert
114 "___ Got a Friend"
115 Colleague of Kent
116 Leader's name that's etymologically related to "chess"
117 Accord maker
118 Allied
119 Latin 101 word

DOWN

1 German/French river
2 Peak near Neuchâtel
3 Jewel at a 50s dance?
4 Revealed
5 European finches
6 Noted Barton
7 "Hud" director
8 ___ Amin
9 90-Down tribe
10 Case worker?
11 Standing
12 10th–12th century dynasty
13 Article in El Diario
14 Weak
15 Rather, to some?
16 Pint of water, say?
17 R.E.M.'s "The ___ Love"
18 Rel. figures
25 One hawking
28 Parts of el día

31 "No man ___ island"
33 All together, musically
34 Washington city on the Columbia
35 Approval sign
36 Something to avoid
37 Kind of pack
38 Cougars or Bobcats, slangily
39 "___ Whoopee!" (1920s hit)
40 Was out
42 Considers, as testimony
43 "The Lady ___"
44 "I'll think about it"
48 Job antecedent
52 John/Rice musical
54 The Little Mermaid
55 Hurt
58 I.R.S. agent: Abbr.
61 Scolding word to a dog
62 Hike
64 About 1% of the Earth's atmosphere
65 Life of a region
66 Infected
67 Greek city-state
68 City west of Daytona Beach
69 Like an angry Mao Zedong?
70 In ___ (stuck)
71 ___ Angels
72 Crocodile tears?
73 Like some cuisine
74 TV prizes
77 An archangel
78 Sentencing times
79 I.Q. test pioneer

by Alan Arbesfeld

82 Western enterprise that goes bankrupt?
85 Belgian city or province
88 Art Spiegelman best seller
90 See 29-Across or 9-Down
92 Long Island town
94 University in Bethlehem
96 Made reparations
98 Curving
99 Actress Luft
100 Kettle's place
101 Barbecue fare
102 Greenland base for many polar expeditions
103 See 103-Across
104 Gulf War missile
105 Annapolis inst.
106 Pound, e.g.
109 Bill's partner
110 Reply of mock aggrievement

ACROSS

1 Nixon's law alma mater
5 Jinx in reverse
10 Artist Chagall
14 Fit
18 Convenient apartment
19 Plantain lily
20 Flea market find
21 Target
22 Good for a wage earner, bad for a tightrope walker
25 Tree in a Christmas carol
26 Tsk about
27 Well in hand
28 1958 #1 song
30 Bit of effrontery
31 Withdraw
33 Tantrum thrower, maybe
34 Eric Clapton's "Layla" alias
35 Lander at Ben Gurion
37 Mark for life
39 Good for a wish maker, bad for a Hollywood agent
43 Tame brew
45 Sets up
47 Bounces
48 Sopranos' home
49 Some party members, for short
51 N.Y.S.E. debut
52 Social reformer Jacob
53 Verve
54 Good for an attorney, bad for a Spandex model
58 Alpaca and cashmere
59 Singer's filler
62 Staff leader
63 "The possession of fools": Herodotus
64 It's done in the form of an S or a Z
65 Endorser, sometimes
67 Common classroom sight
68 Toiletry
69 Less-than-Ruthian hits
70 Separator
71 Monk's garb
72 1960s White House pooch
73 Reins in
74 Good for a magazine writer, bad for a couch potato
77 Aware of
78 Ward of "Once and Again"
79 Prof.'s helpers
80 Small amounts
83 Org. for 1- and 101-Across
84 BMW rival
85 Like some colors
88 "Our Gang" girl
90 Good for a doctoral student, bad for a crime suspect
93 Prayer start
95 Suffix on era names
96 Clarinet paraphernalia
97 Scraps
99 News source
101 Thos. Jefferson's school
102 Mysterious
104 Quick-witted
106 Dumped
108 Music from the Miracles, e.g.
109 Good for a returning traveler, bad for a bridge player
112 Shadow
113 Some beans
114 Show protectiveness
115 "Beg pardon . . ."
116 Chichi
117 Protomatter of the universe
118 Wrangles
119 Fabricated

DOWN

1 Drew aimlessly
2 Bared
3 Stay (with)
4 Benjamin Disraeli, e.g.
5 Kind of line
6 Advantage in hockey
7 Venom source
8 Ways: Abbr.
9 Like lions
10 Joint
11 Not give ___ (not care)
12 Ipanema locale
13 Brings together
14 Snacks for Dorothy on the Yellow Brick Road
15 Good for a scientist, bad for a roofer
16 Cordelia's father
17 Brontë heroine
20 Atelier item
23 42-Down, to Pierre
24 Fleet
29 Some website owners: Abbr.
32 Duty
34 Whistler's tune?
36 Many a roast
38 Seized vehicle
40 "Mule Train" singer, 1949
41 Chisholm Trail stop
42 Chanticleer
44 Medical tool
46 Sonnet component
50 Alluvia
52 Fair attraction
53 Rock singer in social causes
55 Ample shoe width
56 Hoard
57 Symbol on an old quarter
58 1971 hit movie based on the novel "Ratman's Notebooks"
59 Experimental attire?
60 Temporarily out of the office
61 Good for a mail carrier, bad for an electrician
64 Did yard work
66 Gray wolf
67 Gershon of film
68 I or II N.T. book
70 Baseball honcho
71 "Strangers and Brothers" novelist
74 Turns over
75 Spinnaker
76 Porfirio ___, president of Mexico, 1884–1911

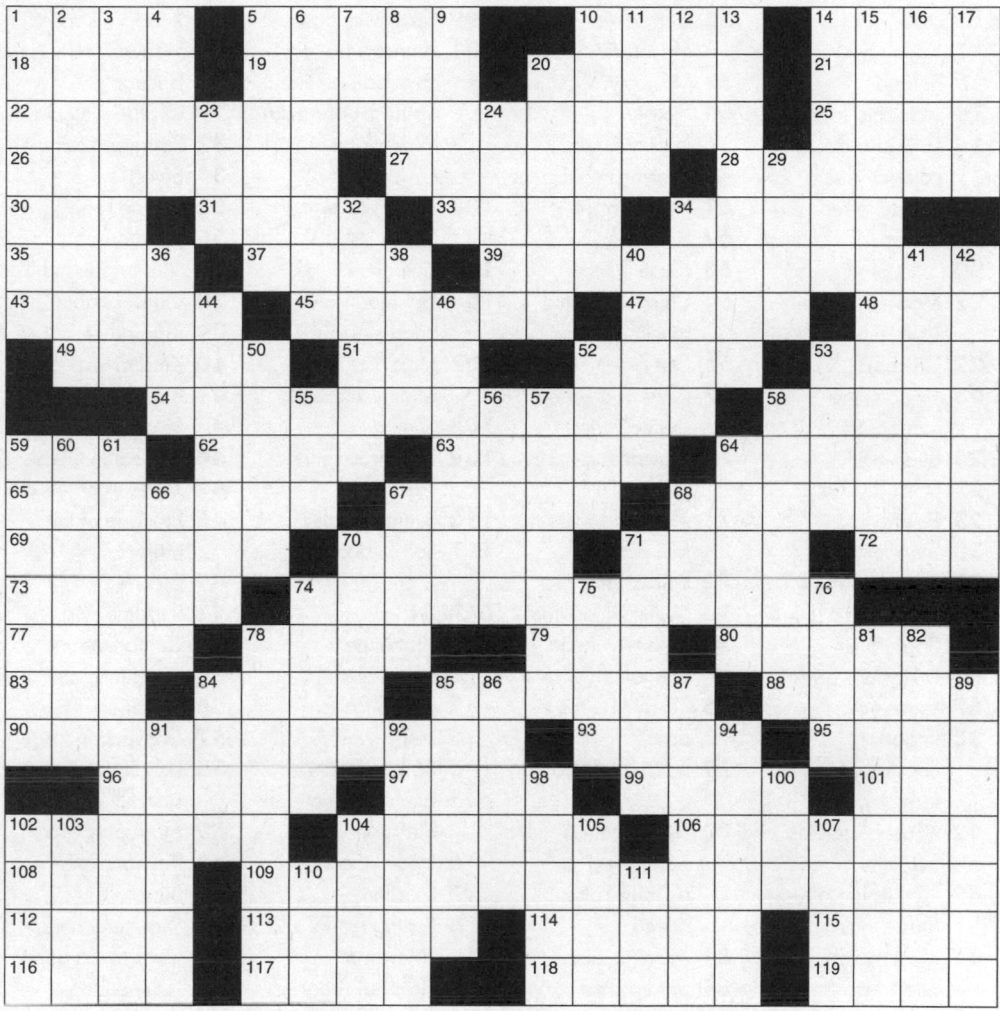

by Arlan and Linda Bushman

78 By surprise
81 Ruckus
82 Like almonds in many recipes
84 Port on a gulf of the same name
85 Wheel maker
86 Give a hint
87 Bowl figure
89 Halls of learning
91 "For sure?"
92 Pre-Bill Hillary
94 Salon devices
98 They're often heaved
100 End-of-sentence abbr.
102 Fictional terrier
103 Din
104 "Don't look ___!"
105 Sporty car feature
107 Soup or sandwich ingredient
110 Shale extract
111 Things laid by a gallina

ACROSS

1 Kid's name
6 Behind
10 Montana tribe
14 Half of a classic comedy duo
19 Ready to be drawn
20 ___ point (never)
21 Monster-sighting spot
22 Car bars
23 "Moon River" composer
25 Bite site?
27 Daring deed
28 Fleece
30 Staggered
31 Threatening sign
32 Looks to the future
33 Shoot a ray
34 Dragster's pride
37 Comes close
38 Important constituent of igneous rocks
42 "Casablanca" actor
43 "Casablanca" music maker
44 Blockbuster offering
45 Pint in a pub
46 "Gotcha"
47 The Joker and Batman, e.g.
49 Bounce
50 Allegiance
51 Mario ___ of the N.B.A.
52 Medical research grp.
53 One who says "one club," e.g.
55 Carmaker Maserati
57 Not very
60 Nixon impeachment hearings chairman
61 No-cal drink
62 Hitchcockian
63 Loose
64 Chip off the old block
66 Got together
67 Point in a space shuttle's trip
70 Provides provender
71 Area of 1940s mil. activity
72 Pair at sea
73 Skater of cinema
74 Mediterranean capital
75 "That'll be the day!"
79 Boxing's Oscar ___ Hoya
80 "My Name Is Asher ___" (Chaim Potok novel)
81 Manhandles
84 Studies late
85 Sends up
86 Plasterboards
88 Needle
89 Hair holder, sometimes
90 "Walk ___" (1964 Warwick hit)
91 St.-Germain's river
92 Windshield option
93 Jacket materials
95 Applause
96 Very fat cats
99 Spray with bouquet
101 Author who covered the Spanish-American War for New York newspapers
104 Court site, with "The"
105 Linen hue
106 Cry made with a head-slap
107 Mass communication?
108 Stink
109 Slip through the cracks
110 Silent signals
111 Bolt to bond

DOWN

1 "Suzanne" songwriter
2 Memo starter
3 Ferry river
4 Scout warmer
5 Like a certain birthstone
6 Understood
7 Feuding
8 Setting for TV's "Newhart"
9 Fictional reporter
10 Wins big, with "up"
11 Ranges
12 10, in a way: Abbr.
13 Spun
14 Gets by
15 Ones with homes away from home
16 Der ___ (Adenauer)
17 In-basket stamp: Abbr.
18 Visibly shaken
24 Reporter's asset
26 Writer Zora ___ Hurston
29 Off-the-wall play
32 Farmyard female
34 Select
35 Private reply
36 Covetous
37 "I'm impressed!"
38 Questionable
39 Big bother
40 Kind of wrench
41 Back in
43 Rap sheet listing
44 Like some threats
47 Takes in or lets out
48 Not one of the majors
49 Escorted
51 Perfume part
53 Cantankerous
54 Innocents, e.g.
56 Gutter site
57 Conversion targets
58 Fabulous storyteller
59 Monopoly grp.
63 Russian range
64 Burn
65 "I'm outta here"
66 Cries like a baby
68 "Duino Elegies" poet
69 It's good at raising dough
72 "For the life ___ . . ."
76 Isolate during the winter
77 Junior's junior
78 Postpaid encl.
79 Kind of candidate
81 Spindle for a grinding wheel

by Harvey Estes and Nancy Salomon

82 "Seascape" playwright
83 Novel banned in the U.S. until 1933
85 Lord Peter Wimsey accessory
87 Very sorry
88 Shred
89 Rock cruster
91 Sex researcher Hite
92 Evidence of sloppiness
93 Gulf of ___ (Joseph Conrad story setting)
94 Push
96 Watch
97 Alliance acronym
98 Salon sound
99 Sounds of understanding
100 Therefore
102 Howe'er
103 Toronto-to-Ottawa dir.

FILM SOUNDS

ACROSS

1 Base for food glazes
6 Waste
11 They're unstressed
17 Company perk
20 Air supplier
21 Appropriate for Halloween
22 Some ducks
23 Decline
24 Nathan and others
25 1980s computer
26 Art fan, perhaps
27 Web address start
28 Cow's favorite movie of 1983?
31 Aquarium fish
32 Guanabara Bay locale
33 Expression of gratitude, briefly
34 Internet market
35 Tropical pitcher plants and such
37 What Fred Astaire danced with
40 ___, Optimo, Maximo (Benedictine motto)
41 Start of a doo-wop phrase
44 Run out
45 Imagined
48 On the Board
50 Point of writing
51 Cat's favorite movie of 2000?
55 Like one battery terminal
59 A boost
60 Part of a dash
61 Attorney Belli
63 Sherpa
64 One-spot
68 Level
70 Not level
72 Haydn string composition
73 "___ It a Pity" (1970 song)
75 Foam toy brand
77 ___ de toilette
78 "It's ___ real!"
79 Snake's favorite movie of 1981?
87 Frenziedly
88 Oh-Wah-___ (game like mancala)
89 A transmitter
90 Game Gear company
91 The Beatles' Madonna, e.g.
92 Nebraska's Cornhusker, e.g.
96 Linesman, maybe?
98 Ancient Italian
102 Sheik's flock
104 Ark contents
106 Measure
108 1936 Cong. measure
109 "___ Rhapsody" (1996 biopic)
111 Frog's favorite movie of 1944?
116 Bolt from the blue?
117 116-Across and others
118 View from Vesuvius
119 Sister of Eva
122 Green-lights
123 Schnook
125 More harsh
129 Desiring
131 Superman's mother
132 President's inits.
133 PC application suffix
134 Hamlet and Gertrude
135 Crow's favorite movie of 1955?
142 Tall runners
143 Romeo and Juliet's home
144 Ante
145 "I swear!"
146 Cartoon art
147 Only now and then
148 Where salts go
149 Grand ___
150 Organ repair sites: Abbr.
151 Title city of a Forsyth thriller
152 Make catty remarks
153 They're tender

DOWN

1 Whiz's musical key?
2 Kennedy colleague
3 Many a boot
4 "Yeah, right!"
5 It's tender
6 Term of affection
7 Sound studio work
8 At first: Abbr.
9 Said "ah"
10 Life saver
11 Native soldier, in old India
12 "See ya!"
13 Modern viewer's choice
14 "___ madly for Adlai" (1952 campaign slogan)
15 Turned up
16 An ID
17 Kitty teaser
18 The Three Stooges had many
19 Rest
23 Sheep's favorite movie of 1991?
29 It's a knockout
30 "Little Red Book" ideology
31 Meting
36 Princess on the small screen
38 Big inits. in check processing
39 French vineyard
41 Popular Russian vodka, familiarly
42 Actor Villechaize
43 One may be secret
46 Curators' degs.
47 Modern music genre
49 Mark consisting of a series of dots
51 Kind of team
52 Step on it
53 19th-century samurai home
54 Perry White, e.g.
56 Worse
57 Cutting down, after "on"
58 Actress Téa
62 Larry of the Black Arts Theater, and others
65 Bee's favorite movie of 1983?
66 Clock std.
67 Colossal, to Coleridge
69 Actor with a mohawk
71 Some ranchers
74 "My ___"
76 Loan overseer: Abbr.
79 Judaism : kosher :: Islam : ___
80 Fine Japanese porcelain
81 They're found in fountains
82 "Decide already!"
83 ___ date: Abbr.
84 Fast sound: Var.
85 Early afternoon time
86 Tour grp.
93 Chiseler
94 Spring locale
95 "What's ___?"
97 Trillion: Prefix
99 N.Y.C. line

by Roy Leban

100 Name preceder
101 Corn order
103 Equilibrium
105 Lack equilibrium
107 Nobody
110 Wing-to-wing measure
112 Reactionaries of 1917

113 Farm sound
114 Drink, informally
115 British verb ending
119 Louisiana music
120 Tailoring machine
121 Cancels
124 Old Blood and Guts
126 More authentic
127 Former Mrs.

128 Fixes at zero, say
130 Mammonism
131 Wool producer
132 Wag
136 First name in mysteries
137 Gym displays
138 Genesis name
139 ___ go at (tries)

140 Honeydew lovers
141 Small salmon
143 Brandy letters

ACROSS

1 Begin
9 Drum set
16 "Howdy"
20 Carefully study
21 Firedog
22 King Harald's father
23 Chef's comment at the poker game
25 Swiss miss, maybe: Abbr.
26 Actor Arnold
27 ___ good example
28 Stuck during winter
30 Fox News host Hannity and others
33 Pardon
36 Announcement at Penn Sta.
37 Brief rule
38 Laundry worker's comment at the poker game
41 At first, say
43 Film director often seen at New York Knicks games
46 1970s Irish P.M. Cosgrave
48 Noted index, with "the"
49 Medal winners
50 Bridge site
53 "Oz" airer
54 Yardsticks: Abbr.
57 Broadway producer's comment at the poker game
61 Football Hall-of-Famer Long
62 "Lord, is ___?"
63 Au courant
64 Indian turnover
65 French possessive
66 Detective, essentially
67 Dodges
71 IV amounts
72 Portion of the iris
74 So as
76 Jackie's #2
77 Reeves of "Speed"
78 Lifer's comment at the poker game
83 Character in Trollope's "Phineas Finn"
84 Well-rehearsed
85 Number after a period: Abbr.
86 One of the Ramones
87 Vegas opener
89 Strong team
91 Life jackets
93 They take big steps
96 Car seller's comment at the poker game
100 Old TV talk show host Kupcinet
101 Speech fillers
103 Ariel and others
104 Took off
108 Loses hearing
111 "I say!" sayer
112 Spring time in Paris
113 Canceled
114 Tennis pro's comment at the poker game
121 Each
122 Landlocked Asian
123 Logician
124 Marine carriers in W.W. II
125 On one extreme
126 Experienced dizziness

DOWN

1 Sticks in the barbecue
2 A hard row ___
3 Kitchen magnet?
4 Word on the street
5 Nail site
6 Prefix with duct
7 Elite group, with "the"
8 Dog's catch, perhaps
9 Body work
10 50-50
11 Year in an Amerigo Vespucci voyage
12 Circle constants
13 Some Dadaist works
14 Who lives forever
15 Wholly
16 Kind of cooking
17 Artist's comment at the poker game
18 Bush and Clinton, once
19 Pay back
24 Den
29 Source of magic dust
31 Canon competitor
32 Piece of music
33 Michigan in Chicago: Abbr.
34 Tenn. footballer
35 Nobelist Root
39 Ancient land of France
40 Soft touches
42 Beloved
43 Asian mushroom
44 Metal craftsman
45 Farmer's comment at the poker game
47 Tommy ___, Olympic skiing gold medalist
50 Jubilation
51 Buzz in space
52 Key letter
55 Circumspect
56 Coasts
58 Carnival's promise
59 Cologne conjunction
60 Walking
61 Suffers from
64 Baked dessert
66 Certain strain
68 Blows it
69 Sun Valley locale: Abbr.
70 O.T. book
73 Former center of Los Angeles
75 Super Bowl side: Abbr.
78 Bus. page news
79 Start of something big
80 Twos in the news
81 Post in a flight
82 Fortune 500 company based in Moline, Ill.
88 Fastener
90 Vowelless number
91 Coaches
92 Walkman batteries

by Randolph Ross

93 Wave, e.g.
94 Some peacekeepers
95 Girl with blue eyes and a ponytail, in a 1962 #1 hit
97 Start of a writ
98 Off course
99 Finish off
102 Subject of the biography subtitled "Visionary Who Dared"
105 Range name
106 Conseco Fieldhouse player
107 Ranks
109 Payoffs
110 Lava ___
115 Simpson case judge
116 Wine aperitif
117 Green brew
118 It's not right to say on a farm
119 Pothook shape
120 Turn bad

43 NAMES, NAMES, NAMES

ACROSS

1 Like the names at 33-, 51-, 61-, 73-, 93-, 101- and 120-Across
10 First alert, often
14 Put on a spit
20 Welcome abroad
21 "That's ___!" (angry retort)
22 "The Music Man" woman
23 Like many driveways
24 A security
25 Stat
26 Dole (out)
27 Further condition to 1-Across
29 1929 Literature Nobelist
30 "Mon ___!"
32 Substitute in the kitchen
33 Author and longtime professor of writing at Princeton
39 Hunters' needs: Abbr.
43 Inventeur's need
44 ___ Awards (annual prizes for African-American achievement)
45 Fruits de ___
46 Bob Dylan song "___ for You"
47 Supplied
48 Boatload
49 Final bid
50 Carol starter
51 Actress whose great-grandfather was a British P.M.

55 Tastiness
58 Soccer star Hamm
59 See 96-Across
60 Bauxite, e.g.
61 Three-time French Open champion
69 "Delta of Venus" author
70 Four CDs
71 Part of a rainbow
72 "___ Gold" (1997 film)
73 1988 and 1992 Olympic track gold medalist
81 Not yet shaped
82 Little hopper
83 Razor-billed birds
84 "This Old House" address
87 "That's ___" (cautionary Roy Orbison song)
88 Since, informally
89 Bar offering
91 Suffix with pluto-
92 Stock market overseer: Abbr.
93 Six-time U.S. Open winner
96 With 59-Across, a knock
99 Stone made of silicon and oxygen
100 They move shells
101 "Slaves of New York" actress
107 Standard deviation symbol
109 Knight from Atlanta
110 President Taft's alma mater
111 Stretches

115 Most basic
116 Annoyer
117 Opposite of chic
118 Minuscule
119 Oil of ___
120 He developed the "Three Principles of the People"

DOWN

1 TV schedule abbr.
2 Greetings
3 Shown again
4 Better
5 Daughter of Poseidon who was the ancestor of a prophetic clan
6 Educational grant named for a senator
7 Pot foundation
8 St.-Honoré, in Paris
9 Spread, as hay
10 Shakespearean haunter
11 Former Expos manager
12 Girl in a Beatles song
13 Stem-to-stern item
14 Drive
15 W.W. I battle locale
16 Woods, e.g.
17 Aretha Franklin's "___ No Way"
18 Wood strip
19 1961 space chimp
27 Wriggling
28 ___ Rios, Ecuador
29 Calculator button
30 Go under
31 Kind of chamber

33 Peter Pan rival
34 Theater turn-off?
35 Busy as ___
36 With all agreeing, after "to"
37 Musical John
38 Bogus
40 Awaiting
41 Circle
42 Pioneer products
46 Moscow's home: Abbr.
48 Spanish muralist
49 Stole
50 Curtain-rising time
51 Doll
52 Grp. pledged to "do no harm"
53 Storage place
54 Dallas hoopster
55 Western Hemisphere city founded in 1521
56 Writer Huffington
57 Mexico's Villa and others
62 Comic superheroes
63 Part of speech: Abbr.
64 Nix
65 Ben-___
66 Cry on opening a tax bill
67 Hints
68 Nog ingredient, maybe
74 N.H.L. Hall-of-Famer who played for Montreal
75 W.W. II battle site, for short
76 "___ Hit Parade"
77 Many a part in "The Pianist"
78 Stand

by Derrick Niederman

ACROSS

1 Submit
7 Latin-American import
13 Wines from Spain
20 Grand Canyon sights
21 More elegant
22 Where the Tombigbee flows
23 Why is Y like a romance novel?
25 Au ___
26 Raiding party?: Abbr.
27 Baby's first word, maybe
28 What may be raised at celebrations
29 Word to a dog
30 Counter offer?
31 Lamb specialty
33 What's C and easy, too?
37 Rest
38 Stains
39 Belts
40 Bow shape
41 Place
43 Something to be cured
46 Some are personal
47 Fund-raising grps.
48 Crosswalk user, for short
49 Many members of 47-Across
52 Unmelodic sounds
54 Dove, e.g.
55 P.D. alert
57 School dept.
58 What describes both screams and napoleons?

62 Far from florid
64 Oklahoma native
65 Biblical judge
66 Deli freebie
67 Hospital staffer: Var.
69 Cover over
71 Winner of 81 P.G.A. Tour victories
73 Appliance rating
74 Attributed
75 Quechua speaker
76 Writer LeShan
77 "Mr. Dieingly ___" (1966 Critters hit)
78 Ping-Pong skills
79 How does "no" describe some baseball caps?
83 Wing
84 Cause of many a blowup
85 Top-drawer
86 "Gotcha"
87 Ship's hdg.
88 Already, in Italy
90 Some are deadly
91 Cash drawer compartment: Abbr.
93 Hero's award: Abbr.
95 Many an Olympian
97 Bass ___
98 ___ Ste. Marie
100 Fundamentals
104 Long time
105 What Stephen King title is suggested by the letter F?
108 Honolulu's former ___ Stadium
109 Study

110 Far out
111 Pisa's river
112 Lord's Prayer start
114 Berlioz's "___ Troyens"
115 All together
118 What science fiction movie do taxes and anime bring to mind?
121 "The flower of my heart," in old song
122 Reddish brown
123 Like Eeyore, in "Winnie-the-Pooh"
124 Fort ___ (Oregon Trail stop)
125 Presses, folds and stretches
126 ___ beef

DOWN

1 Remained
2 Precious
3 Hockey area
4 Directional ending
5 Tricky
6 Old "Happy motoring!" sloganeer
7 Profit-and-loss calculator: Abbr.
8 Junkie
9 Features
10 Florida governor before Bush
11 "How's that again?"
12 Suffix with secret
13 Nuts
14 "Woe is me!"
15 Bodybuilder's target
16 Father of, in Arabic

17 How would you describe both seraphs and unintelligible talk?
18 ___ Island, Fla.
19 Like many nuts
24 Short flights
29 Jam
32 Pompeii killer
34 "___ Teenage Frankenstein," 1957 film
35 Disastrous
36 A gift, for short
42 Little girl's plaything
44 O.K.'s
45 Oscar-winner Matlin
47 Relative of the cod
49 Many New Zealanders
50 Tackle
51 What teen hangout is named by the letters PP?
53 Creep
54 Court cry
56 Losers to the 49ers in Super Bowl XXIII
59 Residents, e.g.: Abbr.
60 "___ Rainbow" (1947 musical)
61 Pearl hunters
62 Travelers' aids
63 Tease
68 Goofed
70 Em, e.g.
72 Thomas Bailey Aldrich story "Marjorie ___"
80 Caught but good
81 Jolly Roger feature
82 Supermarket area
89 Woof

by Nancy Nicholson Joline

90 What nobody doesn't like

91 Old boxer called the Ambling Alp

92 Coached

94 Low-___

95 Kind of nerve or tire

96 It's listed in minutes

98 He said "I exist because I think"

99 Trampled

101 Crooner Michael

102 "Say ___!"

103 Dissed, in a way

106 Farsi speaker

107 Picker-upper

108 ___-Detoo ("Star Wars" droid)

113 Iwo Jima Memorial honorees: Abbr.

116 Ending with plug

117 One of the Cratchits

118 "Don't ___!"

119 Clattery trains

120 Itinerary abbr.

45 LEAP DAY

ACROSS

1 Darkness
6 Pack carrier
11 Application datum: Abbr.
14 Background of Vladimir Putin, for short
17 Route indicator
18 Traveler's woe
19 Island strings
20 Anti-inflammatory agent
21 Striped animal
22 "The Witches of Eastwick" author
23 A full course?
25 Queens contest
27 Daughter of Hyperion
29 Strike, essentially
30 Thesis basis
31 Big inits. in news and culture
32 Four fluid ounces
33 Food company with a sun in its logo
34 Cigarette pkgs.
36 Empire State Building décor
38 Put in
42 Shack topper
45 Sinatra scat syllable
46 Black bird
47 Express views
48 Pry
49 Take off
52 Open, in a way
54 Writing
55 1968 Oscar-winning musical
56 Has trouble with words
57 Smell, e.g.
58 Cuts using a box
59 Long period
60 "It's you ___"
61 Upright at sea
65 Ed.'s inbox filler
68 It's hard, to swallow
74 Just above average
79 "Enough already!"
81 Red-faced
82 Hangout
83 Spot for Roosevelt
84 Apt
85 Parenthetical passage
86 Blows
87 Nus to us
89 Co. in a 2000 telecommunications merger
90 Ripen
92 South Seas monarchy
93 "Frankenstein" props
95 Kiln
96 1991 Gerardo hit "___ Suave"
98 Fall's end
99 VJ's employer
100 "Dang!"
104 Chicken go-with
107 Term. info
108 Minor minder
110 Sights
112 1966 Mary Martin musical
115 Deadly virus
116 Blender sound
117 Reagan military inits.
118 Run with gates
119 Less seen
120 Calendar col.
121 Sinuous sea dweller
122 Administers, with "out"
123 It's a secret

DOWN

1 Biblical woman from Bethlehem
2 Troubled (by)
3 Worry for a wearer of high heels
4 Takes a quickie vacation, say
5 Bud holder
6 Molokai resident
7 Co. name end
8 2001 biopic
9 Achieve significant progress
10 Long-known
11 Challenge, legally
12 Not read something completely
13 Rio ___, part of the Venezuela/ Colombia boundary
14 Swiss abstract painting
15 Takes a turn
16 Like a shepherd's staff
18 Has ever-changing loyalties
20 Seek a lawyer's license
24 Sink a putt
26 Monumental year?
28 Source of spills on hills
32 Channel
35 Lightweight helmet, in India
36 Come out of denial
37 Civil rights, e.g.
39 Snake, for one
40 Vast, in verse
41 Like osmium, more than any other known element
42 48 in a cup: Abbr.
43 As to
44 Twelve
50 "The Whiffenpoof Song" singer
51 Drs.' workplaces
53 Cafeteria worker's hairdo
61 Annoys
62 St. Teresa's birthplace
63 Medical supply
64 Answer continued
65 16th-century start
66 Answer continued
67 Gregg method user
68 Old White House nickname
69 Answer continued
70 Like chrome hubcaps
71 Garage jobs
72 Precitizenship course: Abbr.

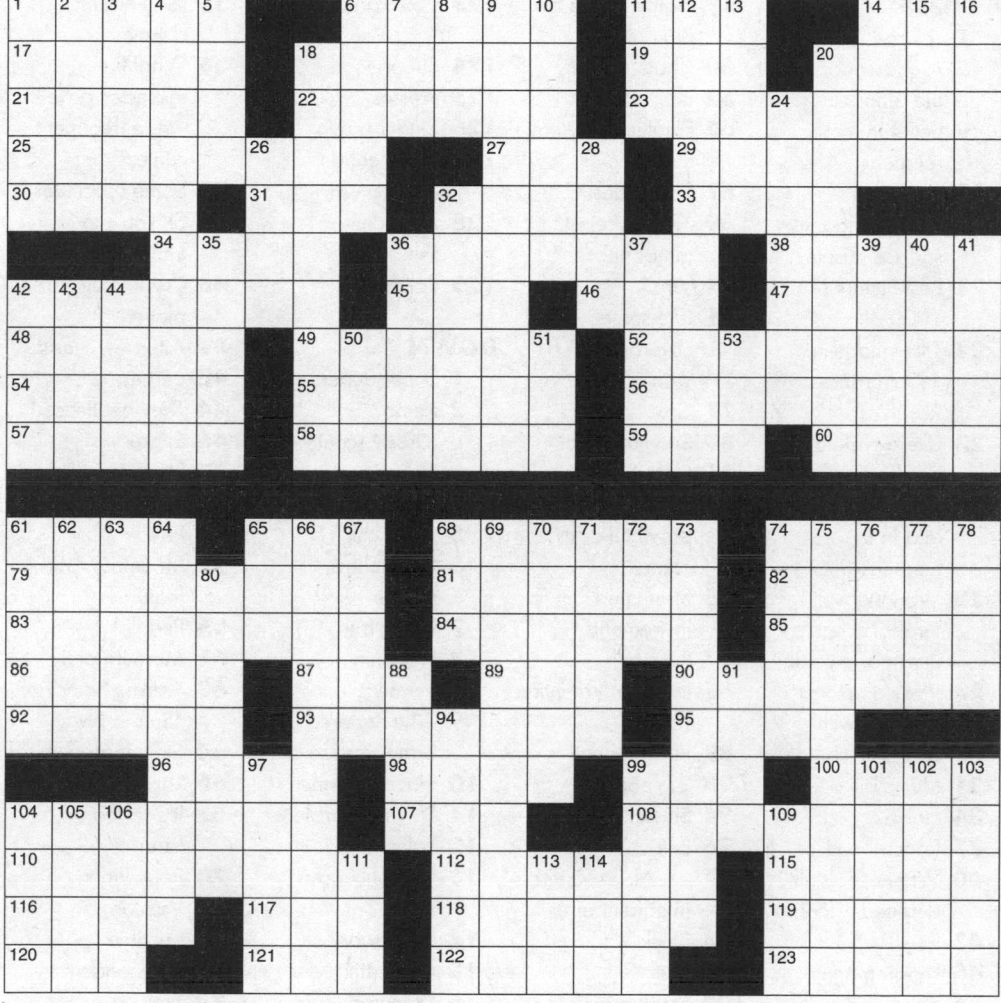

by Patrick Merrell

46 "THAT'S DISGUSTING"

ACROSS

1 "Hurry!"
5 Ambassador of old autodom
9 Belief in most religions
18 Bank
20 Army surface-to-surface missile
21 Best Picture of 2000
22 Title village in a 1979 Francesco Rosi film
23 Like a certain number system
24 What was just laid in the henhouse?
25 Working with turquoise and ultramarine cloth?
28 Invoice amount
29 Connect with
30 Laundry job
31 Music bit
34 Halve
37 Ranch head
40 Where "Falstaff" debuted, 1893
43 Retell
45 Leading figure
46 False god
48 Mideast carrier
49 "A stitch in time . . . ," e.g.
50 Terse tip for a street fighter?
54 Sample
55 Gold-medal speed skater Johann ___ Koss
57 Stripe wearers
58 Bosses

59 Golfer called the Big Easy
60 Chad toucher
62 Places to sit
65 Families may have them
67 Spectacles
69 "The sweetest gift of heaven": Virgil
71 Like some health coverage
74 Wings it
77 Cruelty
80 Shoe material
81 Elaborate
83 Philippine province or its capital
85 Strummed instruments
87 Rare bills
88 Informal Valentine word
89 Bird tendon?
93 ___ poetica
94 Barber's job
96 Bee ___
97 ___ Newspapers (media chain)
98 Stuck
100 Out
102 Small bags
104 Encephalitis cause
105 Actress Polo
106 Snick's partner
108 Pageant judging criterion
110 On easy street
112 Nut taken directly from the freezer?
118 Like bad coffee?
122 Lit

123 Cole Porter's "___ Men"
124 Suppressor
125 Presses
126 Singer Lenya
127 Make out an envelope for
128 After-dinner selection
129 Fall sound

DOWN

1 Super-duper
2 Kemo ___ ("trusty scout")
3 Three-in-___
4 Nicer
5 Some chips
6 Some chips, maybe
7 Union foe
8 Fraternity travail
9 "The Bartered Bride" mezzo
10 Blood's partner
11 Playing marble
12 Fall place
13 Choral concert sights
14 Framework
15 Ore suffix
16 Driving danger
17 Dyne-centimeter
19 Small taxi
20 Trent of Mississippi
26 Go-___
27 Old map. inits.
32 Not the real Martha?
33 Swing wildly
34 Buffalo's AAA baseball team

35 Leaning, in a way
36 What the inspector gave the waste treatment center?
38 Some sculptures
39 St. Louis-to-Indianapolis dir.
40 Crypto.com Arena player
41 Attorney Gloria
42 Bernese ___
44 They get fleeced
46 Sticker
47 Elec. designation
51 Tailward
52 Pried
53 Mountain road features
56 Peddle
61 Museum piece
63 Actress Nancy of "Sunset Blvd."
64 Stew ingredient
66 Threaded holder
68 It's stored on a farm
70 Pope when Vatican City became independent
72 Eats up
73 Rent payer
75 Blasé
76 Yeas or nays
78 Water-___
79 Computer offering
81 Der ___ Herr (the old man): Ger.
82 Fred ___, front man of rock's Limp Bizkit

by Tyler Hinman

84 Fleur-de-___
86 Kind of tank
90 Demonstrated
91 Pollster Harris
92 Holiday revelry
95 Popular chocolate treat
99 Course starter
101 Great Plains capital
102 Jellied delicacy
103 Carousals
106 Track
107 Give the ___ (pick)
109 Chances
111 Turner and others
113 Bring on
114 Tiny organism
115 Biblical verb
116 Cry of Caesar
117 Narc's target
118 "Mad About You" cousin
119 Digital watch part: Abbr.
120 Cousin of inc.
121 Lived

MOONLIGHTING

ACROSS

1 Steps in Havana
6 It may be dripping
13 Mellow, in a way
16 What supers supervise: Abbr.
20 Actor Ryan or Ron
21 Occasional soap opera plot feature
22 Measuring stick
24 Who ran Iran, once
25 Telecom executive's other job?
28 Famous language-signing gorilla
29 Curls up
30 Coast Guard concern
31 Boxing referee's other job?
33 Cure-___ (panaceas)
34 "Hansel and Gretel" setting
36 Puppy's sound
37 Hull enclosure
38 Film's "three caballeros," e.g.
41 Scand. land
42 "Honest" one
43 "Come ___!"
45 Homebody
46 Isn't straight in the middle
47 Ticket word
51 Tip-top
52 Terse
53 Ming thing
54 When repeated, show disdain
56 Zipped through
58 ___ instant
59 Spicy stew
60 Sequel writer's other job?
64 Carole King's "___ Too Late"
65 All-___ Team

67 Stick in the wrong place
68 Overly decorous sorts
70 New Jersey home of Walt Whitman
73 Relay part
74 Part of many cages
75 #1 Danny & the Juniors hit
78 Garbage
79 Quiz show sounds
81 Singer LeAnn
83 Klutzy
84 Meticulously
86 Raiding grp.
88 Quirk
89 Tips off
90 Remains
91 Holds a pose
93 ___ favor
94 2003 Indy winner ___ de Ferran
96 File clerk's other job?
100 Some cobras
104 Like a line, in math
106 Prefix with trash
107 Sean ___ Lennon
108 Nearby star
109 Drink with a straw
110 Biff ___, Arthur Miller character
112 Sharp-tongued "American Idol" judge
114 Something to serve
115 Florida city
116 Liquid Plumr rival
117 Little bird
119 Stick in one's craw
120 Suitable to be ridden, as a horse
121 Like some dollars on currency exch. boards
122 Classified times: Abbr.
125 Causes to go

127 Steady
128 Safari guide's other job?
131 Guitarist Nugent
132 Expecting
136 Famous 50-oared ship
137 Drill instructor's other job?
140 Old Roman road
141 Jupiter, e.g.
142 12-note series
143 Eponymous candy manufacturer Harry
144 "The Thin Man" role
145 Pen
146 Be born with
147 Wows

DOWN

1 Chem. units
2 In a bit
3 Orders come from it
4 Psychiatrist's other job?
5 American standard
6 Letter enclosures: Abbr.
7 Acct. figures
8 Messenger ___
9 Wartime positions
10 Broad neck scarf
11 Break, of a sort
12 Scratch or dent
13 1970s sitcom
14 "Treasure Island" pirate Ben ___
15 "In Memoriam," e.g.
16 Wants for a price
17 Jockey's other job?
18 Go for
19 Shipping units
23 Humorist Bombeck
26 Panacea's targets
27 Implored
32 Per
34 Caesar, for Gaius Julius Caesar
35 Slaughterhouse

38 Chow chow chow
39 Do drudgery
40 Global: Abbr.
41 Worker with a dog
44 When "Route 66" was on: Abbr.
46 Take action against
48 Grocery
49 Standoffish
50 Lures
54 QB's throw them
55 Locale in a Beatles song
57 Zip
60 ___ Pedro
61 Stingy person
62 Circled
63 Ex ___ (from nothing)
66 Hardly a crooner
69 Military adviser's other job?
70 Top-rated TV show of 2002-3
71 Wheat covering
72 Diet doctor's other job?
73 Rap's ___ Kim
75 Old nuclear regulatory org.
76 Make a selection
77 Jar sizes: Abbr.
79 Decathlon equipment
80 "Hurry up!"
82 Manglers
85 James who wrote "The Morning Watch"
87 Spore source
89 Fig. in car ads
91 Gift tag word
92 Animal home
94 Piece of bling-bling
95 So that one could
97 ". . . ___ shall die"
98 Stop at a vineyard
99 Common street name

by Craig Kasper

101 Take to the cleaners
102 Light
103 Hockey's Mikita
105 Forebear of one of the 12 tribes of Israel
109 Deer, e.g.
111 Boat builder
113 Cheri formerly of "S.N.L."
114 Some hippie wear
118 Needlework?
120 Grouse
123 Newsman Roger
124 Bygone blades
125 Ross of fame
126 Joanna of "Growing Pains"
127 Anatomical ridges
129 "David Copperfield" wife
130 Letter-shaped fastener
132 Specialists
133 In full sail
134 Inquisitive
135 ___ belle
138 Big race sponsor
139 Not post-

ACROSS

1 New Deal power project: Abbr.
4 ___ Club
10 Shelter grp.
14 Big lie
19 Trader and restaurant entrepreneur
20 Shout on a ship
21 Gene Cernan was the last man there
22 Later
23 2003 addition to the Museum of Flight
24 Taking the place (of)
25 Offering
26 First distiller to sell whiskey by the bottle
27 A dozen mad bakers?
31 "And away ___!"
32 Part of a cornerstone inscription
33 Down-to-earth ones, in brief?
34 Opposite of dis
35 "Bravo!"
36 Sports photographer's bane
37 It's played with a scrum
39 Let know
41 Minor afflictions
43 Conductor's instruction to a percussionist?
48 Laura Bush's alma mater, for short
51 Boors

52 Xylophonist's need
53 Back
55 Stanford rival, familiarly
56 Calendar abbr.
59 "___ won't!"
60 European spa
63 Popular reality show, with "The"
66 Classic Jaguar
68 Lyre-playing Muse
70 NASA's Spirit and Opportunity?
75 C.D. issuer
76 Prominence
77 Devilish
78 Money-raising grp.
79 Ore. neighbor
82 Down
84 Mountain curve
85 Bagel topper
86 Dweller on the Red Sea
89 Comment after a failure, perhaps
92 Gen-___
93 Having the Space Needle outside one's bedroom window?
98 Cheese made from goat's milk
99 Very large
100 Apples introduced in 1998
104 "Hurlyburly" playwright
105 Like Abner
107 Tycoon Onassis
108 56-Across and others
111 It's surrounded by beaches
112 It means "red" in Mongolian

113 Remark regarding chili preference?
117 Patty Hearst's name in the S.L.A.
119 Hatcher of "Lois & Clark"
120 Where "three men" of rhyme are
121 Yes, in Japan
122 Knockoff
123 With 127-Across, 1930s–'40s leading lady born in Russia
124 Opposite of all
125 N.Y.C. trains overseer
126 Is undecided
127 See 123-Across
128 Smooth
129 Hand writing?: Abbr.

DOWN

1 Lucille Ball or Monty Hall
2 The Preserver
3 Dramatics
4 Dart
5 Indian dignitary
6 Shoreline feature
7 Some tennis scores
8 Actress Perlman
9 Silent
10 More stylish
11 Prefix with graph
12 Average Joe
13 Adams of Yosemite
14 Cabbage Patch dolls, e.g.
15 What divorced ladies want?

16 Vitamin needed for pernicious anemia
17 Player in organized sport
18 Faults
28 Former Virginia senator Charles
29 Showy trinket
30 Language related to Urdu
38 "Whoopee!"
39 Comic Margaret
40 Elementary suffix
42 Syracuse-to-Albany dir.
44 Button material
45 Kofi Annan's birthplace
46 Available, in a way
47 "Alice" spinoff
48 Photos
49 Tough luck
50 Straight
54 Hot summer night?
57 Unneeded
58 Sleepover attire
61 Tums competitor
62 Fight (for)
64 Web address, for short
65 Having everything one needs
67 ___ mai (dim sum dish)
68 H.S. requirement
69 ___ night (annual event)
71 It may be tapped out
72 Brutus's burdens
73 "How ___?"
74 Start
79 Pushes forward

by Roy Leban

80 "Angele ___" (Latin prayer)
81 Ending of some relationships
83 Not taking kindly to
87 Poetic contraction
88 Car starter: Abbr.
90 Actor Danson
91 551, in 551
93 Nonsense syllables in a 1965 song title
94 City in Pennsylvania Dutch country
95 Like pizza
96 "Me neither"
97 Radiate
98 Support staff?
101 Allergy problem
102 Baseballer's wear
103 "Buck Rogers," for one
106 Bits
108 Mazda convertible
109 Four Holy Roman emperors
110 Blackballs
114 Sea flier
115 Hydroxyl compound
116 Mind
118 Loser to D.D.E.

ACROSS

1 Biblical verb
5 Actress Dench
9 Defraud
15 Lawyer: Abbr.
18 Mixed bag
19 65-Across to, regionally
20 Worldly
21 Even if, briefly
22 Start of a humorous definition of 50-Down (with a French "twist")
26 Runs out of gas
27 Abruzzi's locale
28 "Whenever"
29 Misstep
30 Other side
32 Romantically involved with
35 Exuberance
36 Definition, part 2
42 N.Y.C. subway line
43 Badly agitated, with "up"
44 Kitt who sang "Santa Baby"
45 Alternative to café
47 Struggle
49 Grp. involved in a cleanup
52 Spring times
56 Definition, part 3
59 On cloud nine
62 "Rhyme Pays" singer
63 Guys
64 Most-used edition: Abbr.
65 Contrary
67 "That Thing ___!" (Tom Hanks film)
68 On the ball
70 Definition, part 4
71 Unfounded rumor
72 Kruger National Park sight
73 Romance novelist's creation
74 Scatter
75 Tail
76 Close up
77 Bother
78 Definition, part 5
81 Liking a lot
83 Sizable duration
85 Plaintive cry
86 Maximilian's realm: Abbr.
87 Get ready to take more pictures
90 King of France
92 Mauna ___
94 Definition, part 6
103 Picturesque town in 27-Across
104 Priest's subordinate
105 California's Fort ___
106 Hawaiian wedding ring?
107 Stage setters
111 Commodities futures listing
113 River through Grenoble
115 End of the definition
119 He put people on the ropes
120 Fools
121 Initiative
122 Andy's boy in '60s TV
123 "___ Girls" (Gene Kelly movie)
124 Green-lighted
125 Long stretches
126 The fox in Disney's "The Fox and the Hound"

DOWN

1 Traditional remedy
2 Bourbon Street legend
3 ___ Club
4 Lug
5 Part of a political debate
6 More revolting
7 Losing cause?
8 Rashly
9 Garage work
10 Here, to Henri
11 "Queen of denial," e.g.
12 2000 Olympic hurdles gold medalist ___ Shishigina
13 Yellowish brown
14 Wear out by rubbing
15 Gaul invader
16 1964 Irving Wallace best seller
17 Sign at a bicycle shop or boardinghouse
20 Peeping Tom
23 Concerning
24 Salt of a certain acid
25 Rote learning method
31 Beat at the ballot box
33 Laura Bush, ___ Welch
34 Agcy. created by Truman
37 Declarations of disgust
38 Illustrator Silverstein
39 In a corner
40 Slightly
41 Uncertain reactions
45 A good thing to steal
46 Like some witnesses
48 Not the party sort: Abbr.
50 See 22-Across
51 Crazy as ___
53 Guayaquil's land
54 Papal vestment
55 Dull plodder
56 Fishing places
57 "___ Perpetua" (Idaho's motto)
58 Letter ender?
60 Fools
61 Summer wear
66 "1984" figure
67 Deviates at 74-Down
69 It's usually hidden
70 Anatomical foot
71 Loan signer, at times
73 Le Duc Tho's city
74 See 67-Down
77 Hang on to
79 Give out
80 Become friendlier
82 Sci-fi drug
84 Melodic passage
88 Far-away connection

by David J. Kahn

89 Sandra of "A Summer Place"
91 Unhelpful
93 Singer Gorme
94 Ankle-related
95 Player of Priam in "Troy"
96 Popular fragrance
97 Unkempt
98 Enduring marks
99 1953 Best Actor William
100 Syrian city of 2 million
101 Moon of Neptune
102 Like Carnegie Hall
108 In the event it's true
109 Composer Satie
110 Ward of Hollywood
112 Grooving on
114 Kind of check
116 Disingenuous
117 Hurry
118 Letter ender?

ACROSS

1 "Help!"
7 Cry of relief
11 Top spot
15 Time period
19 First
20 Costa follower
21 Sen. Cochran of Mississippi
22 "What can ___ to help?"
23 Blazing
24 Garden figure
25 Dan attacks while . . .
27 Polly punishes while . . .
30 One way to wait
31 Dilly-dally
32 Bona fide
33 Like some Mideast conferences
35 Morals man
37 All-day sch. events
38 Girl's name that means "sorceress"
42 Occasionally
46 Faye rides while . . .
49 Bear: Sp.
50 Fictional rubber
51 Cause of many an accident
52 Doppelgänger
53 Lincoln and others
54 Having the most reason
55 Building regulations
56 Greatest chance
58 Halfway houses
59 West Indies native
60 A fighting force
62 Wild blue yonder
63 Lester bats while . . .
66 Old protest org.
69 Outcasts
71 Coaxes
72 What's left at sea
73 Certain nuts
75 Pip or pit
76 Chewing gum ingredient
78 Daft
79 Give a hand
82 This girl
83 Tutor of the Beatles
84 Question
85 Chad rows while . . .
87 Takes hold of quickly
88 Operatic villains, often
90 March time
91 Certain print
92 Ear problem
95 As found, after "in"
96 Hanukkah serving
101 Some salad items
104 Lenny makes buys while . . .
107 Vic doesn't finger anyone while . . .
109 Bull: Prefix
110 Battlement
111 Bit of infirmity
112 1950s TV's "The Martha ___ Show"
113 South American monkey
114 "The Tatler" writer
115 Try
116 Had down cold
117 "Smart" one
118 Judge

DOWN

1 Sends unwanted messages
2 Talk of the town?
3 Home for the holidays
4 Online shopping center
5 Carey leaves shore while . . .
6 Util. bill
7 Take advantage of
8 Opposite of "Whoa!"
9 Poker phrase
10 "A fickle food upon a shifting plate," according to Emily Dickinson
11 Off-road goer, for short
12 What a feller needs?
13 Food in Exodus 16
14 First name in mystery
15 Gob
16 El Misti's locale
17 Sums (up)
18 Twinkies or cookies, e.g.
26 Amherst campus, briefly
28 Bean of Hollywood
29 Neuter
34 Periodic table abbr.
36 Rework
37 Paige tangles the hair while . . .
39 Robbie takes punches while . . .
40 "Gotcha"
41 Deep in thought
42 Sanctuary
43 Wing
44 Manny leaves guns at home while . . .
45 Cool drinks
46 Foster in the movies
47 Sullies
48 Work, in a way
51 Western settings
53 Money source, for short
55 Checkout clerk's question
57 Class group: Abbr.
59 Quit
60 Fierce one
61 Listen to
63 ___ de coeur
64 Imagist poet Doolittle
65 Lets go
67 1964 title role for Tony Randall
68 Demanding
70 Prefix with benzene
72 Languish
73 Not hold it in
74 Spanish flower
76 Voucher
77 Basil picks fruit while . . .
80 Never, after "in"
81 New Jersey city near Hackensack

by Manny Nosowsky

83 Layout
85 Giant
86 Act of faith?
87 Like a lecher
89 Hole in the wall?
91 Tiny
93 "It was ___ and stormy night"
94 Fictional salesman
95 Antenna holder?
97 A large spread
98 Florida ZIP code starter
99 Naval bases?
100 Opera singer Simon ___
101 Body structure: Abbr.
102 Rehab target
103 Baron in "Der Rosenkavalier"
105 Blues singer James
106 "___ deal!"
108 Darn

51 WE'RE #2!

ACROSS

1 Electrical gizmo
8 Ones hoping to get in
16 Defense Dept. branch
20 Soothe
21 Wild apple source
22 Fourth of July marcher's accompaniment
23 #2 with lots of hits
25 Gymnast Korbut
26 Vulcans and others
27 Roadside sign abbr.
29 Tape format
30 Actor Cage, familiarly
31 Ohio cheerleader's request, twice
32 Rest area?
35 Criticize
37 ___-Globe
38 Responses to babies
39 Boffo show
41 Fall cache
42 "___ been to the mountaintop": King
43 Listens
46 Blight victim
47 Erred on
50 Patient of unknown origin?
51 Partially submerged structures
54 Spy Rudolf and others
55 ___ Lanka
56 Ultimate

57 "The Age of Bronze" artist
58 Old but new again
60 Vet, of a sort
63 Need to pay
65 Overseas address: Abbr.
66 Welcome sign for a producer
67 Litigators' grp.
68 Crystal set part
69 Singer's warm-up syllables
70 Oft-visited part of a pub
71 Department of eastern France
72 Defraud
73 "Suicide Blonde" rock group
74 Legendary reptile with a fatal breath
76 One putting on cargo
78 Turkish title
80 It follows Leap Day: Abbr.
81 Villa ___, Tivoli
82 Story's approach
83 1978 blockbuster movie co-written by Mario Puzo
87 Mug material
88 Every, on an Rx
89 Painting guides
90 Colts, on a scoreboard
91 Little hooters with big peepers
94 Carved dish
95 It may be brought up on charges
96 European peak

99 Change the direction of
101 Nine digits: Abbr.
102 The Way, according to Lao-Tse
103 It's always in sonnets
104 German cry
105 Baker's unit
107 "Generously" bill
111 Locale for Georgia O'Keeffe
113 #2 on a table
117 Destination for visitors to Paris
118 It might give you a fat lip
119 1984 Martin/Tomlin comedy
120 Oboe or sax
121 Rooftop, perhaps
122 Visibly tired

DOWN

1 Indo-Europeans
2 Buy and sell
3 Magnet alloy
4 Long-snouted fish
5 One recently bar mitzvahed, e.g.
6 Too wowed for words
7 Fortifications with double parapets
8 Big plot
9 Newspaper employee
10 India neighbor: Abbr.
11 Fourth after F.D.R.
12 Resident: Suffix
13 One-named designer

14 Reacts with shock
15 Venus's sister
16 Subj. of many a faked video
17 #2 on a stand
18 Soft blanket
19 Thanksgiving dos
24 Green: Prefix
28 #2 on a ticket
33 Skin
34 Tries to get information
36 F.D.R. affliction
38 #2 with lots
39 Final precursor
40 Rear
42 Without purpose
43 Verifiable, as facts
44 A Turner
45 Library regular
47 Cooking wine
48 Portuguese, e.g.
49 #2 for a driver
52 Certain zinger
53 Game on a table
55 Shore dinner entree
59 Wall St. action
60 A for Adenauer
61 Tic-tac-toe loser
62 Mdse.
64 Used to be
68 It's a wrap
74 Makes impossible
75 Bawdy
77 Oscar-winning composer Bernstein
79 Plunder the contents of
80 Certain brew
84 Early space chimp

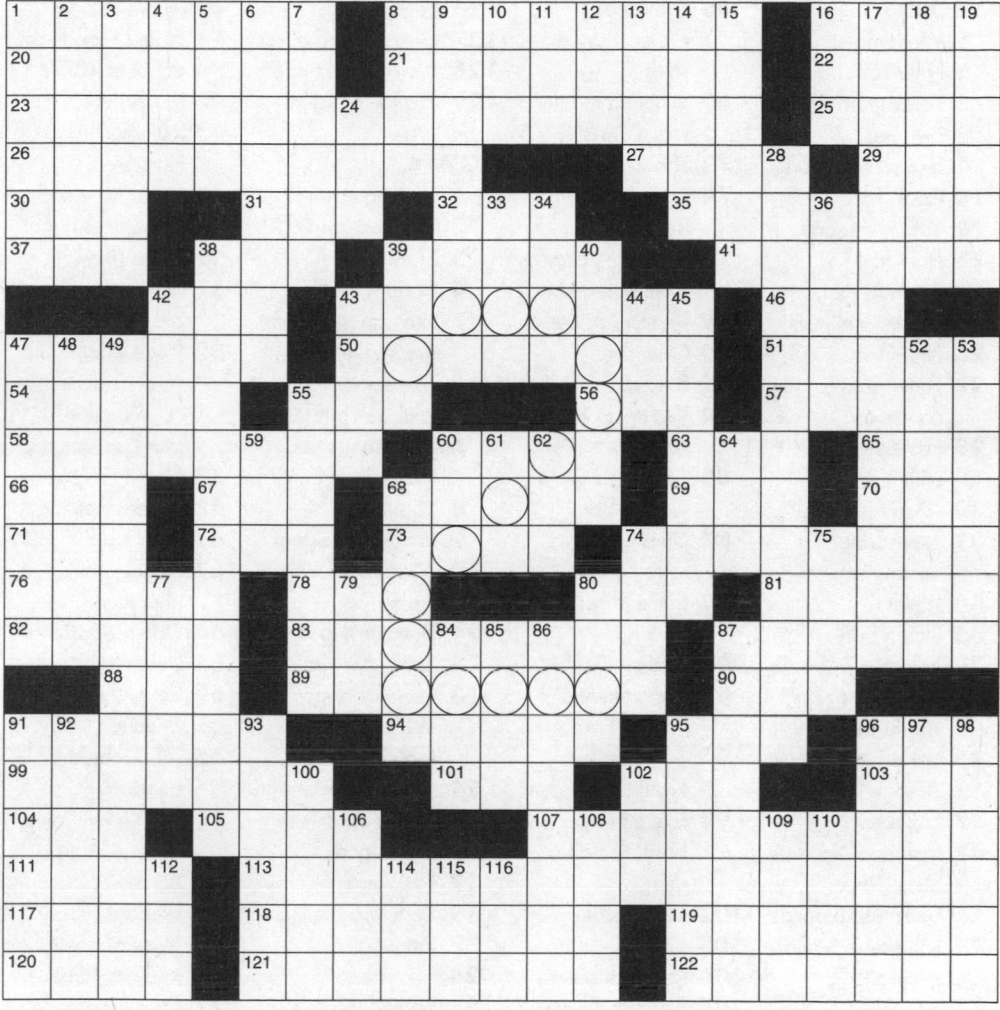

by Patrick Merrell

85 Some HDTV's
86 What something shouldn't be called
87 40-point meld
91 Jesse Jackson, e.g.
92 Concerned ones' assurance
93 Aged potable
95 Unwanted buildup
96 Oxygenate
97 Peanut, e.g.
98 Certain major
100 Deep lake out West
102 X
106 Cut down
108 Let out
109 Had in hand
110 Fiber-yielding shrub
112 Old cartoonist Hoff
114 Inventor Whitney
115 One can't stand having this
116 Braggart's display

ACROSS

1 Wedding staple
5 New Test. book
8 Relay team member
14 Like some orders
18 Cool
20 Suffix with pay
21 Hold fast
22 Footnote abbr.
23 Master violinist?
26 First-place
27 Throw into confusion
28 Increases, with "up"
30 "Don't give up!"
31 Newspaper income source
34 Lifeless
35 Doing battle
39 Ireland's patron saint in a tizzy?
45 Hindu deity
46 Sandra of "Gidget"
47 ___ rule
48 Irish poet Seamus ___, 1995 Literature Nobelist
49 Long-term sewing project?
54 ___ John
55 Equal
56 Actress Davis of the "Matrix" movies
57 It's found in stacks
59 Hamas competitor, for short
60 Health care supplement for seniors
63 Gets rid of
66 Subject of evolutionary study
69 Where a toddler sets a drink?
72 Thaw
74 Penn of "Mystic River"
75 Bob of the comedy team Bob and Ray
79 Mercury or Saturn
80 Offenses
82 Kind of game
84 Realm of Otto I: Abbr.
85 Some Red Cross work: Abbr.
87 Do a cowboy's job?
92 Some gallery offerings
95 Cadge
96 Department of eastern France
97 Swashbuckler Flynn
98 Like a person who has fallen off a diet?
102 Battle locale
103 Iota
104 R.I. clock setting
105 Fed. fiscal agency
107 Runners' goals
110 Reasons for excommunication
117 Slime
118 Order from an old English outlaw to his cohorts?
122 Ocean danger
123 Soprano Farrell
124 Weigh (on)
125 Attendance counter
126 Badge holder
127 Gets 100 on a test
128 Always, to a poet
129 Ocular problem

DOWN

1 Lacking cover?
2 Desert plant
3 Standard
4 Dummy
5 How angry words are spoken
6 Like some textbook publ.
7 "Diamonds and Rust" singer, 1975
8 "___ now!"
9 Neither's partner
10 A.L. and N.L. city: Abbr.
11 Dramatist Ibsen
12 Some are vital
13 ". . . for anger ___ in the bosom of fools": Eccl. 7:9
14 Not a big spender
15 Woodwind
16 ___-edged
17 Las Vegas figures
19 Early programming language
24 ___ cry
25 Something to run for
29 Canadian tribe
32 "Phooey!"
33 Assent in Acapulco
35 It's just south of the Himalayas
36 "___ you are!"
37 Took a bride
38 Bygone greeting
39 Stew ingredients
40 Wave catcher
41 Noted Broadway debut of 10/7/82
42 Klutzy
43 Author Zora ___ Hurston
44 Greek sandwich
46 Tyrannical
50 Longs (for)
51 Sides in an age-old "battle"
52 Place where you're advised "Don't fall in love," in song
53 Noted foursome
58 Boxers seek them
61 Doer's suffix
62 Pioneer cell phone co.
64 Ode preposition
65 Union foes
67 Ott of the Polo Grounds
68 John-John's stepdad
70 2,700-mile-long Russian river
71 Borrowed
72 Lifeboat support
73 Muse of poetry
76 Midwest hub
77 Check for fit
78 Electrical pioneer
79 Disney output
81 Naut. direction
83 Surrounded by
86 Impudence
88 It has six sides
89 Med. plan options
90 Leaf holders
91 Education basics, briefly

by Richard Chisholm

93 Another, in Madrid
94 Dylan Thomas's birthplace, in Wales
99 ___ acid
100 Used car transaction
101 It has six sides
105 Willow
106 Atlas abbr.
107 They're big on Wall Street
108 "A Doll's House" heroine
109 Life savers
111 Famous kicker
112 "The Grapes of Wrath" figure
113 Former Concorde fleet
114 Not genuine: Abbr.
115 Slimy
116 Bygone blade
119 Guitarist Paul
120 "South Pacific" prop
121 It does a bang-up job

ACROSS

1 Mount held sacred by pilgrims
5 "Greatest Love ___" (#1 Whitney Houston song)
10 Unloads (on)
15 Livestock feed
19 Apple product for audiophiles
20 Psychologist's study
22 Bivouac
24 Big name in Art Deco
25 K–12, in education
26 One earning rewards
28 "You . . . will . . . ___!"
29 Warbler
31 "Faint heart ___ won . . ."
32 Firefly's young
34 Former Atlantic City hotspot, with "the"
35 O, for one
38 Common project in shop class
40 Singer James
41 Genetics lab study
42 Very recently
44 Part of E.E.C.: Abbr.
45 Hanoi holiday
47 ___ Electric Co.
49 "Rouen Cathedral" painter
50 Derby
52 Set on
55 Multicolored
57 George's lyrical brother
59 Favorable position
62 Worthy of page one
66 Looped handle, in archaeology
67 Shipped
69 Alphabet trio

70 Safecracker
72 "___ magic!"
73 Transcript stat.
74 Range maker
75 Rowlands of "Another Woman"
76 Puffin, for one
77 Online guffaw
78 Blow
80 ___-ovo vegetarian
82 Arm offerer
84 N.Y.C. drive, with "the"
85 Dennis of the N.B.A.
87 Boy toy?
88 Rev.'s address
89 Kind of special
92 Double-decker, e.g.
93 Sanctioned
96 Michael and others
99 Jumps (out)
100 Shoot the breeze
101 Tip off
102 Daddy-o
104 Former sporty Pontiacs
106 "Tsk, tsk!"
107 Judge Lance
108 Make ___ dash for
109 "Strange Magic" band, for short
110 Sniffish sort
111 Painter Magritte
112 Foreign assembly
114 1996 Beatles hit
118 Spike's greeting
119 Made like
120 Top
122 Green land?
124 ___ living (bring home the bacon)
126 Paris daily, with "Le"
129 Classic cars, popularly
132 High ___
133 Chaotic condition
136 Daughter of Cadmus
137 Retriever

140 Drive away
142 ___-Caps (candy)
143 Formerly
144 Resisting
146 "I'll be back in ___!"
147 Swab
149 Mobutu ___ Seko of Zaire
150 3-Down, for one
157 They're tops
158 Pull an all-nighter
159 Palliate
160 "The Little Clock" poet Wylie
161 Part of a pot
162 "Beetle Bailey" pooch
163 Like some neutrals
164 Guam's capital, old-style
165 Operatic prince

DOWN

1 Party
2 Transfer, as a computer file
3 Artist born April 26, 1785
4 "Gotcha"
5 Klutz
6 Shed stuff
7 Had a little lamb?
8 Subject of a lic.
9 The Fighting Tigers of the Southeastern Conf.
10 Can't stand
11 Locked up
12 12th-century year
13 Janis of stage and screen
14 Troutlike fish
15 Persian cry
16 Garden spots
17 Camper's jelly
18 "Yo!"
21 One of the Islas Baleares

23 Tropical flower in florists' shops
27 Modern, to Beethoven
30 Alcatraz inmate
33 Pink flamingo, for one
36 AARP target
37 Stopped fooling around
38 Person likely to have binoculars
39 Old antisubversive grp.
43 "Star Wars" character
46 ___ kwon do
48 Project's end?
51 To be, to Gigi
53 Authority
54 Corralled animal
55 Doctor's aid
56 Like some estates
58 Writer Quindlen
60 Egg holders
61 Equilibriums
63 3-Down work
64 Plot
65 Monogram on a scarf
68 Like plastic slipcovers
71 St. Peter's station
74 ___ crossroads
75 Lovers' conveyance
79 Downing St. V.I.P.'s
81 Prairie home
83 Unpolished
84 Monk's title
86 Linguist Chomsky
90 Sit-up target
91 Pet shop bagful
94 Jell-O maker
95 Novelist Malraux
97 It helps you get a leg up
98 Peace disturbers

by Elizabeth C. Gorski

100 U.S. general's command
101 Egrets and herons
103 Sit
105 Pinhead
111 Go on and on
113 Actress Gardner
115 Phone no. add-on
116 Time piece
117 Golfers' delights
121 Ring events
123 "Don't think so!"
125 Capacity
126 Total disaster
127 Flip
128 Attacks
130 Garden fixtures
131 Pageant wear
134 Must
135 Big shooter
138 Others, to Jorge
139 1965 Moody Blues hit
141 Classical opener?
145 San ___, Italian Riviera city
148 Kyrgyzstan range
151 "Lord, is ___?": Matthew
152 Motor add-on
153 Singer's job
154 ___ New York minute
155 Junior
156 Part of a chorus line?

54   SELF-DEFINING

ACROSS

1 New Hampshire's state flower
6 Spanish boys
12 Photo ___
15 Hungarian sheepdog
19 Robert of TV's "Vega$"
20 State bordering Arizona
21 See circled squares
23 See circled squares
25 Foolhardiness
26 "Bewitched" role
27 Ancient coins of Greece
28 Visual illusions
29 Kathleen who wrote "Through a Glass Darkly"
30 Tombstone letters
31 See circled squares
35 Liable to snap
36 Computer fodder
37 Car last made in 1957
38 A Verizon predecessor
39 "Absolutely!"
40 Biblical kingdom
42 Unknown element
45 W.W. II general ___ Arnold
46 Pesto ingredient
47 Singer Janis
48 Cabbie's question
51 Dueler's unit
54 "___ him on a Monday" (Crystals lyric)
56 Theme park company
59 One in debt
60 Newsman John

62 Fill up again with inventory
65 "In my dreams!"
68 Where you can hear a PIN drop
69 See circled squares
72 Big or little dipper
73 Melville novel
75 Like the Pledge of Allegiance
76 Quits the Net
78 "When I was ___ . . ."
80 Himalayan myth
81 Furman's partner in brokerage
83 Quod ___ demonstrandum
84 Massage
87 Men
89 Family girl
91 Abbr. in car ads
92 Least polite
95 Kind of cow
96 Failure in bridge
99 ___ low profile
102 Pants part
103 "Pass ___!"
105 Writer Cecil of "The Straight Dope"
107 See circled squares
109 Boston skyscraper, informally, with "the"
110 Nana's mate
111 Bizet opera priestess
112 Impugn
114 Help by confirming a false alibi
115 Worker's advocate, for short

118 Dictionary term for any of the "self-defining" answers in this puzzle
120 See circled squares
121 Spectrum member
122 "Flying Down ___" (1933 movie)
123 "This one's ___!"
124 Compass dir.
125 Fishy sign
126 Sin city

DOWN

1 Clearness
2 Steel factory input
3 Hockey great Eric
4 Cast
5 See circled squares
6 Hit CBS drama
7 See circled squares
8 Shortly
9 Ecuadoran volcano that erupted in 1940
10 Oblast capital SSW of Moscow
11 Impudence
12 How tuna may be served in a diner
13 Coin-operated entertainment
14 Poisonous plant
15 Hardly svelte
16 ___ possidetis (as you possess, at law)
17 Turned on
18 Like winter sidewalks
22 Any "Cheers" episode, now

24 Some apron wearers
31 Not PC?
32 See circled squares
33 "Snazzy!"
34 Fair
36 Pioneer German automaker
37 Title girl in a hit 1925 musical
41 Willow
43 See circled squares
44 Pi follower
46 Wanna-___ (pretenders)
49 "Dallas" family name
50 VCR button
51 Jr.'s exam
52 Firm member: Abbr.
53 See circled squares
55 Instant
57 Eggs on
58 Columbus Day mo.
61 Element of tribal warfare?
63 Ethelred the Unready, for one
64 Classic name in Irish ales
66 Resting place
67 Bulk
70 Baseball's Ron
71 Seeps
74 Tarzan portrayer
77 Meet with
79 Titled Frenchman
82 See circled squares
84 Azerbaijan's capital
85 Store sign
86 They're busy
88 Allowances

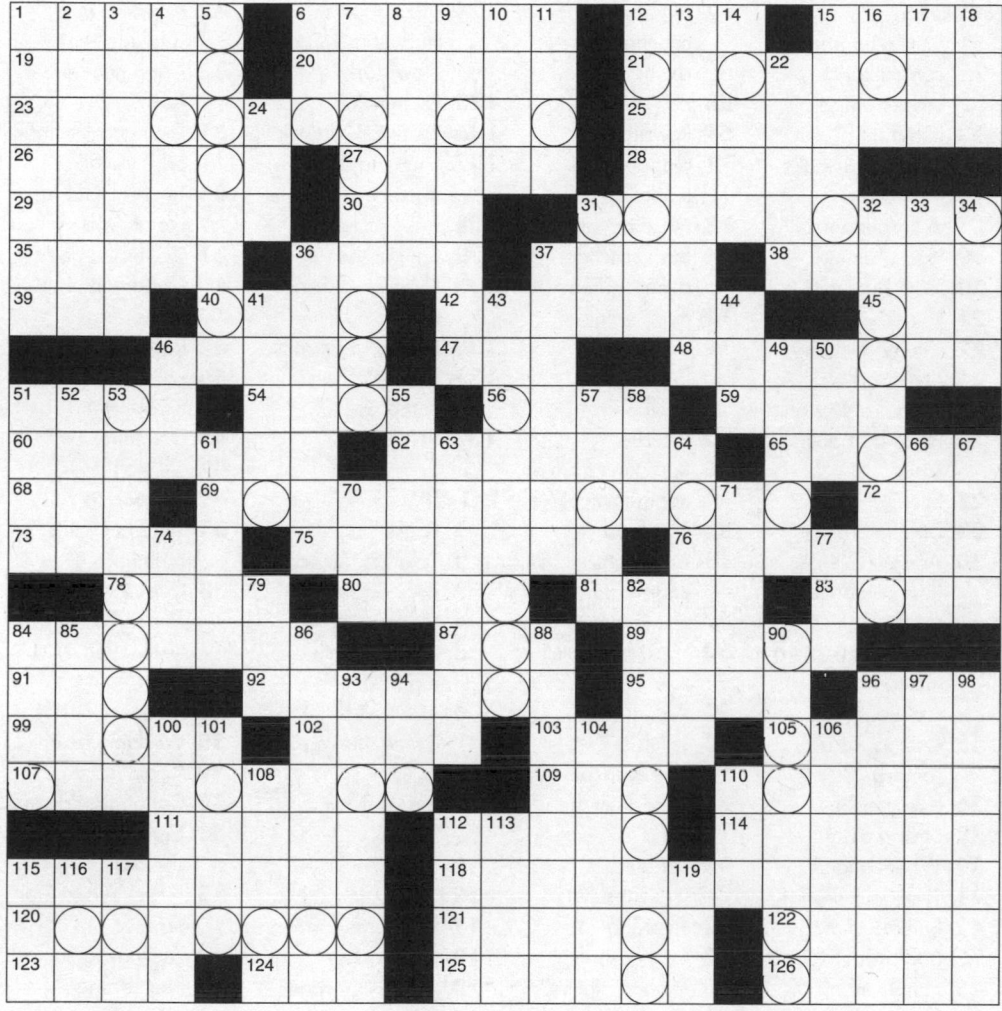

by Derrick Niederman

90 See circled squares
93 Medical disappointment
94 Scotland's Firth of ___
96 1970s sitcom title role
97 Italian shopping mart
98 Russia, once
100 Hairy
101 Insurance worker
104 Like "Aida"
106 Korean car
108 Brings on
110 Day-___
112 Leave out
113 Gershwin's "The ___ Love"
115 Cause of many calls to the police, often
116 Pitcher Robb ___
117 "How Dry ___"
119 Children's author/illustrator Asquith

ACROSS

1 Best Western competitor
7 Ledger entry
12 Need a lift?
15 Bit of cheesecake
18 Metalware decoration
19 Hair dressing
20 New Deal inits.
21 Hurler's stat.
22 Clingy duchess?
24 New York's ___ School of Design
26 Place for booths: Abbr.
27 Slick
28 Double-crosser
30 Andrea ___ (lost passenger ship)
31 Comment about a mixed public reaction?
35 Cutting, as a remark
36 Like peas in ___
38 Strong as ___
39 Wheel alignment
41 That, to a señorita
42 Summa cum ___ (top grads)
45 Family man, familiarly
48 Il or elle, in Paris
50 Some summer workers
52 "___ oui!"
54 Agree
57 Plowing December roads, e.g.?
62 Tea accompanier
63 Some seasonal Florida residents
66 Prohibitory words
67 Start of a counting-out rhyme
68 Pay stub?
69 Rewrites
71 Gogol's "___ Bulba"
73 N.L. East city
74 Bush solicitor general Theodore
77 Fluid overload
79 Weight of a lorry's load, maybe
82 Release
83 Reception from a Roman emperor?
85 Fast-food restaurant equipment
87 ___-Rooter
88 "Don Pasquale" role
92 Annoy
95 Levels
98 Like some blows to the side of the head
99 Pot-au-___ (French stew)
101 The King
103 Casual shirts
105 Moving picture?
106 More advanced, in a way
108 "Restrooms ahead"?
113 See 115-Across
114 South America's Rio ___
115 Modern locale of ancient 113-Across
116 Cut through
119 Brought out
121 Most bookish student in western New York?
125 Pitcher Robb ___
126 Bikini-to-Oahu dir.
127 They may be seen in cameos
128 Juice producer
129 One of the "Star Trek" series, to fans
130 Bygone map inits.
131 "Camelot" composer
132 Seizure

DOWN

1 Pause
2 Take ___ (snooze)
3 Delineates
4 "I ___ Rock"
5 Luth. or Meth., e.g.
6 1966 Michael Caine title role
7 Frank
8 It runs Down Under
9 Lowest parts
10 "___ care"
11 Like some farmers
12 Gatekeeper
13 Actress Gardner
14 Flower smeller?
15 Barbarian songwriter?
16 ___ Army (links group)
17 Herod's fortress
19 Intrusive
23 First Lady of Jazz
25 Groundskeeper's order
29 Surgeon general under Reagan
32 Adjective in a "Ripley's" entry
33 Asian peninsula: Abbr.
34 They may be final or physical
36 Tomb of ___, in Najaf, Iraq
37 Go for the gold?
40 Quadrennial games org.
43 Eagle of the sea
44 Possible reason for a poke in the ribs
46 Domestic
47 ___ noir
49 As soon as
51 Alfred Nobel's birthplace
53 Caesar's March 15 destination
55 Bond
56 Staggers
58 Wedding belle
59 Virgin Isl., e.g.
60 Cartoonist Edward
61 Candidate's declaration
63 "The Voyage Out" novelist
64 Feeling worse
65 Foul-tasting dessert?
70 ___-Hawley Tariff Act of 1930
72 Eye site
75 Arch with a point
76 Viking competitions?
78 Noted wine area
80 It means everything
81 As required, after "if"

by Charles M. Deber

84 "___ the conquered!": Livy
86 Lambert Airport locale: Abbr.
89 Identical
90 Cross shape
91 Goal-oriented guy
93 Holyfield of the ring
94 Hillock
96 Whistle blower, for short
97 Font lines
99 Arouse
100 Big roll
102 Pair of lamps, maybe
104 Dweller on the Danube
107 Article in Die Welt
109 El ___
110 "El ___" (1983 film)
111 Linney of "The Truman Show"
112 Reason (from)
117 Yeasty brews
118 Herbaceous plant
120 Dash widths
122 Part of a business report, with "the"
123 Bank deposit
124 Word repeated before "away"

ACROSS

1 ___ Maine
4 Literary biographer Lord David ___
9 Colonnade tree
12 Strongly recommended
18 Actress Zadora
19 1988 comeback hit for the Beach Boys
20 Flirting with a patient, e.g.?
22 Slop trough site
23 What the mother of a dozen kids says just before turning out the light?
25 Hostility
27 Make big, as hair
28 Open house org.
29 "Let's hear it"
30 Caring grps.
32 Give out
34 Ending of a firm's name
36 V.I.P. on Al Jazeera
37 Alter ___ (another exactly the same)
39 Plant production
42 "Just the thing!"
44 Defers
47 Headquarters
49 Pillow filler
50 Delhi tongue
52 Have a "Star Wars" character preserved?
55 Straighten out
57 Worry
58 1994 "S.N.L."-based bomb starring Julia Sweeney
62 Hosp. workers
63 Miracle-___
64 Razor maker
65 Pulp
67 Actress Hatcher
68 "Get off the stage!"
69 Lively fish dance?
73 Long time
74 Bowed (to)
76 Next in line
77 "___ Kapital"
78 Food label no.
79 Lap dog
80 Musical premiere of 1805
82 Symbol of pride
84 Island purchase?
86 What the impatient reader of English essays requested?
89 Patches up
90 Brief romance
93 Out fishing, possibly
94 Making a big hit
96 Relaxes
98 Champagne classification
100 Euro pop?
101 Cast wearer's problem
104 Largish deer
105 Gershwin title character
107 In the past
109 Zen achievement
111 "Some Words With a Mummy" writer
113 Nonlethal firearm
116 Priests, e.g.
117 Phrase describing an offerer of sympathy?
121 Kind of charge
122 Royal rebuke?
123 Woos
124 Formula ___
125 High-hats
126 W.W. II spy org.
127 Benders?
128 On the warpath

DOWN

1 Advantages
2 Light show
3 Give either a wholly good or bad review?
4 Marsh marigold
5 Stretches (out)
6 Venez. neighbor
7 World bankers' grp.
8 Ball game
9 Dame ___ Everage
10 TV role for 67-Across
11 Fictional sleuth Travis
12 Purchase from the frozen foods section
13 Archaeological find
14 Delicate cut
15 Rendered immobile
16 Magnify
17 "i" piece?
19 Music compilation seller
21 Heart, e.g.
24 Oilman Leon who owned the New York Jets
26 Poet portrayed in "Il Postino"
30 1920s–'30s Winter Olympics star
31 About six centuries hence
33 Pick up the tab
35 Geom. point
38 Disapprove of
40 Opposite of hinder
41 Playboy's wear
43 In the lead
45 Is a rat
46 Sewing shop purchase
48 Tempter
50 Self-effacing
51 Suitable for rainy days
53 Like corsets
54 Campaigns in the Mideast
56 Kind of flour
59 Drum that makes tiny bird sounds?
60 Nearby
61 Touches
64 Brought forth
66 Paint remover
70 Jewel case inserts
71 Hidden drawback
72 Supermodel Campbell
75 Uses a harrow
81 Spy in Canaan
83 Din
84 Enemy pilot in a dogfight

by Patrick Berry

85 Softies show it
87 Bill Wyman, in the Rolling Stones
88 "A good breakfast, but an ill supper": Francis Bacon
90 ___ du Diable
91 "Bottle-nosed" creature
92 Object of the 1981 hit "Woman"
95 Holiday spots
97 Greek sea god
99 Elton John's "___ Song"
102 "Body Heat" actor Richard
103 Not explicit
106 ___ voce
108 Sweater style
110 They may be bitter
112 Kellogg company brand
114 As follows
115 Is amused by
116 "Look ___!"
117 Work units: Abbr.
118 Legendary Giant
119 Boatload
120 Clamor

ACROSS

1 "The Lucy-___ Comedy Hour"
5 Preppy sportswear label
9 Set in concrete, so to speak
14 Lhasa ___ (dogs)
19 Airline info, for short
20 French film director Clément
21 Oldsmobile sedan
22 Surgeon's insert
23 1997 action film about a spa duo?
26 Devonshire dad
27 Saturn's largest satellite
28 Journalist Lindstrom
29 Statistical measure
31 Filly, but not a billy
32 Candidate's goal
33 Latin hip-shakers
36 Former queen of Jordan
37 Neck feathers?
38 1981 thriller about bygone blade holders?
42 Return addressee
45 Dash alternative
46 Safety org.
47 Hatch
48 Yoplait competitor
50 Grasped
53 Butler of fiction
56 Spill producer
57 1985 teen movie about morning washup?
61 Turf
62 Biblical gift
63 Thug
67 Journal
70 "Awake and Sing!" playwright
73 Removes from power?
75 Wonder Woman, for one
77 Scads
79 Philip who wrote a 1975 C.I.A. exposé
80 1983 tearjerker set at a salon?
85 Over
89 "60 Minutes" correspondent
90 "ER" roles, briefly
91 Consider extremely funny
92 Start of a Beatles title
94 Suit makers' org.?
96 Novelist Tan
97 Draft letters
98 1998 war film about a beard?
105 Yom ___ (Jewish holiday)
106 Standout
107 Woman's shoe type
108 Ad ___
111 Hip-hop's Dr. ___
112 They're effervescent
114 Aries or Taurus
115 "Shucks!"
116 Pianist Claudio
118 1987 British film about a balding man's lament?
123 Cold forecast
124 Frostflower
125 Brewer's stock
126 Sushi fish
127 Singer Nelson and others
128 Assents
129 1940s foe, with "the"
130 Slow-cook

DOWN

1 One who is thrown a ball
2 Divisions politiques
3 "Three Pieces in the Shape of a Pear" composer
4 Babylonian love goddess
5 A theocratic republic
6 Kind of state
7 Even (with)
8 Casual wear
9 Wide's partner
10 U.N. workers' grp.
11 Neighbor of Colo.
12 French rocket launcher
13 Exiled dictator with a palindromic name
14 Bad-mouth
15 Class-conscious grp.
16 Puts a price on freedom
17 Small and insignificant
18 Barely ran
24 Charge dodger
25 Olivia ___ of "The Wonder Years"
30 Favor
33 Clever comment
34 Away
35 Turn on
39 Defense type
40 Gloaters' cries
41 Sports bar staples
42 Name provider
43 Gung-ho
44 Sternutation
49 Bull or Cav
50 It's above the horizon
51 Jimi Hendrix's do
52 Charge
54 Ticker tape?: Abbr.
55 Corps de ballet
58 Egyptian god of the universe
59 Bundle
60 Marceau's everyman
64 Wool producer
65 Some pistols
66 Gemini rockets
68 Go over
69 Connects with
71 Outsiders
72 Fax function
74 Small paving stones
76 Techno-funk band with the 1991 #1 hit "Unbelievable"
78 Pitches
81 Burn
82 Circle
83 Group of companies
84 Formal pronoun
85 Prepare for later, in a way
86 Couldn't stand

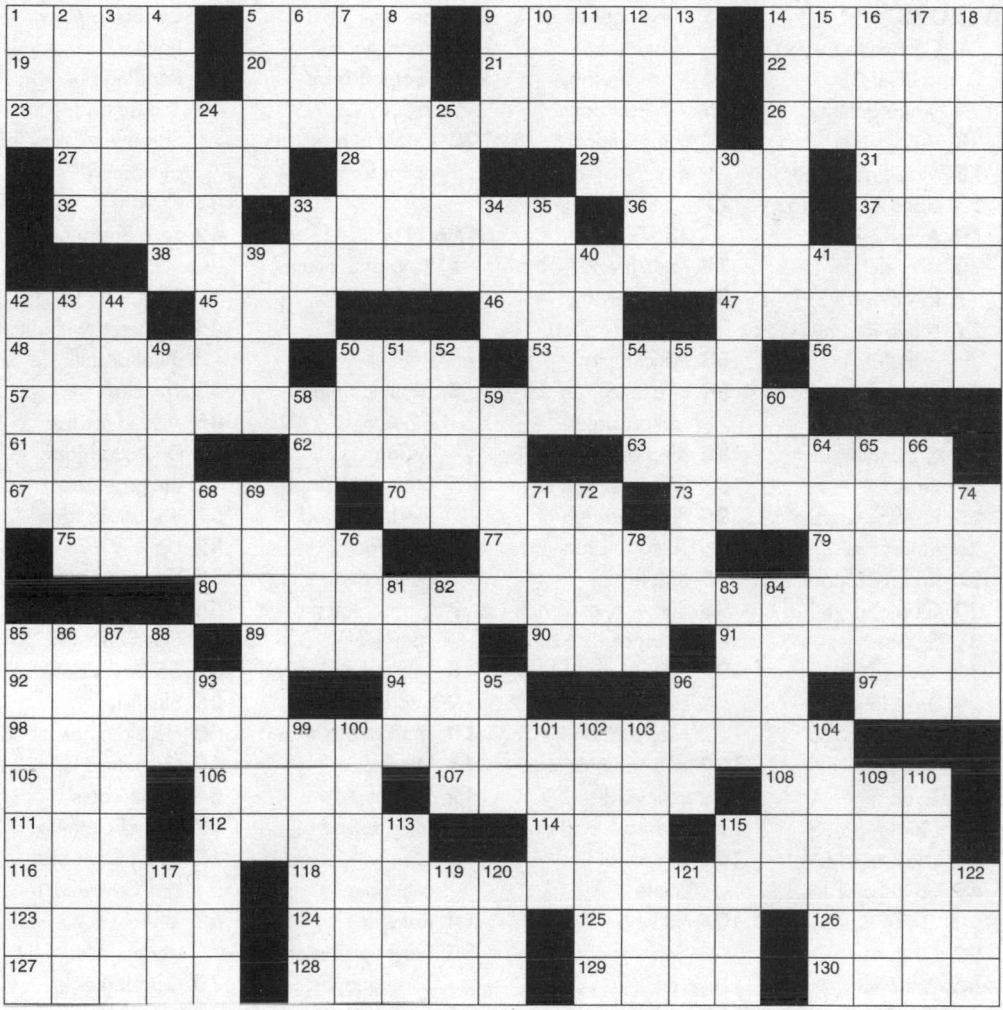

by Deb Amlen and Nancy Salomon

ACROSS

1 Carrier to Kyoto, in brief
4 Strike gently
8 Voice
15 Map lines: Abbr.
18 Liberal D.C. group
19 Actor Morales
20 Woodcutter in folklore
21 Leave in a hurry, with "out"
22 Start of a quote by 102-Across
24 Carpenter, at times
25 Present opener?
26 Inner: Prefix
27 Impose (upon)
29 Quote, part 2
31 Slobber
33 "Wassup?!"
35 Base lines
36 Lab sights
37 Whiskey ___
39 Spat
43 Quote, part 3
48 Least ruddy
49 Sayings of Jesus
50 "Take ___!"
52 Stretches
56 Pell-mell
57 Solidifies
58 Fragrance used in perfumes
59 Fix at the blacksmith's
61 Szczecin's river
63 Conoco rival
65 Monet oil "Vétheuil en ___"
66 Quote, part 4
71 Father's talk: Abbr.
72 Furnish
73 Greek goddess of war
74 More squirmy
75 Where troops camp after a day's march
77 ___ Rebellion of 1857–59
79 Tex's friend
82 Annual May event, for short
83 Insect nests
84 Stroke in calligraphy
85 Kind of membrane
87 Quote, part 5
94 River through Toledo, Ohio
95 Kindle
96 Showing evidence of fright
97 "The Boondocks" cartoonist McGruder
100 Like some college volleyball
101 Theseus' land
102 Source of the quote
107 Ed who played Santa Claus in "Elf"
110 Abbr. on an envelope
111 Whistler's whistle
112 Pigged out
114 End of the quote
116 Collectibles source
117 Upwardly mobile type
118 "Mi chiamano Mimi," e.g.
119 Letters of success
120 Snitch
121 Pooh-pooh
122 "Potpourri for 1,000, ___"
123 Count in a full count

DOWN

1 King of Scotland, 1567–1625
2 Keats, to Shelley
3 Exciting time at 82-Across
4 A pop
5 Stars and Stripes land, for short
6 Chalupa alternative
7 Kind of torch on "Survivor"
8 Waited patiently
9 World Cup cry
10 Martial arts expert
11 "Peek-___!"
12 Half of a TV alien's send-off
13 One with a handle
14 Rake in
15 New version of a song, maybe
16 Doltish
17 Pares pounds
21 A field may have one
23 Patterned fabric
28 Demonstrates
30 Ruthless boss, perhaps
32 Letters on a cognac bottle
34 "___-hoo!"
37 ___ breve
38 Orders to plow horses
39 Reading pen
40 "Sense and Sensibility" director, 1995
41 "Yes"
42 Eero Saarinen's ___ Terminal at J.F.K.
44 Prepared without meat or milk
45 The cloth
46 Added for free
47 Drove to hiding in the ground
51 It's just an idea
52 Up
53 Like some traits
54 Spanish highway
55 See 57-Down
57 55-Down donkey
58 Blemish
60 Heraldic border
62 Go extinct
64 Accelerated
67 Line of clothing
68 1924 Olympics star Gertrude
69 Internet annoyances
70 Quarterback Manning
76 Fund for a little fun
78 Toll road
80 Maple genus
81 Rip off
84 Good name for a flight attendant?
85 Advertising figure with a cane
86 Narrow strip

by Brendan Emmett Quigley

88 Place for a turret
89 Spanish bear
90 To be, in Toledo
91 Like the best-looking teeth
92 Land measure
93 Endlessly
97 Label on a certain advertising photo
98 Oranjestad's island
99 Rushed
100 Humor, with "to"
101 1970s sitcom
103 Blasts with a ray gun
104 Get ___ (bronze)
105 ___ Noël
106 Make way?
108 Sweet 16 org.
109 Peer
113 ___ whim
115 Line on a cash register receipt

ACROSS

1 Lock up for a long time
9 Bordering area
14 Tests for some coll. seniors
18 Modern times
19 Rear
20 Easy two-pointer
22 Where to color cartoons?
24 End of ___
25 Drivers' org.
26 Abbr. before some state names
27 Place to walk, for short
28 Tot
30 No string bean
32 Nile slitherers
34 Gas: Prefix
35 "May ___ frank?"
36 Musical notes
37 Demand more cartoon ideas?
41 Wall St. hiree
42 Follows
43 T size: Abbr.
44 Desires, with "after"
45 Every other quarter
47 Nightspot
50 Immigrant's sch. course
51 Means of finding cartoon signatures?
54 Fed. loan group
57 Rested (on)
59 Large number suffix
60 Slangy greetings
61 On/off points: Abbr.
62 One with lots of bucks?

63 Sign on an elementary school door
66 Wrecks
68 "The Time Machine" race
69 Stale
72 Wowed
74 City WSW of Copenhagen
75 Rembrandt van ___
76 Making lots of circles in a cartoon?
80 Russian assents
81 "You better believe it!"
82 Pogo and others
84 Up's partner
87 "Today" rival, for short
88 Title town in a John Denver song
90 Special ___
91 Aspiring cartoonist's problem?
95 What good R.N.'s dispense
96 Like Haydn's "The Fire" Symphony
97 "Cool"
98 A sci.
99 Chicken's place
102 Kicks up one's heels?
104 Pedal pusher
106 Here, to a 108-Across
108 Lady abroad: Abbr.
109 Pass
110 Cartoon dialogue?
115 ___ Hawkins Day

116 Like some rotations
117 Nowheresville
118 Word after he and she
119 In again, after being out
120 It "kills" some people

DOWN

1 Super bargain
2 Boaster's comment, in a cartoon?
3 Underground grp.
4 Commuter headaches
5 Hero aviators
6 Becomes pallid
7 Rep.
8 Quick assent
9 HBO sports series
10 Arduous chore
11 Union symbol
12 Carbohydrate suffix
13 Popular drink mix
14 Sword lilies
15 Money in Port Elizabeth
16 They're shut at night
17 Guarantee
18 Common rhyme scheme
21 Kitchen gadgets
23 N.L. team starting in 1969
29 Assn.
31 Hard-hearted
32 Miss ___ Evans of McCullers's "Ballad of the Sad Cafe"

33 Sneak
34 Bureau
37 Construction beam
38 English literary pseudonym
39 Food thickener
40 Capek play
41 Wanting as much change as possible?
42 Campers' milieu
45 North African native
46 Instant: Abbr.
47 Aristocracy
48 "Well, look here!"
49 Grant, as a title
52 Monopolist
53 Hindu title
54 Cartoons displayed on easels?
55 Many Christmas trees
56 Weigh
58 Pasta name suffix
61 Jeanne, e.g.: Abbr.
64 Traveler's alternative to J.F.K.
65 ___ Sec.
67 Some roulette bets
70 ___ Palmas
71 Yoakam who sang "Honky Tonk Man"
73 Goes blindly
76 Set off
77 "___ la Douce"
78 Around
79 Phone abbr.
81 Good laugh
83 Standout performance
84 Writer Walker and others

by Patrick Merrell

85 Screwy
86 Anthem with two sets of lyrics
88 Hurt
89 Farm enclosure
92 Marsh

93 1980s Defense secretary Weinberger
94 Classic Harlem theater
95 Sibelius's "Valse ___"

100 Havana, informally
101 Knockouts, so to speak
103 Third-century year
104 Cross condition
105 When repeated, a cry of approval

106 Summer treats
107 Pointed end
111 Feller
112 "___ a date!"
113 Moo ___ pork
114 Wrong

60   ROGET AND ME

ACROSS

1 New Deal agcy.
4 Brit's exclamation
7 "Race Horses" artist
12 Home in the mountains
18 Apple pie order?
20 Be bombastic
21 "My ___" (#1 hit for the Knack)
22 Thrift shop transactions
23 Wave to
24 Folks
25 Immovable armada?
27 Abandons Congressional workers?
29 "Battle Cry" author
30 Temple figures
32 Pope's work
33 Suffix with press
34 Football Hall-of-Famer Ford
35 Exhibition of lamps?
38 Sanction
40 File
44 Hugo, for one
45 ___ Lanka
46 It may be dammed
47 Like some milk
48 Had an epiphany?
52 Send home, in a way
55 Works on the edge
56 Grow
57 Braxton of song

58 Make up?
59 Parti-colored
60 Bring out
62 "M*A*S*H" Emmy winner
63 Suit material?
64 Level
65 U.S. rocket with a name from Greek myth
66 Chop finely
67 River to the Seine
68 Where you might take a lorgnette
70 Solomonlike
71 Mr. Television
72 Hand-me-down
73 Itch
74 Not present fairly
76 Farm implement
77 Antares, e.g.
79 1962 hit with the repeated lyric "A little bit softer now"
80 Hard to believe
81 Have a bug
82 Bark back
83 "Ma Jolie" artist
86 Barely make headway
89 Sensible tax?
91 Lummox
93 Rhyme time?
94 King or queen
95 Unkind response
97 Poetic plaint
98 Makes fun of laceworkers?
103 Dependable move for a gymnast?

105 Quarantine
106 2003 Best Actress nominee Watts
108 Resistance to change
109 Gave comfort
110 Believe in
111 Satanic disguise
112 Captivate
113 Suit material
114 Word of greeting
115 Joey ___ & the Starliters

DOWN

1 Mom, dad, three kids and luggage, e.g.
2 Jumped over
3 W.W. II battle town of Italy
4 Play Pebble Beach, say
5 Newbery Medal-winning author Scott ___
6 Twice-secured
7 Name holder
8 Slip a cog
9 Certain Celt
10 Suit to ___
11 Distinguish
12 Great divide
13 Prop for a Marx brother
14 Compass
15 Chaise ___
16 Records
17 Scottish drinking cups

19 Photo studio supplies
21 "Inside the Third Reich" writer
26 Palace resident
28 Not binding
31 Like topiary
36 Nincompoop
37 Two-faced
38 Victoria's Secret purchase
39 Writes down the names of cads?
41 Dirty tool?
42 Annoyed
43 Acct. bonus
45 Proverbial battlers
47 Utter
48 Diamond plane
49 Facing
50 Maroon
51 Flustered state
52 Long way to go?
53 Kay Thompson character
54 Analyzed
55 Wrinkle with age
56 Dish served with kraut
59 First anniversary gift
61 Cow
64 Kind of treatment
69 Beyond the pale?
70 Pleasure trips
71 Jazz's ___ Fleck and the Flecktones
75 Lady's man
76 Egg holder
78 Up to, briefly

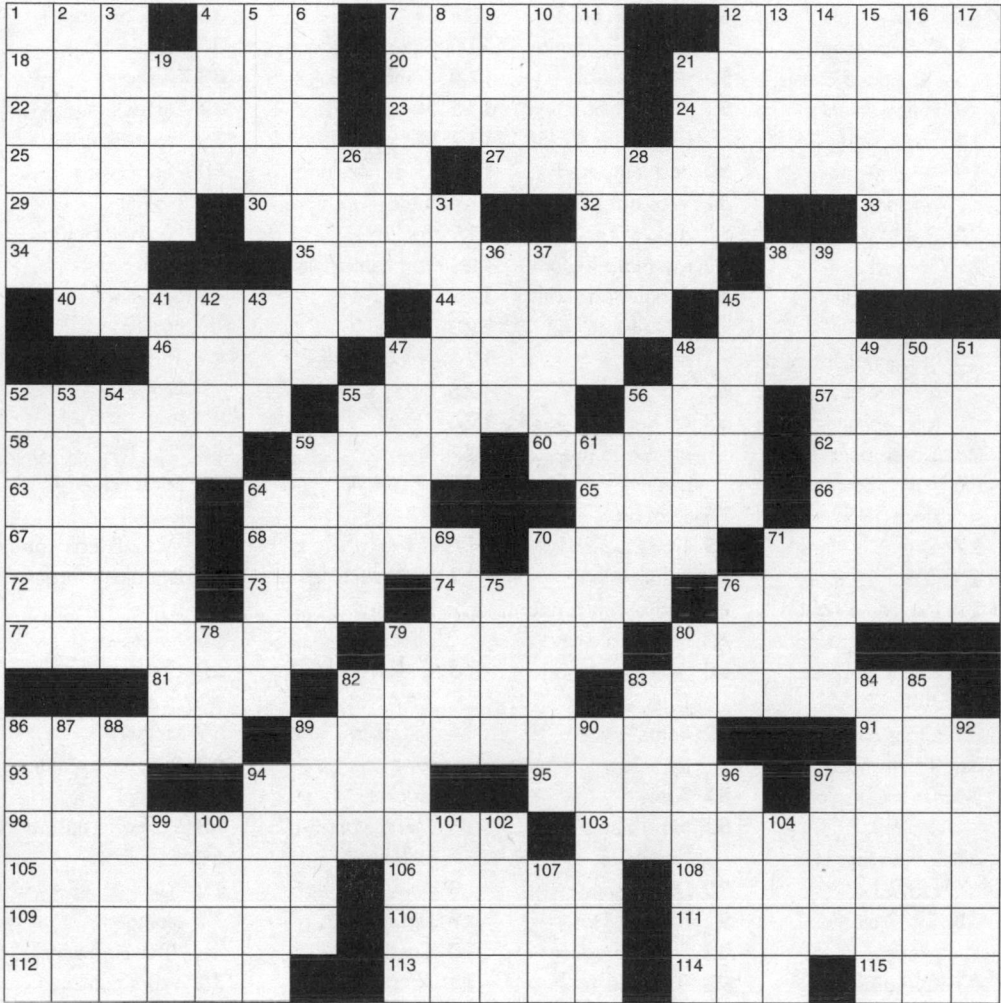

by Richard Silvestri

79 Principal charges?
80 Sushi bar offering
82 Nature
83 Answer to a charge
84 Paid respects to
85 Iridescent
86 Red shade

87 Justification
88 Neighbor of Namibia
89 Full
90 Kind of inspection
92 Will matter

94 Play (to)
96 Soprano Fleming
97 Soc. Sec. supporter
99 Criticize severely
100 Crunchy munchie
101 Reddish

102 Go bad
104 So
107 "No ___"

ACROSS

1 Club of song
5 "___ good cheer!"
9 Follow intently
14 Score sign
19 "In principio ___ verbum"
20 Gold's is 79: Abbr.
21 Spread
22 "Mule Train" singer, 1949
23 Newsman famous for inventing folksy similes
25 Green pear
26 Fast food chain since 1964
27 Online business
28 "Rose ___ rose . . ."
29 Welcome sight after a big storm
31 Kerry or Gore: Abbr.
32 Clear cover
35 It's stranded
36 Crumbly salad topping
37 When taps is played
38 1948 election group
41 Old air letters
44 Verne's circumnavigator
45 1948–52 Olympic track gold medalist Zátopek
46 Grid goals, for short
47 1987 self-titled million-selling album
48 One getting strokes?
50 Street on old TV
52 Rock's ___ Band
55 Is a guest of
57 "The ___ Sanction" (Trevanian book)
60 Bad-tempered
61 Was not off one's rocker
62 Mermaid feature
65 Shout made with an outstretched hand
66 Pro ___
67 Leader of the pack hidden in this puzzle?
74 Jazz bit
75 Trade punches
76 Balance due
77 Suffix with cannon
78 Panhandle city
80 State bordering Tibet
82 Some are in the 90s
85 Some
87 Nevil Shute's "___ Like Alice"
90 Dude, once
91 Spy ___ Hari
92 Spray producer
95 To be, in Toulon
96 Place to get conked
97 In the least
98 Setting for a Disneyland attraction
101 ___ magica (alchemist's work)
102 Rime
104 Chaps
105 Locations, old-style
107 Once owned
110 Sitter's headache
114 Bambi's aunt
115 Mindful (of)
117 Cut back
118 Goes here and there
119 Trick
121 Port containers
122 Winning
123 "Oops!"
124 Palace resident
125 Bomb trial
126 Quays
127 Phnom ___
128 "Phooey!"

DOWN

1 Quit claiming
2 Make an allocution
3 Old rival of 41-Across
4 Longfellow's bell town
5 Cricket club
6 Moral standard
7 Unfair
8 Awhile
9 Didn't sink
10 Cassiterite
11 Add-on
12 Irish dramatist Hugh, who won a Tony for "Da"
13 Old Danish king who conquered England
14 Glowers
15 Weight in gems
16 Zodiac sign
17 "Only Time" singer
18 Song ending?
24 Claims
30 Back on board
33 Thankless
34 Cast out
37 Disraeli, e.g.
39 Nonreaders
40 Peer Gynt's mother
42 Football Hall-of-Famer Ewbank
43 Showing signs of culture
44 This is its brothers' keeper
47 Box
48 "Hey!"
49 Slickrock Trail locale
51 What E. coli eat
53 Doodler's target
54 It goes by rail
56 Smidgen
58 Commemoration at a seder: Abbr.
59 Loaded
63 Res ___ loquitur
64 Kissers
68 Vatican treasure
69 "___ first . . ."
70 "Qué ___?"
71 Home of "The Sopranos"
72 What comes to mind
73 Hotbed
78 Dr.'s magazine
79 ___-Ude (Trans-Siberian Railroad city)
81 Hole producers
83 Claws
84 Rentals: Abbr.
86 It. is there
88 Prepares for editing

by Manny Nosowsky

89 Drink of forgetfulness
93 Ice machine
94 Echo
98 Most like a ghost
99 "Nor heady-rash provoked with raging ___": Shak.
100 Charm
103 Pen chorus
106 Early priest
107 Cartoon character with a helmet
108 Showground
109 Relinquish
110 Spot remover?: Abbr.
111 Rear end, in a fall
112 No longer carry
113 Cough syrup amts.
116 Charge
120 Sound of satisfaction

HEAR! HEAR!

ACROSS

1 Locale for Bo-Peep
7 Noted ennead
12 Sigmoid
19 Offered as proof
21 In concert
22 Current flowing in the direction of the wind
23 "Long live the king! Long live the king!," for example?
25 Pertinent
26 "Oh, puh-leeze!"
27 Saturn, e.g.
29 Ambient music composer Brian
30 Addition signs
33 1940s–'50s leader with a palindromic name
34 1962 war epic, with "The"
37 Mixture
38 Cotton pod in Santiago?
40 Persian pleasures?
44 Blockheads
45 Seminary graduate
49 It can be picked out
50 Prefix with natal
51 Advance, slangily
53 Load
55 Latin lover's word
56 Author Bret's deceptive move?
60 Missing, in a way
61 Washout
63 Witty Bombeck
64 Movie mogul Marcus
65 Amoeba, e.g.
66 Chatterbox
68 Sit (down)
69 Down in the dumps
70 Levee feature
71 ___ lot (gorged oneself)
72 Washington locale, with "the"
73 Bookstore sect.
74 Hebrew leader: Var.
75 Footnote abbr.
76 Bridal procession area?
79 F.D.R.-era agcy.
82 Chatterboxes
84 Code signals
85 Former California fort
86 Frick collection
87 Work ___
88 Popular music magazine
90 Consistent moneymaker
92 Quiet before lions attack an animal herd?
98 Home of 3-Down: Abbr.
99 Vulnerable area
102 She famously married in Gibraltar on 3/20/69
103 Addict
105 Flying Cloud automaker
106 Island east of Java
107 Lacking a sponsor
109 Decorative shelters
112 Herb for one at the Round Table?
117 Kick up a notch
118 "Er . . ."
119 Feature of the stratosphere
120 Abandons
121 Sore spots
122 Curt

DOWN

1 Fellah
2 Old English letter
3 Town in 98-Across
4 "The Count of Monte Cristo" setting
5 Chess pawns, e.g.
6 Bridge positions
7 Name with Dan or San
8 Earning one's keep, say
9 Parisian silk
10 Side in the War of 1812: Abbr.
11 Goodbye gala
12 Swamp
13 Judo master
14 Plenty ticked, with "up"
15 ___ Z
16 Spoke (up)
17 Suburb of Minneapolis
18 Spurious aircraft
20 ___ 180
24 Bungle
28 Letter attachments: Abbr.
30 Ski lodge fare
31 Door attachment
32 Dieter's morning routine?
34 Unwilling
35 Certain cameras, for short
36 Place to set cups
39 Bath accessory
41 Guaranteed to get
42 Wren's sound
43 "___ lied!"
46 Outcry from an eccentric group?
47 Weak hit
48 "Would you look at that?!"
51 Boardwalk diversion
52 Ceremonial splendor
53 Couple of the week, e.g.
54 Unfamiliar
57 Carter and others
58 Concedes
59 Unedited
62 Old-fashioned water conduit
66 Catalan composer ___ Nunó, who wrote the music for the Mexican national anthem
67 In the box
68 España, por ejemplo
69 ESP, they say
70 Kid carriers
72 Flirty wife in "Of Mice and Men"
73 Spring sound
74 Razor brand
77 Explain to
78 Summer Games grp.
80 Drudge
81 Battling

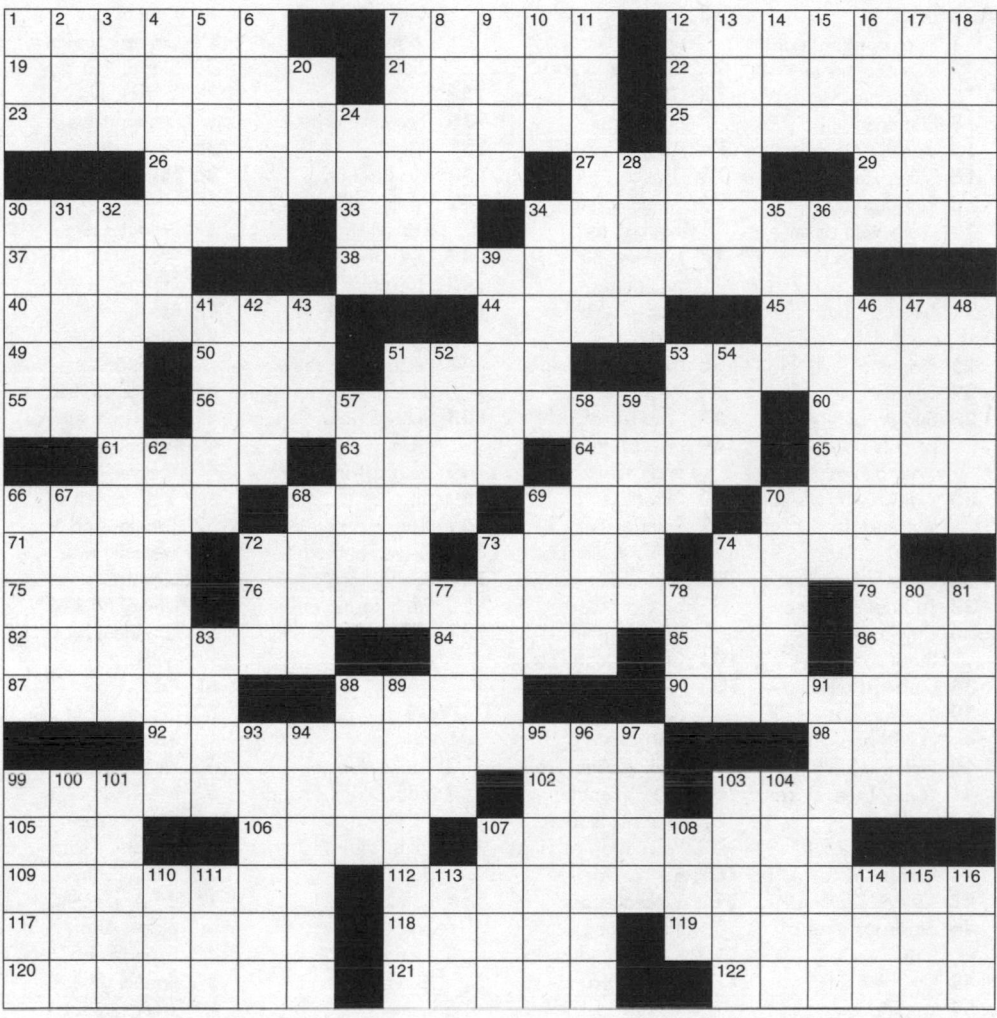

by Peter Abide and Steven Kahn

ACROSS

1 Rock band with an electrical name
5 Asian new year
8 Stationed (in)
13 Varnish ingredient
16 Batter's box
20 Ring figure
21 Prefix with center
22 Thrill to pieces
23 "Exodus" role
24 "Like ___ out of . . ."
25 Bingeing
27 Succeed
28 Subject of Stefan Fatsis's book "Word Freak"
30 Artisan who works with metal
31 "Bali ___"
32 Square measures
33 Teasdale and Lee
34 City in a George Strait country hit
38 Guitarist Allman
39 "___ his kiss" (1964 pop lyric)
40 Gel in a lab
41 "Only Time" singer
43 Cellist Rostropovich, to friends
45 Cute ___ button
46 Starts, as a roll of film
49 On the right
51 Laid up
53 Jeanne ___
55 Rockies resort
56 Fathers
58 Domino-shaped fig.
59 Dungeons & Dragons spellcaster
60 Disintegrated, as cells
62 Pulled off
64 Pastoral sound
65 See 45-Down
66 Finger
67 + end

68 Legendary maker of a 96-Across
71 Calendario page
72 "Rhinoceros" playwright
74 Airline to Sweden
75 Drollery
76 Something to exercise in
77 Nutmeg State collegian
79 Stars and stripes, and others
83 Long-distance inits.
84 Was idle
87 "The Turtle" poet
89 Noughts in noughts-and-crosses
90 Actor Bert
91 Ruler amts.
94 Literary alter ego
96 Item commissioned by George Washington
101 Charge to the limit
103 "Man, do ___ a drink!"
104 Abridges
105 "Ally McBeal" role
106 1990s Senate majority leader
107 Polynesian carvings
109 Buffalo, for one
112 Vincent Lopez's theme song
113 K–12, in education
114 City with a Volkswagen plant
115 Org. with a lab
118 Martial arts expert
119 Scott Turow's first book
120 Reagan-era program: Abbr.
121 Nickname in which "A" stands for Alex
122 Shiraz native
124 Sight from Bern
126 Bowl stats: Abbr.
127 Pine product
129 Innateness

131 Wife of the Duke of Cornwall, in Shakespeare
133 Fills up
135 These, to Jorge
137 Drifts
139 Persona non ___
142 White-collar worker
144 Gym bag stuff
145 Marriage, e.g.
146 Underworld figures?
147 Person who shows discrimination
148 Spread on a dinner table
149 ___ upswing
150 Jiffy
151 "Luncheon on the Grass" and others
152 Pea jackets?
153 Pre-V formation
154 1992 Wimbledon champ

DOWN

1 On
2 Traffic director
3 With 86-, 17- and 91-Down, how to "illustrate" this puzzle
4 Bob of broadcasting
5 National park in Newfoundland
6 Some foils
7 Rank
8 Solicit
9 Hello and goodbye
10 Leopards are spotted here
11 Online commerce
12 "___ Freischütz" (Weber opera)
13 Unit of punishment
14 Rainbowlike
15 Juggling, e.g.
16 Beach shelter
17 See 3-Down

18 Kind of force
19 Giverny summers
26 Storm, to a captain
29 Whatsoever
34 Eastern titles
35 Dr.'s orders
36 Historic Virginia family
37 Black beauty
39 "Forget it!"
40 Improvises
42 Motionless
44 Dick Cheney's predecessor
45 Part of 65-Across
47 Red Cross effort
48 Penpoints
49 Tootsie
50 Scale notes
52 Tanglewood Music Festival town
54 Grant
57 Unit of hope?
59 "Buddenbrooks" author
61 Came down
63 No longer under consideration
65 Flea market tag
66 Mr. Fix-It
69 China's Lao-___
70 On one's ___
73 Slangy suffix
76 P.T.A. meeting place: Abbr.
78 Expert finish?
80 Farmers' beans
81 Things in pots
82 "Oh, my!"
83 Cosmo or S.I.
84 All ___
85 Former gov. Schwarzenegger
86 See 3-Down
88 Cut up
90 Baryshnikov's birthplace
91 See 3-Down
92 Prepared, as cider
93 Picks up?
95 Hairy Himalayan

by Elizabeth C. Gorski

97 Botch
98 Columbo and others: Abbr.
99 Vest pocket
100 ___ Hubbard
102 Prefix with phobic
107 Actress Garr
108 "Finished!"
110 How jams are stored

111 Have the nerve
115 Michelangelo works
116 Setting for many a joke
117 Mistakenly
121 Basketball stat
122 Dragged on?

123 How vending machines give change
125 Yuletide cupful
128 Creepy
129 Author Calvino
130 Really bother
132 Bouquet
133 Pyramid scheme

134 Lowlife?
136 Station
138 Food card
140 Till section
141 Italian wine area
143 Price abbr.
146 Popular a.m. show

ACROSS

1 Dust picker-upper
8 Off one's game
16 It's in a blind
20 Semisweet sherry
21 Big rubber exporter
22 ___ platter
23 Makes sacrifices on behalf of an old telecommunications company?
25 Kyoto treaty subj.
26 Summons from the boss
27 Growing old
28 Young and Simon
29 Shooter Adams
30 2001 film for which Jim Broadbent was named Best Supporting Actor
31 U.S.N. clerk: Abbr.
32 Auto introduced in 1928
33 In bounds
34 One ___ (kids' game)
35 Do some restaurant work
36 Used as sustenance
37 West ender?
38 Deceive
39 Fathers and grandfathers
40 Serving from a garçon
41 W.W. II nickname
42 Soft stuff
43 See 44-Across
44 With 43-Across, comic book superhero

47 Secret store
49 Dramatic procession
51 Euclidean subj.
52 Sailboat poles
53 Some Xing crossers
54 Where to get down
55 Prefix with plasm
56 Dense fog
58 Important, in a way
60 Tennis champion Roddick
61 Teams
63 Taper, for short
64 Wicked
65 Closely monitored hosp. areas
66 Slightly sour
68 ___ Field, where the Rockies play
69 IBM competitor
70 1.85 kilometers/hour
71 Mad ones are bad
72 Weapon handle
73 News subjects
75 Puts down, in brief
76 ___ Hari
77 Result of a certain sacrifice, for short
80 Cold-blooded ones
82 It's in the winter air
83 Part of a racetrack
84 Psychologist Piaget
85 Subj. that's for the birds
86 One of Alcott's "Little Men"
87 He has manors
88 Gets the mood of
89 Large pipes
90 Cheapen
92 Adoption agcy.?

93 Relative of a Winnebago
94 Pac-12 gossip column?
96 Cookie holders
97 "On the house"
98 Deep
99 Verb with thou
100 More highfalutin
101 Pests

DOWN

1 Long time
2 Property seller
3 Goes ahead
4 Like some biology majors
5 Pulitzer Prize dramatist Tad
6 Buckeye sch.
7 It's licked on a stick
8 "Everything's under control"
9 Holes in the head
10 "___ well"
11 Impertinent relation?
12 French schools
13 "___ hooks" (crate sign)
14 In perfect condition
15 Reward, as a dog
16 Risked a fine
17 How Desi kept track of his daughter?
18 Its last mission was #17
19 Certain Sooner
24 Untamed
28 Partner of Evans in journalism

32 Plastic for beer bottles?
34 Response to an awful pun made by actress York?
35 Gymnastics coach Károlyi
36 Talked up
38 Relish
39 Dallas five
40 Ones doing art finishing
41 "Blondie" dog and others
42 Repaired, as roads
45 Monopoly purchases
46 University associated with the Carter Center
47 2001 Economics Nobelist Michael ___
48 Malign the labor movement?
49 College units
50 Place for rings
51 Go on a lucky streak
52 Home of the Alhambra
57 Lacy frills
59 ___ Gay (W.W. II plane)
62 Have an accident with a vacuum and a household pet?
63 I do's, e.g.
67 What goes around
70 Smallville family
72 Submitted

by Randolph Ross

74 Most likely to stop at a mirror
76 Cuban patriot José
77 Farm work
78 Severe form, as of an illness
79 Working on commission
80 Spotted insect
81 The "g" in e.g.
82 Hogan dweller
83 Deadbeat
84 Kidded around
86 Battery brand
87 Fencing move
88 Cost
90 Popular insecticide
91 Loughlin of "Full House"
94 Wee ___ (small fry)
95 Rock musician Brian

AMBIGUOUS JOB RECOMMENDATIONS

ACROSS

1 Gambit
7 Kind of day
14 Fix permanently
20 Emphatic yes
21 Heir, in legal terminology
22 The way things stand now
23 Recommendation for a chronically absent employee?
26 Sham
27 Volkswagen model
28 Photo lab abbr.
29 Goes out
30 MSN competitor
31 Solo
36 Recommendation for a dishonest employee?
45 Spiral-horned antelope
46 Fair-hiring letters
47 Actor Tognazzi of 1978's "La Cage aux Folles"
48 Passing concerns?: Abbr.
49 Early sixth-century date
50 Keys who won five Grammys for her debut album
52 Showy flower
55 Records
56 Like some ears
57 Polite denial
59 Adroit
62 Tram loads
63 Recommendation for an employee who stole petty cash?
69 Wallop
70 White or Red follower
71 Stately stand
72 Recommendation for an employee guilty of sexual harassment?
82 Son of Seth
83 Gin flavoring
84 Extinguish
85 Family-friendly card game
86 Memo opener
87 Dirty
90 Buffet warmer
93 Orbit, for example
94 __ mind
97 Chinese "way"
98 Computer key
100 Dairy pitcher?
101 Recommendation for an employee who was chronically drunk?
106 Set upon
107 Tee off
108 Incentivize
111 Letters at sea
112 Dark area
115 N.Y.C. cultural attraction
119 All-purpose ambiguous job recommendation
125 Not inclined
126 Mercury, for one
127 Power in old movies
128 Least
129 Lives
130 Silences

DOWN

1 Short row
2 Top 5 song by Sarah McLachlan
3 Bop
4 "The washday miracle" sloganeer, once
5 Notorious Amin
6 Flimflam
7 Thai currency
8 Settled
9 Minolta digital camera
10 Fell
11 Santa __ winds
12 Plural suffix
13 Abrogate
14 Family of five, say
15 Saskatoon-to-Winnipeg dir.
16 Storage problem
17 Decorative needle case
18 "Good one!"
19 Expresses disapproval
24 Moisturizing lotion
25 Empty, as an apartment
30 "__ quote . . ."
32 Egg
33 "We cannot all be masters, nor all masters / Cannot be truly follow'd" speaker
34 Some low-risk investments, briefly
35 Some Windows systems
36 Moor
37 "Dallas" matriarch
38 Good-hearted soul
39 Dad's bro
40 Collar attachment
41 Ancient region bordering the Aegean
42 Targets of baking soda
43 Double star in Orion
44 Affectionate, slangily
51 Robes may touch them
53 Surrealist Max
54 Specialty shoe width
55 Miserable
58 Having eight pins, as an electrical connection
60 Lets go
61 Marks in Spanish class
64 Really big
65 Key preposition
66 Muck
67 Radiate
68 Fed. money overseer
72 Ponder
73 Opposite of get-up-and-go
74 Computer network menaces
75 Dobbs or Rawls
76 Soup choice
77 Raccoon relative
78 Spicy cuisine
79 Novelist Fannie
80 Certain navel
81 Responded to a cattle call
88 Start fishing
89 Leaf feature
91 Like some patio furniture
92 Two-time U.S. Open champ
94 Gives the nod
95 Trawling gear
96 The Cradle of Texas Liberty
99 Saloon floozie, slangily

by Seth A. Abel

102 He declined the 1964 Literature Nobel
103 Brilliance
104 Brought out
105 Spirit
108 Went from bank to bank?
109 Smooth over
110 Not-so-straight shooter?
113 Barn locks?
114 Some lunch orders
115 Nonunion employees: Abbr.
116 "Oops!"
117 Greedy cry
118 Treasonous Aldrich
120 Curve shape
121 It's surrounded by eau
122 Mayo, por ejemplo
123 Record label inits.
124 Manhattan sch.

66 CUED IN

ACROSS

1 Common website sect.
4 Revolt
10 Do some copy work
14 "Phooey!"
18 20-Across forerunner
19 Vast
20 See 18-Across
21 Like a blue rose
22 "Is ___?"
23 Description of an 18th-century writing desk?
26 Jefferson player in "Jefferson in Paris"
28 Barren
29 Singer ___ Rose
30 Hit
31 French eye
32 "This is serious!"
35 Oil shipment: Abbr.
38 Old dagger
39 Mrs., abroad
40 Intelligent like Groucho Marx?
42 Ones calling the shots?: Abbr.
44 Cut
46 Gives with confidence
47 Charles after whom a sports field was named
50 Sawed gourds, so to speak
54 Move it
55 Small change
57 Like the botanist Linnaeus
60 Verdi's "___ tu"
63 Spots for 42-Across
64 Be a director
66 Woods along a fault line?
70 It's a scream
71 Advertising supplement
73 Twisted yarn
74 Johnny with the 1980 #1 country hit "Lookin' for Love"
75 Constant tic?
78 Marvin Gaye's "Can ___ Witness"
79 Some M.I.T. grads: Abbr.
80 A, B and C in D.C.
81 Establishes
83 Kind of comb
85 Whip but good
88 Nicole Kidman or Tom Cruise, e.g.
90 ___ Dam on the Sacramento River
91 Needle
96 First word in "Send in the Clowns"
98 Time of anticipation
99 Geologist's entire collection?
103 FedEx rival
105 Prefix with distant
108 Instant
109 Problem in a plane cabin
110 Burned up
111 University of Kentucky's ___ Arena
112 Tops: Abbr.
114 Vein contents
115 Stroll
117 Crusading knight's story?
122 Hoover, e.g., in brief
123 Cracked open
124 Baltic resident
125 Getting ready to play seven-card stud
126 Sorority letter
127 "Saturn Devouring His Children" painter
128 Thinking prefix
129 10-, 11- and 12-year-olds
130 Kind of room

DOWN

1 Some military maneuvers
2 Film genre
3 Fast break result, on the court?
4 They might precede blows
5 Cooks' gadgets
6 Replacements for missing teeth in dental arches
7 Slippery as ___
8 See 116-Down
9 Toast to one's health
10 Producing more chills
11 Library stamp
12 Grp. that launches investigations
13 Worn ___ frazzle
14 Heart
15 Transport that runs on tracks
16 It may be bookmarked
17 State with only three counties: Abbr.
19 On one's ___
24 "Forever, ___" (1996 humor book)
25 Al Jazeera employee
27 One of the Wayans brothers
33 Indian bread
34 Neck of land: Abbr.
36 Kind of part
37 Former records
40 Lodge
41 Freakish
43 Blockhead
45 One way to take things
47 Foils
48 Airborne Rangers gear
49 Expressionless
51 Not opt.
52 Cabinet dept.
53 Thoreau and others
56 "Thong Song" rapper
58 Piece supporting the rudder
59 Ax wielder
61 Start to tremble?
62 "There!"
65 Doctor's prefix with -ologist
67 Greek cheeses
68 City SW of Kansas City
69 ___ coil
72 "Time ___" (old sci-fi series)
76 Moving
77 Actress Cattrall of "Sex and the City"
82 Do perfectly
84 Pothouse
86 Clip
87 "The Pianist" extra

by Brendan Emmett Quigley

89 Newspaper's choice for public office
91 Brightness measurements, for short
92 Have second thoughts
93 Bettor's spot
94 Feather's partner
95 Getting there
97 Add for free
100 ___ be different
101 Seasons
102 Vampire of fiction
104 Hardly long-distance runners
106 News briefing
107 Syrup in the medicine cabinet
110 Outpouring
113 Additional, in ads
116 With 8-Down, course that includes Shaq.
117 Broom rider
118 Spanish eye
119 QB Manning
120 End of a demonstration?
121 Tucson-to-L.A. dir.

ACROSS

1 Make a quick left, say
4 Confusion
8 Subject of the documentary "As I Was Saying"
12 A black key
17 First word of "Wooly Bully"
18 Brooks from Tulsa
19 ___ nova
20 They're taken in court
21 B & B
22 Having a line of symmetry
23 Spenser player on TV
24 Get rid of
25 The candidate was accused of having a ___
29 Spotted
30 More than 70% of its exports are fish: Abbr.
31 Like some monuments
35 The candidate tried to cover it up and was ___
41 Early times, for short
44 Record exec Gotti
45 Shoebox letters
46 Membranes
47 Funds ran low in the candidate's ___
55 Old Dodge
56 List ender
57 Victory: Ger.
58 Some summer babies
60 Preceder of Alamos or Altos
61 Sublet
64 Frigid finish
66 Big overhead?
67 The candidate called reporters in for a ___
74 "The Fog of War" director Morris
75 Relative of a gull
76 "You've gotta be kidding!"
77 It's watched in Ont.
80 Invent
81 Make over
83 Bad: Prefix
84 Avis adjective
86 At the convention the candidate ___ . . .
92 Words after duke or shout
94 Something flipped
95 Big ox
96 "I told you so!"
97 . . . and ___ . . .
105 Drink from India
106 Wrapped up with
107 Do little
111 . . . and later lost the election in key ___
117 Tourist center's name
120 North of Virginia
121 Show as an encore
122 Short order, for short
123 Army of the Potomac commander, 1863–65
124 Has an opinion
125 Bats
126 Flap
127 Legendary luster
128 Greek house
129 Pampering places
130 Call on

DOWN

1 Influence, slangily
2 Bug
3 Adjective with chance or fortune
4 Large, in commercial lingo
5 Bana who played the Incredible Hulk in film
6 Bad reception
7 Shoddy goods
8 Blue matter
9 Words before "were"
10 Way up
11 Enthusiastic
12 Dishes
13 Broken down
14 P.O. piece
15 "Bingo!"
16 A small dose: Abbr.
18 Square dance partner
19 Trump, e.g.
26 Medicine watchdog grp.
27 Service charge
28 It's hot in Cannes
32 High country
33 Cy Young Award winner Mike Scott, for one
34 Some coll. seniors take them
36 Actress Carrere
37 Prefix with state
38 Stock market figs.
39 Bill: Fr.
40 Informal assent
41 Sharp
42 Spanish saint
43 False flattery
48 Commoner
49 "Soul Food" actress, 1997
50 Brecht collaborator
51 Indian tourist city
52 Madrid daily
53 Astin of "Lord of the Rings"
54 Teatro Costanzi debut of 1900
59 Sullivan had a really big one
62 Tiny fraction of time: Abbr.
63 Lose on purpose
65 Sinus specialist, briefly
66 The New Yorker cartoonist Edward
68 Emporium suffix
69 Soft ball material
70 14 years before the Magna Carta
71 Slate and Salon
72 Opposite of día
73 Certain security, briefly
77 Like a new dollar bill
78 Wash
79 Bad business partner
82 Repeated interjection in the Rolling Stones' "Miss You"
85 Shop that fixes collision damage
87 QB Manning
88 Archaeological enterprise
89 Looks up to
90 1990s Indian P.M.

by Randolph Ross

91 As loud as possible, in music
93 It may be political
98 Addams Family cousin
99 Leave home
100 Tool for melons
101 Japanese Beatle?
102 180's
103 Get in shape
104 State with two time zones: Abbr.
108 In the box
109 One of the Fitzgeralds
110 Block legally
112 Zeno's home
113 Expensively decorated
114 Bank contents
115 Does a job for parents, maybe
116 Encouraging word
117 Type widths
118 Shade of green
119 Be-bopper

TAP, TAP, TAP

ACROSS

1 Quite a story
5 Fahd and Saud, e.g.
10 Way to get noticed
14 Barrage
19 Besides
20 "I pass"
21 Melville novel
22 Actress Zellweger
23 Sub firers
25 Arrive at the airport
26 Had a row
27 Noted Vegas casino with an Irish name
28 Cubed roots?
29 Hot spots
30 Billingsgate
32 Reverse progress
34 Primitive business dealing
35 Worked a garden
37 Afore
38 Like some races and hopes
41 Jackie's second
42 Seat that may spin
44 Hiker's aid
46 Poker announcement
48 Boston airport
51 Can. province
52 Conspires with, perhaps
54 Son of Ramses I
55 Take a shot (at)
56 Assume
58 Baseball line score letters
59 A Baldwin
60 Cardinal competitor
61 Prince Valiant's son
62 Plural ending
63 Fugitate
64 Metric base
65 Call for help
69 ___-di-dah
70 Parts of l'Océanie
72 Informal wear
73 Loop transports
74 Get around
77 Claim
78 Hirt and Gore
79 Twist up
82 Policy at a ladies' club
83 Yacht material
84 Almost touching
86 Steps down to a river, in India
87 Having heat?
88 On the line
90 Teacher's org.
91 Lumberjack
93 Dutch city
94 Beckett title character
95 W ___ (finale of an encyclopedia)
97 Hardly a brainiac
99 Acted badly
102 Some airport shuttles
104 Thug
105 Moral code
108 "The Prince of Tides" star
109 "Mark of the Vampire" actor
112 Tail
113 Flood survivor
114 Summer wear
118 "___ Report," influential Indian document of 1928
119 Crucifix letters
120 "The Dragons of Eden" author
121 Apartment
122 Sixth-century B.C. storyteller
123 Org.
124 Come to ___
125 "Uh-huh"

DOWN

1 Bolt down
2 3-Down antagonist
3 See 2-Down
4 Renege
5 Et alia
6 Playboy
7 "Fernando" group
8 Ones with combs
9 Manhattan's east/west arteries: Abbr.
10 Whistle-blower, at times
11 Squarely
12 Loudness units
13 Take baby steps
14 One who can't get over something
15 Split
16 Docket phrase
17 Comics target
18 British finales
24 "___ est percipi" (Berkeley principle)
28 Pop
30 Burr and Copland
31 Marilyn Monroe contemporary
32 Nonsense
33 Van Gogh work
34 Model material
35 Cushion site
36 Man's tie feature
38 "Hard-boiled" writer
39 Cosmetics name
40 Clear for takeoff?
43 Atlanta-based channel
45 August birthstone
47 Without payment
49 Mountain social
50 Glower
53 Precisely, after "on"
57 Urging from Santa
65 "Go on!"
66 Adores
67 Panel illumination
68 Attends to a detail
69 Mellow Horne
70 Luggage attachment
71 Not just mislead
72 Add
75 One of rock's Ramones
76 Broke up
79 Starts to become tiresome
80 "The Banger Sisters" co-star, 2002
81 When people hate the heat in Haiti
85 Laypersons
89 Mug
92 Basketball stat
96 Composite flower
98 It's widely worn on the feet
100 Food flavoring brand
101 Enthusiastic agreement abroad

by Bill Zais

102 Prefix with economics
103 Blessings
105 2002–3 erupter
106 Corner
107 Derisive laughs
109 Not yielding much
110 Itch
111 Fed
114 Org. for hikers
115 Shot putters?: Abbr.
116 20-20, say
117 Sault ___ Marie

ACROSS

1 North Sea tributary
6 World Cup chant
12 Lightning sound
15 Govt. security
20 "JFK" actor
21 Ill-fated
22 Bounty competitor
23 Songwriter Greenwich
24 Start of a quip by 58-Across
28 "No More I Love You's" singer, 1995
29 4 on a fax machine
30 "Holy Toledo!"
31 Like some queens
32 ___ many words
33 "Ta-da!"
36 Actress Zadora
37 Ones above 48-Acrosses
38 Modern in Munich
39 Quip, part 2
45 Change from an R, say
47 Turning points
48 See 37-Across
49 Bit of gel
51 Yoga position
53 Birth-related
55 Levels
57 For dieters
58 Source of the quip
61 Quip, part 3
64 Sang-froid
65 "Dear ___ . . ."
67 ___ signum (here is the proof)
68 Opening word?
69 Pool wear
71 Meat-and-potatoes
74 Audience
76 "Say ___" (1940 Andrews Sisters hit)
77 Former French president Coty and others
79 Quip, part 4
81 Late start at work, maybe
83 Remove, as from a habit
85 It's bad in France
87 Thrown off
89 Potluck dinner staple
93 Brand of writing implements
95 Buzzed
97 Top part of a form, usually
99 Where to see le soleil
100 Quip, part 5
104 Quip, part 6
106 In a bottle for a long time
107 Major employer in Hiroshima
108 Krupp works city
110 "Lord of the Rings" letters
111 Calls for silence
112 Word before an old name
113 Ural River city
114 Least likely to attack
117 Quip, part 7
123 Camel, e.g., for short
126 Saunter, e.g.
127 Certain baseball positions: Abbr.
128 Leaves in the dust
129 Kind of bean
130 Celts play it
132 Elite Eight org.
134 Eskimo knife
135 Plays, in a way
137 End of the quip
142 "The Tattooed Girl" author
143 Gumbo thickener
144 Big event sites
145 Its capital is Oranjestad
146 Bleep out
147 Antiprohibitionist
148 Places for buttons
149 Bandleader Kay

DOWN

1 Like some rebates
2 Ancient ascetic
3 Like drivers with records, maybe
4 Sheet music symbol
5 Puzzlemaker Rubik
6 Quaint
7 Judge's study
8 Asylum seeker, maybe
9 Where "Quiet!" may be heard
10 Where Samson defeated the Philistines
11 Boston hrs.
12 Coors product
13 Fanlike
14 Buddy
15 It might be up to its neck in hot water
16 Like bruises
17 Actress Chase
18 Property law topic
19 One of two Virginia signers of the Declaration of Independence
22 1970s–'80s Robert Urich show
25 Plus amount
26 They have it coming
27 City with a radio station that has the same call letters as the city's name
34 Milliner's sale
35 Flush, now
36 Burrito meat
37 Dame's introduction
39 Scottish hillside
40 Workout target
41 Like a suit with a vest
42 Down too much
43 Company with a good track record?
44 Japanese mat
46 Listed
50 "Venerable" English monk
51 Kindergarten stuff
52 Daytime show
54 Target Al Jazeera viewer
55 Active ingredient in marijuana
56 Old protest grp.
57 General under Alexander the Great
59 "Don't gimme that!"
60 Hit man?
62 PC troubleshooters
63 Badlands sights
66 Goat's cry
70 Cygnus star
72 Put on
73 ___ Sheraton (old hotel company)
75 Took the reins again
78 Golf legend Gene
80 Migratory fish
82 Indian bread
83 Shipping concern
84 Catch
86 Acclaimed
88 Flag lieutenant
90 Saguaro
91 Actress Campbell
92 Saloon selections
93 Bake sale grps.
94 Moon lander, for short
96 Ultrasecret org.
98 Critical innings
101 "Shut your mouth!"
102 Grazing groups

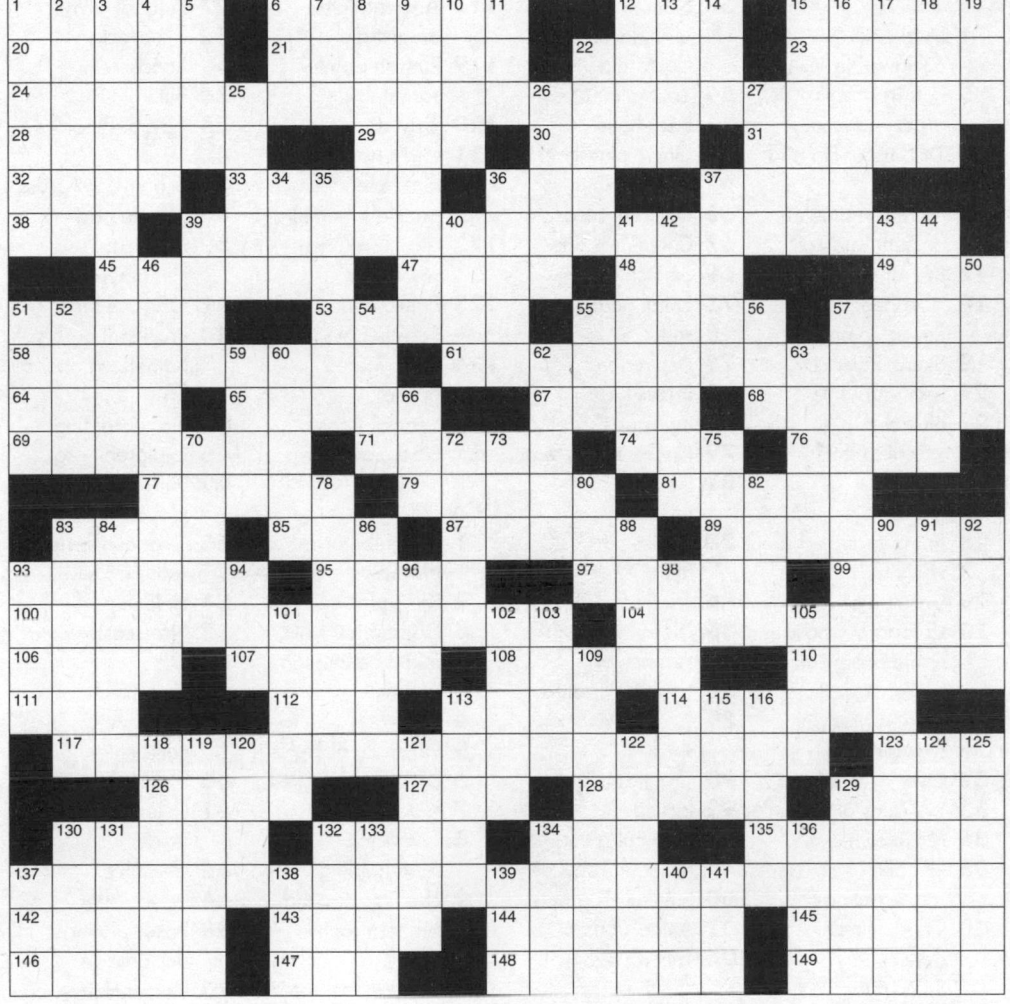

by Brendan Emmett Quigley

THAT'S FUNNERY

ACROSS

1 Dual elec. designation
5 Puts in proper order, nautically
9 TV boss of Flo and Alice
12 Modern home of ancient Knossos
17 Brave
18 "Orphée, Le Repos" painter
19 Skunk River city
21 Less taut
22 Blue dye
23 Winning bird colony?
26 Mexican muralist
28 Some grandkid spoilers
29 Crosspiece
30 Company whose name is pig Latin for an insect
31 Tolkien Moria warriors
32 Over
33 Williams of Boston
34 Mayo to mayo
36 Invitation from a rogue nation?
40 Chorus line dances
42 Silas of the Continental Congress
43 Eliot Janeway subj.
47 Civil rights leader Medgar
48 Manipulative sort
52 Lodge member
53 Sheen formed with age
55 Self-titled WB sitcom
56 Artemis's twin
58 Steinbeck's birthplace, in California
59 Young 'un at a hash house?
63 Grave plunderer
65 Forensic ID
66 Restraint cord
67 Chem., for one
69 Smitten
71 Email address suffix
73 Aspirations
75 Prizes for manicurists?
79 Cricket teams, e.g.
81 It's broken at mixers
83 Eagles hit "___ Eyes"
84 Studly
85 Diner cuppa
86 Advent song
88 Lawn ball game
89 "___ sow, so shall . . ."
90 "Pagliacci" role
92 Incited
94 Result of a cat hitting the sauce?
100 Suffix with grape
101 Aetna's bus.
104 Thoreau work "Faith in ___"
105 Suspenseful part of "Survivor"
106 Over
108 Some teens just hanging out
110 Clear, in a way
111 Strongbox
114 Request to hear a certain audiobook genre?
117 "La Dolce Vita" setting
118 Ancient Roman magistrate
119 Finnish painter Järnefelt
120 Troy story
121 Girl's name (or a hint to this puzzle's theme)
122 Like a weather-worn face
123 Emulate the Beastie Boys
124 Endangered goose
125 Year of Boris Godunov's birth

DOWN

1 Month before Nisan
2 Kid's plea
3 What a few volts might be enough to do?
4 Star
5 Playmate of Piglet
6 Like some patches
7 Kiddie racer
8 Cause for nose-holding
9 The Say Hey Kid
10 Modern rock genre
11 Parisian art district
12 Artful
13 Martha in denture ads
14 Apply with might
15 Josh
16 Was off
18 Preschooler's medium
20 Endeavored
24 Demolished, in Derby
25 Experience
27 Punjabi royals
32 Like clocks with hands
34 Bitter
35 H.M.S. Pinafore force
37 Sch. in 19-Across
38 Frigate part
39 Mythical Himalayan beast
41 Origami bird
44 President Bush's hometown after a fire?
45 Go ___ outing
46 Explorers' org.
49 Buffalo hockey player
50 Org. concerned with PCB's
51 Holds up
53 Newscaster Zahn
54 O.K.
57 French school
58 Matsushita competitor
60 Lucy's pal
61 Lake Geneva feeder
62 Uh-huh's
64 New staffer
68 Poker player's declaration
70 Heroic trait
71 St. Petersburg's river
72 "Boola Boola" singers
74 Out of it
76 Prefix with tourism
77 In big bits
78 Cutting
80 Perspective
82 Focus of one who's willing?
85 Wag

by Cathy Millhauser

87 Mil. amphibian
88 Good, in Guadalajara
90 Scourge of the African savanna
91 Kvetcher's cry
93 Took a second?
95 Impaired
96 Bloke's "Well, well!"
97 Tech expert, in British lingo
98 Hepburn's "The Lion in Winter" co-star
99 Medicated shampoo brand
101 Drive
102 Silents star Nita
103 Gotten rid of
107 Violinist Zimbalist
109 Cy Young award winner Sparky
110 Trapdoor
112 Pianist Gilels
113 Punjabi royal
115 Time gone by
116 West of "Go West, Young Man"

ACROSS

1 Gets used (to)
7 Mies van der ___ (German-born architect)
11 Early education
15 Oceans
19 Deliver, as music or water
20 Windows alternative
21 Wind (up)
22 Heat in a hurry
23 Fort Bliss city
24 Fall mo.
25 Opera's ___ Te Kanawa
26 Knitting ball
27 Litigant
28 With 34-Across, elated
31 Group of religious proselytizers
33 ___-de-Marne (French department)
34 See 28-Across
36 Swain
37 Had something
39 Computer-sharing setup
40 Natterjack
42 Running-shoe maker
46 Noted company headquartered in Times Square
48 Full count
50 Source of ambergris
52 Actor Penn
53 "We know drama" sloganeer
54 Arm bones
56 She played Sally in "When Harry Met Sally . . ."
57 Kid
58 Anka's "___ Beso"
59 Reclined
60 A modicum of modesty
64 Seat of Allen County, Kansas
65 "___ say!"
66 See 72-Across
67 Municipally partitioned
68 Streaming video maker for the Net
72 With 66-Across, where some hunters aim; with 75-Across, when hockey players rest
73 Fast-food franchise
74 Skating jumps
75 See 72-Across
76 Information booth handout
77 "It seems to me," in computerese
78 Bus. card info
79 Author Sholem
80 Slice (off)
83 Mai ___ (drinks)
84 Artist Rembrandt van ___
85 Menial
87 How to address a lt. col.?
88 Popular alternative press magazine
89 ___ Park, Colo.
92 Spare tire
93 Bloviates
95 Sell door-to-door
97 King Harald's capital
99 "Rock and Roll, Hoochie ___" (1974 hit)
101 Comics dog
102 Round top
104 See 112-Across
107 Like
108 Arm guard
112 With 104-Across, despicable
113 "Toodle-oo"
115 ___ Minderbender, villain in "Catch-22"
116 Tampa paper, for short, with The
118 "Beetle Bailey" creator Walker
119 Titillating
121 Foe for El Cid
122 Adm. Zumwalt
123 End in ___
124 Go through again
125 Aardvark fare
126 Not natural
127 Call for
128 Made square

DOWN

1 Mimics
2 See 37-Down
3 Attracts
4 Dived for treasure?
5 Sequel to "Angela's Ashes"
6 Schnozz
7 Corroded
8 Info in a used car want ad
9 Mudhole lover
10 Shake down
11 Parrot's cry
12 Clink, at sea
13 Chocolate substitute
14 It might be put on a web site
15 See 43-Down
16 Where to wear a lei, maybe
17 Gumbo pods
18 Be inclined
29 Rink org.
30 Current
32 Enclosure with a ms.
35 Doo-___
37 With 2-Down, ancients
38 Flowers named for a Swedish botanist
41 Father ___, famous priest to lepers
43 With 15-Down, undoubtedly
44 Shootin' Annie
45 Folds, presses and stretches
47 Misgiving
49 It may be see-through
51 Something to see through
55 "Cool" sum
61 Attach, as a patch
62 Ticked
63 Some are Jewish
66 Flier around a lighthouse
67 Breezes
68 Cry from a laggard
69 Giver (or receiver) of alimony
70 With 71-Down, in secret
71 See 70-Down
72 Understand now, as someone's tricks
73 More than odd
75 M.D.
76 Co. with a butterfly logo
78 Took first?
79 Not manual

by Manny Nosowsky

80 St. Augustine's language
81 See 82-Down
82 With 81-Down, like some recoveries
86 Ontario is on it

90 It's left of F1 on a PC
91 Untidy one
94 France of France
96 Pretty sad
98 Kind of show
100 Go (for)

103 Too soon
105 Government issue, for short
106 "Ta-da!"
108 Madame Bovary
109 Emblem of Great Britain

110 Printer's mistake
111 Cost for a dozen, in a phrase
114 Scored very well on
117 Hunk's or babe's asset
120 Gun

AT THE COMPANY PICNIC

ACROSS

1 Grp. with forces
5 City along the Finger Lakes
11 One on a PT boat, maybe: Abbr.
14 Letter amount
18 Actress Lena
19 Former Philippine leader
20 One who keeps changing rooms
23 The software installer brought . . .
25 Crosses
26 Employer of speakers
27 Obsolete
29 Korean-American author Chang-___ Lee
30 Org. whose annual convention many authors attend
31 "Crikey!"
32 Wild land in Africa
35 The copy-room worker brought . . .
39 Dreamlike
42 Gobblers
43 Now, to Nino
44 The financial analyst brought . . .
48 N.Y.C. airport
49 West Coast fossil find
50 Where Douglas MacArthur returned, famously
51 Style for Eubie Blake
55 Daughter of King Minos
57 Lou Gehrig's disease, for short
58 Below the surface
59 Colony member
60 The office supply manager brought . . .
64 "Likewise"
66 Sanctions
67 The network technician brought . . .
74 Take, at a concert
78 Ones who think too much
79 Several periods
80 Hot torrents
83 Stews
84 Parts of some plots
87 Approach quickly
88 Law enforcement hqrs.
89 The secretary brought . . .
91 "Well, look ___!"
94 Subway purchase
95 Lead-pipe cinch
96 The mailroom clerk brought . . .
99 Keyed up
100 Deficiency
103 Rapper Tone-___
104 TV schedule inits.
105 3:00
108 Heading
110 Despicable
114 The packaging supervisor brought . . .
117 They feed the kitty
118 Often-followed car
119 Notch
120 Mil. honors
121 Flagstaff-to-Tucson dir.
122 One thing to consider
123 Overwhelm, at a comedy club

DOWN

1 Note on a Chinese menu
2 Prince Valiant's love
3 By the clock
4 "___ off?"
5 Qualified fellow's boast
6 Wash. State's Sea-___ Airport
7 Buckingham Palace inits.
8 Cause of much bellyaching?
9 Endure
10 Syrian president
11 Geezers' queries
12 Part of a bid
13 Ticks off
14 Literary inits.
15 Comedian Philips
16 Foe of Kit Carson
17 Slide used with a dress shirt
21 Sport with masks
22 Section at Blockbuster
24 Upbraided
28 A, in Morse code
33 Mrs., in Mallorca
34 Mint, e.g.
36 Mint
37 Kvetches, maybe
38 "You don't say"
39 Throw out
40 Rap sheet listing
41 Allow to see
44 Dish eaten with a spork
45 Gold medalist Lipinski
46 Geishas draw them
47 Easily-scratched mineral
48 Cagney's TV partner
51 Meal
52 Manhattan, e.g.: Abbr.
53 TV diner owner
54 1920s–'40s Yankees manager Barrow and others
56 Fragrant liquids
58 Pile maker
61 Major civic bldgs.
62 Breath-losing sound
63 How far dictionaries go
64 Dressed to the nines
65 Anatomical passages
67 It keeps an eye on TV
68 ". . . goes, ___ go"
69 Common cartoon tattoo
70 It may be shaken by a court
71 Put another way
72 Port on a lake of the same name
73 Smooths
74 Range
75 Mideast's Gulf of ___
76 Noted 26-Across brand
77 Tallinn native

by Patrick Merrell

81 Bar container
82 Skier's pull
84 Kind of traffic
85 Calendar abbr.
86 Arrange
89 Ones doormen recognize
90 Grazing land
91 Company with a duck in its ads
92 "What a shame"
93 Millionaires' "toys"
94 ___ corpus
97 Raison d'___
98 Skater Cohen
100 Last Supper item
101 Humane org.
102 Bothersome
106 Women
107 Drainpipe part
109 Cemetery sights
111 Non-Rx
112 Monopoly foursome: Abbr.
113 Lao-___
115 Kerry's locale: Abbr.
116 Foreign policy grp.

73 FURNISHING TOUCHES

ACROSS

1 It's carried while on deck
4 Unmitigated
10 Aromatic oil, often
15 Razor brand
19 Green grp.
20 Old British coin
21 Dog originally bred to herd cattle
22 Start of a conclusion
23 Outdoor furniture that can fly you to the moon?
26 Lose one's resistance
27 Actress Sommer
28 Business card abbr.
29 Kid with a new home
30 Cartoon canine
31 Writing tables made from foam rubber?
34 Tight group?
35 Co. name ender
36 Scout leader?
37 Financial adviser, for short
38 They may be in black-and-white
39 John or Christine of Fleetwood Mac
41 Magniloquent
44 Lays down the lawn
45 M-1 rifle inventor
46 Fastens (to)
49 Variety show fillers
50 Adapt musically
51 Went through channels?
52 Quarrel
53 Of living organisms
54 Joseph of "Citizen Kane"
55 Vehicles designed to transport china?
59 Cry of surprise
60 Interstate highway fixtures
61 Soccer star Hamm
62 Question for the hotel housekeeper in the morning?
66 Damon, to Pythias
69 Confronted
70 Diploma holder
71 Unwilling to say much
72 ___ Norman (military nickname)
74 Diane of "A Kiss Before Dying," 1991
75 Walks breezily
76 Member of an Indian religious minority
77 Hood rods
78 Drawing help
79 Pavilion locales
80 It's got a point
81 Flight
82 Photographer Adams
87 Packed away
88 Simpleton
89 Whether to fold out or remain as a couch?
92 Isn't serious
94 Sign of trouble
96 Eastern way
97 Squealed cries
98 "No more!"
99 Bookcase seller's farewell to buyers?
102 Dairy aisle buy
103 Disdain
104 Skull Valley dweller
105 "I kissed thee ___ I killed thee": Othello
106 Cultural gathering
107 English assignment
108 Rent payer
109 Thérèse, e.g.: Abbr.

DOWN

1 Forlorn
2 He cursed Cassandra
3 Append
4 Inference from an ID
5 Like dirt roads
6 Fit to be tied
7 "The ___ of Confucius"
8 Not clichéd
9 Godzilla creator Tomoyuki ___
10 Repeat
11 They're seen around bars
12 Colorful seashells
13 Avian colonists
14 Hillocks
15 Prefix with sphere
16 Humorous tale involving a settee?
17 Coat repair job
18 Go before
24 Set aside
25 They get burned nowadays
32 Doorstep cry
33 Mole
38 "Fairly well"
39 Atlanta train and bus system
40 Food writer Claiborne
42 Farm team
43 Supplied
44 Sword bearers
45 Get bigger
46 ___ Stadium, home of the Pro Bowl
47 Furniture launched from the starship Enterprise?
48 In good shape
49 Actress Christina
50 Supports
51 Boat for shallow water
52 Resist cheerfulness
53 Brought up
55 James of "Misery"
56 Chopped
57 Pair on Wayne Gretzky's jersey
58 High school org.
60 "Follow me!"
63 Unarmed figure?
64 Heavy reading
65 Depression-era drifter
66 Cherry bomb stem
67 Gung-ho
68 Investment choice: Abbr.
71 "For Me and My ___"
72 Talks about
73 Purchase at a government auction
74 Hill or valley, e.g.
75 Certain Indonesian

by Patrick Berry

77 Nice guy
78 Battle of Britain grp.
80 Grip firmly
81 Exit the system
83 Song sung on doorsteps
84 Security risks
85 William ___, baseball commissioner before Bowie Kuhn
86 Rent payer
88 Dragon's head feature
89 "I just had an idea!"
90 Big name in dolls
91 "Over There" songwriter
93 Soft or sweet follower
95 "Unfaithful" director Adrian
100 4 x 4, for short
101 Tolkien creature

ACROSS

1 Many Bob Marley fans
7 Criticized severely
13 Call it quits
20 No holds barred
21 Big Ten team
22 Cause for delay
23 The Good Witch of the North
24 Key of Mozart's Symphony No. 40
25 "This is serious!"
26 DNA sample for lab analysis?
28 Fixes
29 Civic group
30 Football Hall-of-Famer Ford
31 Cause for an R rating
32 Continue
35 "L.A. Law" actress
36 Librarian?
42 Big name in watches
44 Al dente
45 On the ball
46 Pressure unit equal to one newton per square meter
47 Good-for-nothings
50 Checkout procedures
51 Venom
52 Saucers may hold them
53 Zeno, notably
54 Noted 2000 guest at Camp David
55 Sidekick of radio, TV and film
56 Airline's exercise program?
58 "___ Blue"
61 Atlanta's ___ Center
62 TV Land showing
64 Up
66 Revolutionary Guevara
67 Lab instruction?
69 Recently nicked?
73 Hollywood's Hawke
75 N.F.L. team named after a poem
77 Gifts on October birthdays
78 Uncovered the most
79 Regatta
81 Beatnik's exclamation
82 Wine vessels
83 Proceed without a game plan
84 "___ yourself!"
85 Rear
86 Shakespearean forest
87 Dictator's snide remark?
90 Poet's monogram
93 Popular soup ingredient
94 It may get glossed over
95 1863 German invention, for short
96 Holdings of some banks
97 Lady of honor
100 Pajama sellers?
106 "God willing"
108 Ring of color
109 "Want to grab a bite?"
110 Neanderthals
111 Tourists' counterparts
112 Favorite daughter of Zeus
113 Garbage dump, say
114 "Shame!"
115 Sales reps' goals

DOWN

1 Uneven
2 Cause of hereditary variation
3 Spring toy
4 Softens, with "down"
5 Maker of the A4, A6 and A8
6 1972 Wimbledon winner Smith
7 London landmark
8 Popular candy bar ingredient
9 Crack
10 Touch
11 Hydroxyl compound
12 Life-or-death
13 Underhanded one
14 Dance version of a record, say
15 First family's home
16 Slightly
17 Midwest cook?
18 News inits.
19 Honeybunch
27 Graduates, briefly
31 "Was that so hard!?"
33 Dove competitor
34 Honeybunch
36 Mister in Milan
37 Grps.
38 Part of an Atkins breakfast
39 Look forward to
40 Italian alternative
41 Some transp. stocks
42 Leg part
43 City just north of Lake Nasser
44 Leg ends
46 Spanish beach
47 Baker's unit
48 Peerless
49 Playboy's agenda?
50 Time on the job
51 Teed off
53 Writer/illustrator of the story "Gertrude McFuzz"
54 Smoking result
56 Bush whack?
57 With time to spare
59 Full moon, e.g.
60 Dings
63 Give the heave-ho
65 "Goodness gracious!"
68 Goodly
70 Tale end
71 With celerity
72 Leveled
74 Sting, of sorts
76 Puffed up
78 Creator of 23-Across
79 Switch
80 Leprechaun's land
81 Dernier ___
82 Domain of King Minos
84 Thwack
87 2002 film about a virtual actress
88 Movie shots
89 Expose
90 Mega-retailer based in Minneapolis

by Kyle Mahowald

91 Breastbones
92 Snap courses
94 Vision-improving device
96 "Tiny Bubbles" singer
98 Makes like
99 Try it
100 Estonian or Lithuanian
101 Olympic archer
102 Knock down
103 Just so
104 Self-proclaimed "The Big Aristotle"
105 You might go for a spin in it
106 Kind of beer or bag
107 Stable staple

Overheard in Underground New York

ACROSS

1 A bit cracked
5 Rick's love in "Casablanca"
9 Nest part
13 Focus of Seward's Folly
19 Account receivable?
20 "Don't look at me"
21 Perfect
22 Some people are grabbed by them
23 Certain horse race
24 Skier Picabo finishing 11 places down from the bronze?
27 See eye to eye about
29 According to
30 Courts
31 Part of H.R.H.
32 Travel ways
33 Gets trounced
36 Splitting point
37 Order to nab a New York newspaper nerd now?
42 Rebels
43 "Why not?!"
44 Wing
45 "This isn't a joke"
48 Memo heading
49 Use needles
50 Critic's pan of a Jim Morrison rock concert?
55 Ones in need of a metamorphosis
56 Wee wee?
57 Gray matter
58 Dressing part
60 Unite formally
61 Rips into
65 Bullfight figure
66 Some words on the subject?
67 Indication of previous damage
69 College in Cedar Rapids
70 Insight
72 Promise from a prolific wedding dress designer?
78 Ring
79 It details what's left
80 Plants of the water lily family
81 Strong and sharp
83 Often-dried fruit
84 Pinkerton, in "Madama Butterfly," e.g.
85 Cry when an Oakland player's iron-on arrived?
91 Evan of the Senate
92 "Put your purse away"
93 Bath set?
95 Skater Midori
96 Saucy
98 Energy
99 Worth something
101 Sign promoting a dance studio's nice moves?
106 Darkens
107 Mendelssohn's Violin Concerto is in it
108 Apple piece
109 48-Down holder
110 Pulse alternative
111 Two-and-a-half presidential terms
112 24-karat
113 Annoyance
114 R & B's ___ Day & the Knights

DOWN

1 Constellation's brightest point
2 Lingo
3 Trading places
4 Dirty
5 Dope
6 Crackpot
7 Good name for a worrier?
8 Prepares, as snack kernels
9 Why some people travel far to attend church?
10 Suffering
11 Place to stay
12 Smarten up
13 Besides
14 Weightlifters build them, for short
15 ___ financing
16 "You listen to me"
17 Tissues
18 A.L. West player
25 Feeler
26 Greedy ones
28 Philippine president deposed in 2001
33 Lenya of song
34 Foe of the evil Gargamel, in children's entertainment
35 Top of the art world?
36 Totaled
38 Because
39 Labor
40 Audience participation bit
41 Coupling
45 Siena's home
46 One of the Jackson 5
47 "Men always hate most what they ___ most": Mencken
48 See 109-Across
49 Sharp
50 Thick piece
51 Sierra Nevada, e.g.
52 "It's not TV, it's ___"
53 Dormmate
54 Tempting ones
59 Suit spec
61 Iona College athlete
62 Boston retired his number 4
63 Stooge
64 Place for reeds
65 Bromo alternative
67 Beck's holder
68 Controversial danglers
70 Stage coach user, possibly
71 Brief shower?
73 What "O" stands for in publishing
74 Spin
75 Correct
76 "___ My Hat in Haiti" (Fred Astaire song)
77 Prefix with -gram

by Joe DiPietro

81 Simultaneously
82 About freezing
83 Feature of a certain pen
84 Bands together
86 Some December deliveries

87 Keep in check
88 Move in the direction of
89 Richardson of Nixon's cabinet
90 College support group

91 Went by Raleigh, say
94 Some R.S.V.P.'s
96 Trudge
97 Orphan of literature
99 Lyric poems

100 Exploit
102 ___ lab
103 Lean meat source
104 Certain swingers try to make it
105 Suffix with excess

ACROSS

1 Pilotless plane
6 Shows disapproval
10 Pre-1989 Eurasian political divs.
14 Think things over and over
18 Less typical
19 Bullet accompanier
20 Boarding announcement
21 "Nope"
22 Book about Rosa Parks?
25 Subject of a giant statue at Rome's ancient Colosseum
26 Was
27 Fate
28 College quarters
30 Austin of "Knots Landing"
31 Book that gives a brief glimpse of the future?
34 Popular fast food chain, informally
35 Dr.'s posting
36 San ___, Calif.
37 Milne marsupial
38 Peek-___
39 Oysters ___ season
40 Head of England?
43 Heads for
47 In the vicinity
50 Book about Ararat or Vesuvius?
53 New Test. book
54 Ethel Mertz, e.g.
56 Start for starter
57 In utero
59 Book that's a paean to a painter?
62 River of Lyon
63 Shock's partner
64 Year in Italy
65 Bandleader Fleck
69 Ref's call
70 Dubai dignitaries
72 Diet and exercise book for the upper legs?
78 Is content with not taking any action
81 ___ Appia
82 Carefully distributed
83 Cry of contentment
84 Book about the National Hockey League?
88 Lets the fingers do the talking?
89 Shredded
91 Chiang ___-shek
92 Monthly bill: Abbr.
93 Best sellers
94 Exciting periods in the N.B.A.
96 Leaves a mark on
99 Org. that does studies
102 "Take one!"
103 Book about a female that a married gander fooled around with?
106 Members of a span
107 Sudden descent of water
109 Miracle-___
110 Some stockings
112 Jim Davis dog
113 Book about a mutiny?
116 Van Eyck and Vermeer
117 Home with a view
118 What's needed for a Teutonic tango
119 Raison ___
120 Long ones are risky
121 Locker
122 Small change?
123 Arafat of the P.L.O.

DOWN

1 Big name in 1980s TV talk
2 One who doesn't just stay
3 They're followed
4 "___ say more?"
5 It was in old Rome
6 Morsel
7 Tropicana Field locale, informally
8 Prefix with flop or plop
9 Appear corrupt
10 Green squares
11 Remove along a track
12 A little advance work
13 Suffix with trick
14 Auto extra
15 Book of recipes people kvetch about?
16 They're found in the banks along the Seine
17 Pronoun following a preposition
20 Help with homework
23 Irish author/ director Christopher ___
24 Ordinary guy
29 Minstrel show character
32 Related
33 Eve's opposite
36 Uris's "___ Pass"
38 Province of Saudi Arabia
39 Course correctors
41 Magazine founded by Bob Guccione
42 Reset number
44 Day break?
45 Ripped, as a box
46 French river or department
47 PC key
48 Resident of New Providence island
49 Book about hang-gliding?
50 "The ruler of the universe"
51 City between Boston and Salem
52 Frankfurter link
55 Ex of Artie and Mickey
58 Tubside bottle
60 Part of the works
61 Go back
66 Brontë heroine
67 Be biased
68 Tsp. or tbsp.
70 Actor Morales
71 Gymnast's assistant
73 Fertilization targets
74 Barnyard noise
75 Baby's early word
76 Gets a promotion
77 Vietnam War-era org.
79 When some game shows air: Abbr.

by Randolph Ross

80 Connect
85 Actor known as "Scatman"
86 Baltic resident
87 Soup before sushi
90 Nickname for Michael Jordan, with "His"
92 Tom ___, 1962 A.L. Rookie of the Year
95 Transition
97 Ice cream flavor
98 Currently
99 Puts out
100 "Great" czar
101 "Jeopardy!" offering
102 Wannabe surfer
103 Milo of "The Verdict," 1982
104 Basics of education
105 Bananas
106 First words of "Waltzing Matilda"
107 School of martial arts
108 Six-sided state
111 Lamarr of film
114 Inside info
115 Be entitled

77

LOVE CONNECTION

ACROSS

1 Wire material
5 Train and bus overseer, for short
8 Hurry-scurry
11 A moving experience
19 Oodles
20 Belt tighteners
22 Noted Madonna role
23 Submarine
25 Morning
26 Pedicure place
27 Mimosa family tree
28 "Some Girls Do" author ___ Banks
29 Ike's monogram
30 Matchsticks game
31 College in Poughkeepsie, N.Y.
34 Air letters?
36 St. Louis Gateway Arch architect
41 Name hidden in seven other answers in this puzzle
45 Cuddly TV alien
46 Bring in
47 Sings with swings
48 Psychoanalyst Fromm
49 Grazing ground
50 Dumps
53 Bit of comedy
54 Gifted person
55 Eleniak of "Baywatch"
58 Lashes into a fury
60 Puts on a long face
62 Quagmire

64 "O, beware, my lord, of Jealousy!" speaker
65 Cast
67 Till section
68 Notable discovery of 1799
72 Ennui-inducing
75 Strike zone?
76 Capital on the Caspian Sea
77 Diminutive advice-giver, familiarly
81 Place to meditate
83 Rap singers, generically
86 Analyze
87 In the know
88 Dr. Seuss's "Horton Hears ___"
90 According to
92 Guacamole, for one
93 Standard pick-up line?
94 Seating sections
96 Squeezed (out)
98 Daughter of Cadmus
99 Utopia
100 Eastern bloom
103 Game elements: Abbr.
104 Went over the top, in a way
106 Word after good and bad
107 Cartoonist Keane
109 Innocent
112 One of the Nixons
115 Letter-shaped fastener
118 Study of the atmosphere

121 Chess and tennis, mathematically
123 Pub order
124 Synthetic fiber
125 Major, for one
126 Irons
127 Deli slice
128 "Like ___!"
129 Parts of a line: Abbr.

DOWN

1 Slangy dissents
2 Zeno of ___
3 London had the first one in 1851
4 Gave up a seat
5 Mgr.'s degree
6 Salade niçoise need
7 Electrician's favorite rock band?
8 Pianist de Larrocha
9 Point
10 Part of the Dept. of Labor
11 Pajama-clad exec
12 Ab ___ (from the start)
13 Blue or white fish
14 They're waved at the Olympics
15 Groups of 100
16 Opera "Moses und ___"
17 Bird with a dagger-shaped bill
18 Feminizing suffix
21 Skater Michelle's family
24 Look of disdain
31 Summer coolers

32 Nay sayer
33 Result of a racer jumping the gun
34 "The Crucible" setting
35 Olds model
37 Wiring experts: Abbr.
38 Bank posting
39 Kind of leader
40 Slope
42 Douse, maybe
43 Current locale
44 Discards
48 Summer setting in Pa.
51 1978 cult film by David Lynch
52 Nestor
56 "The Stepford Wives" actress, 1975
57 Lenten symbol
59 Barely managed
61 Dullard
63 Ward of "Sisters"
66 Takeover artist
69 Knock
70 Author Janowitz
71 Big D.C. lobby
72 How grade schoolers are grouped
73 Mooed
74 Marble
78 State Dept. worker
79 Poison
80 Stickers
82 Game pieces
84 Crescent-shaped tract of land
85 Zaire's Mobuto Sese ___

by Elizabeth C. Gorski

89 Clear off
91 Certain tel. no.
95 Requirement for surprise
97 Completely clean
100 Quality, in a Ford slogan
101 Do after dark
102 ___ Center
105 Open-back shoes
108 Building supports
109 "Li'l Abner" creator
110 Prince, e.g.
111 Perry's creator
112 Russian monarch: Var.
113 "The Last Time ___ Paris"
114 Camera setting
116 Olin of "Chocolat"
117 Slight reproaches
119 Eur. language
120 Time line markings: Abbr.
122 Kitten's cry

78

YOU WILL BE MISSED

ACROSS

1 More than high
6 Page
10 Russian name meaning "holy"
14 Lord's workers
19 Where the lion spared Androcles
20 Transition in logic
21 Godsend
22 Somewhat, after "of"
23 Laird or thane?
25 Ex-Dallas coach's daytime show?
27 Sweetie
28 Additionally
29 Web mag
31 Cultural breakdown
32 Blackthorn
33 Word with beetle or movie
34 "What, again?!"
36 Denver summer hrs.
37 Diamond cutter's pace?
41 -: Abbr.
42 What traffic cones may show
43 Ear malady
44 "Thimble Theatre" name
45 Spinner
47 Girl in "The Gondoliers"
48 Iciness and wetness?
53 Rap's Dr. ___
54 Loads of
55 First name in fashion
56 Working out well?
57 "Bed-in" participant, 1969
58 Traveler's aid
59 Prioritizing by army medics, e.g.
61 Benevolent witchcraft
65 What Wordsworth did before he got hip?
70 Giants on the sports page
71 Liking a lot
72 Bronze metal
73 Bite for a bark beetle
74 Prefix with metric
76 Do
77 Tiptop
79 A caliph of Islam
80 Games, games and more games?
85 One in a booth, maybe
87 In pigtails, e.g.
88 Wrongdoing
89 Bridge problem
90 Exhibition area
91 Dirt disher ___ Smith
93 Why water got diverted in the garden?
96 Newsman Bradley and others
97 Quick note
98 Results of a wrong turn, perhaps
99 Tidy up, in a way
100 Falling star
102 It may be cradled
104 Like one smitten
105 Answer sheet
108 Nickname for a pushy priest?
110 Young female marchers?
113 Skin ailment
114 Fictional Jane
115 ___ Sea (inland body of water)
116 Milking a cow, e.g.
117 Lavender, for one
118 Set foot (on)
119 Park Ave. address part
120 Banana oil, e.g.

DOWN

1 Flirt, in old slang
2 It's a gas
3 It's a gas
4 Quarterback's error: Abbr.
5 Alabama's state flower
6 Not so great
7 One-named artist
8 Gray
9 Prophesied
10 Require
11 Part of F.S.L.I.C.
12 Liking a lot
13 "Then what?"
14 Decline
15 "The sign of extra service" sloganeer, once
16 School pal, maybe
17 "Sorry, no can do"
18 Workplace for Michelangelo
24 "A Lesson From ___"
26 Ended a call in London
30 More than daze
32 Goes down
33 How to palm a card
35 Mainz mister
37 Note
38 God, with "the"
39 Sage
40 In next to no time
42 Obtained from milk
46 Oolong tea exporter
48 Karel ___, writer who coined the word "robot"
49 Stopped working, as medicine
50 Native's opposite
51 Relative of a mallard
52 Like brioche
54 Natl. Nutrition Mo.
58 Abbr. in a salutation
59 "Pagliacci" clown
60 "All gone," for a tot
62 Took everything from, with "out"
63 Fellow's place
64 Popular
66 Most like a bone
67 Art ___ (7-Down genre)
68 Ancient Spanish kingdom
69 ___-pack
75 100 centesimi, once
77 Make ___ (clench)
78 French door part
80 Cracks
81 Western artist Remington
82 140 British pounds
83 Presider over banquets of those slain in battle
84 In unison
85 Abnormality
86 Quick O.K.: Abbr.

by Manny Nosowsky

89 Corrugation
92 Gentle blow
93 Liked a lot
94 Egg warmer
95 Mortal
97 For dieters, in ads
101 Garden spot

103 Knight in shining armor
104 Sculptor ___ Lorenzo Bernini
105 Ball of string?
106 To be, in Brest
107 Belgian river

109 Hanoi holiday
111 Ending with honor
112 Responses of enlightenment

ACROSS

1 Went down to second?
5 Did laps
9 Place for table umbrellas
13 Like oxfords
18 Common website link
19 ___ Minor
20 Famous mausoleum site
21 Powdered soap brand
22 Locket shape
23 Friend barges in while gent is making amorous overtures; ref declares . . .
26 ___ Hold 'em (poker variant)
28 R & B singer Bryson
29 Two-time loser to Ike
30 Fact-check
31 "You betcha!"
33 Hysteria curber
34 Late philanthropist Joan
35 Widespread reaction
36 Fellow forgets to shave before kissing girlfriend; ref cites him for . . .
42 Some bow ties
43 Compliment to the chef
44 "If only ___ listened!"
45 Acquisitions person
47 Right away
49 Looks over
53 The Great White North
54 Popular brand of stationery

56 Dance floor remains empty at debutante party; ref rules it a . . .
57 Tennis call
58 Join hands?
59 Smooth
60 Big inits. in movies
61 Freestyle jumps
64 Handsome marriageable man enters room; ref signals . . .
66 A neighbor
68 One end of the spectrum
69 Multitude
70 Duke of 63-Down
71 Farm call
72 Gorgeous lady enters room; ref signals . . .
75 Tito Puente's specialty
76 Reading site
80 Name used in indignant questions
81 Lincoln or Ford
82 Secured, as carpet tacks
84 Suffix with dual
85 Revenue sources
86 At a loss
87 Guy gets grabby on first date; ref penalizes him for . . .
94 Suffix with period
95 Naval base?
96 Rock's Mötley ___
97 Salon options
98 Wallace who wrote "Ben-Hur"
99 Unseen character in a Beckett play
100 First name in gossip
102 1930s have-nots
106 Lovers embrace passionately in

public place; ref declares . . .
110 Unmeaningful
111 It's often found in a bar
112 Railroad chartered in 1832
113 Balladeer's aid
114 Iditarod race destination
115 Radiant
116 Russet-colored liquors
117 Release
118 Icky stuff

DOWN

1 Ruined
2 Score of zero
3 Theater company that thinks big
4 Guy acquires girl's phone number but waits too long to use it; ref signals . . .
5 Eat late
6 It precedes a cast party
7 Weigh
8 "Mississippi ___" (Denzel Washington film)
9 Shade provider
10 Contract negotiator: Abbr.
11 Come unglued
12 Body part repaired by tympanoplasty
13 Folk singer McKenna
14 Remain
15 9-Down material
16 Leftover
17 "A merry heart ___ good like a medicine": Proverbs

21 Normandy campaign objective
24 Strong support
25 Thrash
27 Surrounds with trees, say
32 Focus on
35 Edit for TV, maybe
36 Potentially insulting
37 Writer Ephron
38 Bright time
39 Birmingham-to-Montgomery dir.
40 Tom Clancy hero
41 Typical Rick Moranis film role
46 Overhauled
47 Magic wand tip
48 Last part of a paint job
49 Phnom ___
50 Comedian Mort
51 Island off the Tuscan coast
52 Opening
55 Got off
56 Tennis ball fuzz material
59 More than a twinge
61 Synagogue cabinets
62 Fictional princess
63 Rugged biblical land
64 Infraction
65 Magazine contents
66 Hype
67 Man refuses to supply photo on Internet dating service; ref cites him for . . .
69 Pentecost figure
71 Like some hooks
73 Shiver's cause

by Patrick Berry

74 Sky box?
75 Tousle
77 Gladsheim palace resident
78 Traded blows
79 Front and back
81 "Madame Bovary" subject
83 Refuse
85 Everywhere
87 Sparkly mist
88 Prescribed
89 A6 or A8 maker
90 Talks back?
91 Hurler Hershiser
92 Throw for a loop
93 Night guard's problem
94 Actress Massey
99 Eat indelicately
101 Detractor
103 Role model
104 A Muppet
105 Dribble
107 Blowhard's trait
108 Speed
109 Avenge oneself on

GRIDIRON GLOSSARY

ACROSS

1 How one must win in volleyball
6 Like most bicycle tires
11 World Service provider
14 King of comedy
18 Element #5
19 Stradivari's teacher
20 Breeder's interest
22 What one gets from the hot dog vendor when paying with a $5 bill?
24 Who we are
25 Mesabi Range wealth
26 Under cover?
27 A stone may have one
28 Not allow
30 Platinum blonde cheerleaders?
34 Basic learning, for short
35 Tom, Dick and Harry
36 It's murky
37 Singer Baker or Bryant
39 Carpet type
41 Horror maven Craven
42 Clears
46 Home viewers' HDTV's?
51 Where the Danube ends
53 Words before ghost or doctor
54 Some fancy footwork
55 Manage, with "out"
57 Of lesser size
58 Star followers
60 Ill-treats
62 One who flies south in the winter
63 Most popular beer brands at the concession stands?
69 Easily bribed
70 Bids one club, e.g.
71 Marineland performer
72 Time for a spring roll?
74 1990 Broadway one-man play
75 33-Down output
78 Lodge sign
82 Led
84 Trash talk?
87 Babysitters' charges
88 Sinker's call
90 Eye part
91 Molokai colonist, once
92 Tufted tweeter
95 E and G, e.g., in D.C.
97 "Halloween ___" (1983 flick)
98 Rule barring players from dating cheerleaders?
104 Stuart monarch
105 Mo who unsuccessfully ran for president in 1976
106 Some pats
107 Flout the Volstead Act
109 Associated with
111 Untackled players?
115 Mukluk attachments
116 "And if that weren't bad enough . . ."
117 Sea inlet: Var.
118 Many ages
119 Part of E.S.T. : Abbr.
120 Payments made before a deal is completed
121 Politico Kefauver

DOWN

1 Jul. 4 happening
2 2-Down reader, right now
3 Track event?
4 Cause of wrinkles
5 Aware of
6 Large decks
7 Spectral image
8 Bleated
9 ". . . , ___"
10 Hägar creator Browne
11 Store restriction
12 Neighbor
13 N.Y.S.E. listings
14 Subject of much praise
15 Été reading
16 Lend ___
17 Fits snugly
20 Overseas whistle blower
21 Longtime record label
23 Start of Massachusetts' motto
26 Hosp. workers' org.
28 Picks at random
29 With 86-Down, 2002 British Open winner
31 1997 Aaliyah hit "The One ___ My Heart To"
32 Impulse
33 Name on many a children's book
35 Laugh syllable
38 Ones on a bench together
39 One in 100: Abbr.
40 Sot's sound
42 Connected two computers, say
43 Permanently
44 Cuts carbs, maybe
45 1986 #1 Starship hit
47 What a sphere lacks
48 Home of Al-Azhar University
49 Chair filler
50 Arctic gull
52 Work done to scale
56 One with a pole position?
59 More fit
60 Rx prescribers
61 Russian export, familiarly
63 Cool
64 Loose, as stones
65 Choose
66 Roman imperator
67 Sufficient, informally
68 Beforehand: Abbr.
69 Third piece
73 Gum
75 Head warmer?
76 Suffix with oct-
77 Troop grp.
79 Fresh from the oven
80 ___ ten (long odds)
81 Unsettling
83 Child's puzzle
85 Detonator
86 See 29-Down
89 Refined
92 Jousting contests

by Patrick Merrell

93 Snacks packaged in trays
94 One evidently not filing a flight plan
95 Monkey Trial defendant, 1925
96 Having four parts: Prefix
98 Prize money
99 Gland: Prefix
100 Where a do is done
101 Certain side dishes
102 Chicago-based critic
103 Hopeless
104 Auspices
108 Bio
110 Geezers' interjections
111 Old "Up, up and away" sloganeer
112 Dearie
113 Thrice uno
114 '60s campus grp.

ACROSS

1 Woeful
4 Checks the growth of
8 Japanese porcelain
13 Turkeys
18 One that's similar
20 Pressed
21 Studio feed
22 Major nickel exporter
23 Large place where elks gather?
25 Where squabbling neighbors live?
27 Positions
28 Off the wind
29 Driving aid
30 Starchy fixin's
32 Kipling pack leader
35 Spread managers
37 Large amount of money
40 Partner, with "the"
43 Mason's request?
45 Hendrix of '60s music
46 Public rap
48 For ___ an emergency
49 Prefix with linguistics
50 Large bills, informally
51 Red Cross course, for short
53 1970s fad participant
56 Clark's companion
57 Encouraging words
61 Muscat native
62 Defunct pro sports org.
63 Genetically improved grain?
65 Typesetters' needs: Abbr.
67 "___ pray"
69 Impertinent types
70 In a stack
72 Merriest
75 Actress Thurman
76 Copy illegally
77 Milk: Prefix
78 Everyday
82 Dryly said
83 Town on the Humboldt River
84 Complaint that one didn't get enough presents?
88 ___ lab
89 Couple abroad
90 Edwards, for one
91 Adjutants
92 Marcher's woe
93 Wing
94 Primatologist's study
98 Housed, as a student
101 Cattle prod?
106 Clock's slowing down?
109 Directly
110 Tea biscuit
111 Overturns
112 Personal interview
113 Not easygoing
114 Chutney fruit
115 Bubkes
116 "As if!"

DOWN

1 1930s Brazilian import
2 "For want of ___ . . ."
3 1-Down, e.g.
4 Do, say
5 Soviet Physics Nobelist ___ Tamm
6 Stout sites
7 City named for an Indian chief
8 Dies ___
9 Shed
10 Nest builder
11 Heir, usually: Abbr.
12 Inane
13 Walkers on hot coals
14 1930s–'60s power couple
15 God attended by two ravens
16 The Panthers of the Big East
17 Some beans
19 Akin to
20 "O.K."
24 Muskogee tribe
26 Bawl out in no uncertain terms
30 Spelling of Hollywood
31 Claude who starred in TV's "Lobo"
32 Malarial episodes
33 White wine apéritifs
34 First mate
35 Undergrad degs.
36 Decoration from Eliz. II
37 Atoll with no electric lights?
38 French companion
39 Fashionable dress
40 Year the emperor Frederick II died
41 Start fresh
42 Skiing documentaries?
44 Hoover rival
45 Artist from Barcelona
47 Hole puncher
49 Vast amount
51 N.L. or A.L. team
52 They ripple on bodybuilders
54 Small fry
55 Apt. units
57 Talk a blue streak?
58 Legal thing
59 Name meaning "she-bear"
60 Hallmark card text, often
63 "___ pasa?"
64 Parseghian of Notre Dame
66 Begin, as winter
68 However, briefly
70 Tools of the Seven Dwarfs
71 Numerical prefix
72 Ran in the rain
73 Film composer Schifrin
74 Jet enhancer
76 Part of R.I.P.
79 Asian ending for "land"
80 Grunts
81 Drink suffix
82 Upper limit
84 I.Q. tester Alfred
85 Corrosion-resistant metal
86 Everyone in Dixie
87 Nuclear measure
90 "Little Shop of Horrors" girl

by Con Pederson

92 Former White House adviser Scowcroft
93 Bits of energy
94 Heaps
95 Cliff climber's tool
96 Prefix with metrics
97 Contest with many traps
98 Abject failure
99 Fairy tale start
100 Fusses
101 Blab freely
102 Prefix with China
103 Skye neighbor
104 Impecuniosity
105 Greek portico
107 No. cruncher
108 Knowledge

ACROSS

1 Special team
6 Chi-Town paper
10 Get lost
15 Dumptruckful
19 "Twelfth Night" role
20 Mrs. Chaplin
21 "Ta-da!"
22 Word processor command
23 March trailer
24 Haltingly
26 Kind of bike
27 Used up
28 Space flight's starting point
29 Nice-smelling gifts
30 Rhode Island's motto
31 Colored a bit
33 Shake
34 Rights of passage, e.g.
36 Cook's exhortation
38 McCartney title
40 Despot of yore
41 Portion of a ton: Abbr.
44 Aerosol output
45 Hems and haws
46 Totaled
50 Agreeable
52 F.D.R. power project
53 Made book marks?
56 Extra cost in mail order
57 Choler
58 Fights dirty, in a way
59 Martinique, e.g.
60 Street of mystery
61 Pro pitchers
63 Rod attachment
64 Some votes
65 Mock plea for civil language
69 Mix up
70 Came to
71 Pricey
72 Cut
74 Russert once of "Meet the Press"
75 Needed a doctor
76 Stale
77 Scarface portrayer
78 Like some income
80 South-of-the-border shout
81 Got a slice of
83 Obscure
84 Comic Gilliam
85 "Rush Hour" star, 1998
86 Heartbeat, so to speak
87 Abbey ___
90 Fortune 500 inits.
91 Invoice word
93 Coin of the realm
97 Sewed up
99 Perfumes with a joss stick
104 Open
105 First child
106 Waxed bombastic
108 Supermodel Campbell
109 Slave of opera
110 That, to this
112 Values on a scale of 0 to 100
113 Ship part
114 60-Across's boss
115 It's not good
116 Ties up
117 Highlands tongue
118 Plain writing
119 Hawk
120 "I Am Woman" singer, 1972

DOWN

1 "Cease" at sea
2 Painter Fra Filippo ___
3 "Two Women" Oscar winner
4 Black bird
5 Stored (away)
6 Words before and after "or not"
7 King's champion
8 Ahead
9 Puts on the hook?
10 Elm and Peachtree: Abbr.
11 Ship provisioners
12 Roadside pull-off
13 Oil worker
14 Imbroglios
15 Like Wittenberg University in Ohio
16 Continuously
17 Crack
18 Some stadium features
25 Best-selling 1974 detective novel
32 Yankee nickname of old
35 Niles's ex on "Frasier"
37 Cry at the card table
39 Investment option, briefly
41 Under the table
42 Serendipitous
43 Make fit
47 All over
48 Looking good on the tube
49 Lyrical lines
50 High degree
51 Clothes closer
52 Something good
53 Saturday night special
54 Truly enjoyed
55 Firms
57 Penned up
58 Like cattle on the range
61 Burn ___ in one's pocket
62 Faked out, in the rink
64 Some relations
66 Mattress type
67 Surprise
68 ___-Pei (Chinese dog)
69 Pitiful pencil
73 King of the boxing world
75 Combat gear
77 Wall Street scare
79 Terrier type
80 Giant of note
81 Witchy woman
82 Showboater
84 John Hancock and others
85 Thinking outside the box
88 Mammy Yokum's creator
89 Old phone user
92 Many an agent
93 Rich dessert
94 Comparatively gritty
95 Holds, with "over"
96 Hot rod propellant

by Harvey Estes and Nancy Salomon

98 Rattletraps
100 Green
101 Did a cobbler's
job
102 Fix
103 Wuss
107 Compaq competitor
111 Potent potable

ACROSS

1 Causes of bickering
6 "Rock'd the full-foliaged ___": Tennyson
10 Solar event
15 See 24-Down
19 Prayer recipient, maybe
20 Binge
21 1962 tennis Grand Slam winner
22 Sudden clouding-over, maybe
23 Step 1 of a Thanksgiving dinner
27 Thatcher's place
28 One of the angels on "Charlie's Angels"
29 Mount
30 Undersides of overhangs
34 Interpret
35 Cared for lovingly
38 Elevate
39 Extended time
40 Young hog
41 Step 2
47 Walks
48 Send off
49 Game equipment
50 Work of Homer
52 Cooling treats
53 Look-alike
54 Opponent of Stalin
55 Work of Juvenal
57 The "one" in the phrase "draw one"
58 Ray who founded McDonald's
59 Actress Flockhart
60 Step 3
66 Blue Diamond canful
67 "Phooey!"
68 Tirade
69 Elements of a biblical miracle
70 Cooling treat
71 Sawbuck halves
72 Beach sandal problem
76 Spill producer
77 Santa ___
78 Creepy crawler
79 Having the toilet paper roll put on the "wrong" way, e.g.
80 Step 4
85 Responds to gravity
86 "Dies ___"
87 Loosens
88 Make retroactive
92 "Laugh-In" segment
93 Plate
94 Register
95 Procrastinator's promise
96 Show windedness
97 Step 5
106 "___ Rock"
107 Matrimony
108 Perfidious
109 Hello or goodbye
110 Polar expedition, e.g.
111 Competed in a rodeo event
112 Genesis maker
113 Like some jackets

DOWN

1 Line in geometry
2 U.N. agcy. dealing with jobs
3 Sore throat producer
4 Blacken
5 Western heroes
6 Spirit of a people
7 Be idle
8 Time to get back to work: Abbr.
9 Police action
10 Not static
11 Macaulay's "___ of Ancient Rome"
12 Actress Gardner
13 Officiate, briefly
14 Big real estate firm
15 Vagabonds
16 Desert V.I.P.'s
17 Poetry
18 Over
24 With 15-Across, need, slangily
25 Small goose
26 Certain sorority member
30 ___ bar
31 Sight-related
32 Hole in one, assuredly
33 Small wind instruments
34 Fasten again
35 1970s sitcom title character
36 Dynamite
37 British rule in India
39 Approve of
40 Card
42 Stair posts
43 Putdown of those with whom one disagrees
44 ___ point
45 Imitative
46 Spanish point
51 Burn
53 Oversees
54 Much-heard
55 Composer Saint-___
56 Gobs
57 Ruin
58 Winter celebration
59 Nickel and dime
60 High
61 Vocally
62 Insect stage
63 Interlaced
64 Cavity fillers
65 Three-in-one
70 Item with syrup
71 Homecoming project
72 Chanson de ___ (medieval poem)
73 Balsam, e.g.
74 Brown group
75 Kid
77 Set
78 Hospital supplies
79 On the dot
81 "You'd never have guessed, but . . ."
82 Singing syllable
83 Photography brand
84 Having second thoughts about
88 Suit
89 Something to be lent, in phrase
90 Twinkie filler
91 Photography brand

by Kumar Balani

92 Valid
93 1972 pop hit with a never-ending chorus
95 Sole supporter?
96 Fussbudget
98 "___ Father . . ."
99 Mattel game
100 Lace (into)
101 Hello or goodbye
102 Inventor Whitney
103 "My boy"
104 Café alternative
105 Depressing

ACROSS

1 Family-friendly ratings
4 Natl. Grapefruit Mo.
7 "How Dry ___"
10 Fragrant hair ointment
16 They may go for big bucks
18 Fat substitute
20 Ones fit for kings and queens?
22 Attractions at the Thanksgiving parade in old Pennsylvania?
24 Disturbs
25 Volcanic rock
26 Holder of an insect's DNA?
28 Big Ten rival: Abbr.
29 Not waver from
32 Chantilly's department
33 Go after
35 Not likely to pose nude
36 Recipe amts.
38 Many a vacationer's need
44 Fab Four film
45 Fraternity letter
46 "Don't bother!"
48 Longtime Dolphins coach
49 Syndicated advice column from a couch potato?
53 Kind of garage
55 Mattress filler
56 Kooky Kovacs
57 Leaves after a meal?
58 Complain
59 Weight
61 Dublin hangouts
63 Opinion piece
64 Reverse image?
68 Deduce
72 Dress material for a ball
74 Make-up person?
75 "The Lion in Winter" star, 1968
76 What the Lincoln Memorial faces
79 Poets' feet
83 Two years before Claudius was murdered
84 Undo a secession
85 Office manager's oversight of felt-tip pens?
89 Captain's order
90 Adam's first wife, in Jewish folklore
91 Article in France-Soir
92 Captain of 1960s TV
95 Handles
97 ___ the Great (boy detective)
98 Parlor transaction
99 Fundamental physics particle
100 Disney or Whitman
102 Pitcher
104 "Oz" network
105 Background of roses, irises, etc.?
112 Woody vines
114 Stew morsel
115 Ones using "the facilities"?
118 Cordial
119 Season, in a way
120 "Now, about . . ."
121 Does greenhouse work
122 Suffix with expert
123 Actor Vigoda
124 Carrier to Oslo

DOWN

1 Composer of "Oedipus Tex" and "A Little Nightmare Music"
2 Opaque watercolor technique
3 The "surf" in some surf 'n' turf dinners
4 Strength
5 Seasonal worker
6 Ann Patchett novel "___ Canto"
7 Author Calvino
8 So SoHo
9 Neither fem. nor neut.
10 Prepares, as a surface for painting
11 Prefix with -pod
12 "Serpico" author
13 Violist's clef
14 Judge
15 Latin 101 verb
17 Cousin of reggae
19 Pushover
20 Arrondissement resident
21 Bruisable things
23 Berlin-born Sommer
27 Drawing site
30 Italian noble family name
31 Exodus figure
34 Neurology, oncology, cardiology, etc.
36 Round stopper, for short
37 Fries or slaw
39 Archipelago unit: Abbr.
40 "I'm serious!"
41 Bazooka part
42 Portoferraio is its chief town
43 You can catch them on a beach
45 Raison d'___
46 Building support
47 Linda in 1990s news
50 Singer Tucker
51 ___-American relations
52 French fire
53 Three, to Amati
54 Craven who directed "Swamp Thing"
60 Fifth of a scale
62 Snake, by nature
64 Unit of wisdom?
65 Pilfer
66 Of the flock
67 1983 World Series champs
69 Stupidity
70 The "E" of R.E.O. Speedwagon
71 Stimpy's cartoon pal
73 Cambridge sch.
75 Leftovers for Fido
76 New newts
77 Skin care item
78 Postpaid encl.
80 Suburban Philadelphia area
81 Notes hit by divas
82 "___ ain't broke . . ."

by Elizabeth C. Gorski

86 No-goodnik
87 Resident: Suffix
88 The pucks stop here
93 Diva Peters
94 Site of King Minos' palace
96 Wide-eyed young 'uns
98 Western actor William et al.
99 Dr.'s orders
101 "The Man Who Mistook His Wife for ___" (Oliver Sacks book)
102 Profession
103 Rinse, as with a solvent
105 Bug, to so speak
106 Director Wertmüller
107 Leave off
108 Flatten, in Falmouth
109 But, to Brahms
110 Pad ___ (noodle dish)
111 Ref. volumes
113 "So you're the culprit!"
116 Plane watcher: Abbr.
117 Barrister's deg.

ACROSS

1 Sharp-billed diver
5 Home of Russell Cave Natl. Monument
8 Mediterranean resort island
13 Made off with
18 Sicilian mount
19 Frank Delano Roosevelt's phrase "New Deal" came from a book by . . .
21 Like the north wind
22 Theodore Roosevelt, who was never known as the modest type, is the only U.S. president ever to give an inaugural address . . .
25 Homer Simpson outburst
26 Camera lens setting
27 Ocean floor
28 Fort Smith-to-Little Rock dir.
29 Target MTV viewer
30 Horned viper
33 One-armed bandit
34 Special treatment, for short
37 Puts through again, as paper in a copier
39 "When ___ hear from you?"
41 Extremely significant
43 Eggs
44 Kingston resident, e.g.
46 Self-titled WB sitcom
47 Together, musically
49 One-named singer/actress
51 Abound
52 1994 Peace Nobelist Peres
54 Go bad

55 Some fund-raisers
57 Global divide
59 911 responders, for short
60 Below-the-belt
61 Really beats
62 Sorority letters
64 Hate
66 Architect of Spain's Miró museum
67 Early sixth-century year
68 "Stormy Weather" singer
70 It's due in Venice
71 Love
73 Like weightlifters
75 Enter
76 States positively
78 Baroque piece
79 Revolutionary Trotsky
80 1997 Demi Moore title role
81 Circus reactions
83 Work ___ many levels (succeed)
84 Tracy's mom, in "Hairspray"
85 Needle case
86 Dirty Harry, e.g.
88 Maven
89 Bears, on Wall Street
92 Country singer Black
93 Some Diego Rivera works
97 Tax
98 Glove
100 Ushered
101 One going to the dogs?
102 Rum ___ Tugger ("Cats" cat)
103 It may be hard to keep
105 Newspapers
106 Road map no.

107 Calvin Coolidge lived up to his reputation as a man of few words when he . . .
114 Sweden's largest lake
115 George W. Bush, as a managing general partner of baseball's Texas Rangers, traded away . . .
116 Without ___ (unprotected)
117 The only U.S. president whose vice president ran against him to succeed him was John . . .
118 Get rid of
119 Ace reliever Robb
120 Understands

DOWN

1 More lascivious
2 Slothful
3 Presidents 117-Across and 44-Down both died the same day in 1826 . . .
4 "Ixnay"
5 Tickled
6 Coffee orders
7 Bad lighting?
8 Suffix with odd
9 Anguilla is part of it: Abbr.
10 Writer Fleming
11 Takes a jog
12 Pot creators
13 1976 uprising site
14 Stepped (on)
15 Anthem contraction
16 Young fellow
17 QB Manning

20 Cover, in commercial names
21 Cat sound?
23 Have a spot ___
24 Rock's Van ___
30 Object
31 Roofer, at times
32 Works at
34 John Quincy Adams, as U.S. secretary of state, was the man who actually drafted . . .
35 Ronald Reagan is the only U.S. president who was also president of a . . .
36 The Kennedys, e.g.
38 Nevertheless
39 Peace interrupter
40 Rocks, so to speak
42 See 56-Down
44 A U.S. president who was also an architect, musician and inventor was . . .
45 Yanqui
47 Annoyed no end
48 A labor-saving device invented by 44-Down was the . . .
49 French vineyard
50 Kind of cab
52 Grinder
53 Discuss, with "over"
56 With 42-Down, college course, slangily
58 Comforters
61 Twist
63 Drug-yielding plant
65 Pour
67 Demand payment
69 Long lookers
72 Hip-hop's Dr. ___
73 Number five iron

by David J. Kahn

74 N.B.A.'s ___ Ming
77 Go belly-up
78 "Relax, man!"
80 Medieval romance tale
82 Like some stocks and drugs: Abbr.
86 Nolan Ryan, notably
87 Object

88 "___ Porridge Hot"
90 Some heads of state
91 Costa ___
93 Strip off, as blubber
94 Look over again
95 Discount store
96 Fuses, as ore
99 Strained

101 Obsolescent refrigerant
103 Fruit holder
104 Sprint
105 Hoops stat: Abbr.
107 Robt. Byrd's home
108 "Far out!"
109 ___ roll

110 Diminutive, in Dundee
111 Type widths
112 Largest county of Nevada
113 Comic

86 Years On End

ACROSS

1 Fan's sound
6 One of the Brothers Karamazov
12 Collapsible lid
20 Ran very slowly
21 Like most sonnets
22 Multiply like an amoeba
23 Amazed telegram recipient's cry?
25 One who gets a reaction
26 In order
27 Jerk
28 Letter getter
30 "Dennis the Menace" airer on old TV
31 One going down fast
33 PC key
36 Palliate
37 Indian butter
38 Midshipmen's gridiron gains?
41 Fairylike being of myth
43 Where a lot of fed. govt. workers live
45 Playwright Peter who wrote "Marat/Sade"
46 TV Guide data
49 Water, chemically
50 Ignored, as authority
52 Calling "chicken," perhaps
53 Colorful circle
55 Saw out of the blue?
58 Supporting
59 Got milk

61 Correspondence
62 Famous murder defendant of the 1920s
63 Silent authority?
64 Unstimulating
67 Lengthy sentence
68 Carol contraction
69 Silent army
71 Some multiplayer deals
73 "You don't say!"
77 Book before Esther: Abbr.
78 What a local news broadcast leads with?
81 Announce
82 Darkening
84 Impetuously, perhaps
86 Gloomy guy
87 "Don't worry"
88 Clinton's first secretary of defense
90 Relatively rare
92 Falls behind, in a way
93 Tramp class?
95 One of 12 popes
97 "See ya"
98 Namath put it on the map: Abbr.
99 Grounds for a good night's sleep?
102 Table scrap
103 Befuddled
106 Land's end?
108 Kind of theater
110 "Darned if I know"
112 Result of a vacuum cleaner mishap?

116 One tooting a horn
117 Joins in
118 Busted
119 Diving areas
120 Hate with a passion
121 Primary strategy

DOWN

1 Blows away
2 Ding Dong alternatives
3 "The Compleat Angler" author Walton
4 Strong Greek wine
5 Nutritionist's fig.
6 Goes belly up
7 Raymond of "Dr. Kildare"
8 Chats online, for short
9 Course list abbr.
10 Baltic port
11 Cool brews
12 "You don't even want to know the alternative!"
13 Canada's Point ___ National Park
14 Polish
15 Wedding fling?
16 Bird: Prefix
17 Cost of a mail-order bride?
18 Building material
19 Clipped
24 Get bug-eyed over
29 Gorgons
32 Cold weather protector
34 Took care of
35 Tread stealthily

37 Alfred E. Neuman feature
39 7' 5" Ming
40 Made fancy
41 Little digit
42 Lake tribe
43 Mrs. Copperfield
44 Order to a power plant worker?
46 Small types
47 Cheney's predecessor
48 Hoity-toity one
49 Prince of Broadway
51 Kite aid
52 Nourished the mind
54 Early Nebraskans
56 Bro
57 Jackie's second
60 Coarse
62 Moonshine maker
65 Pledge of allegiance
66 ___ gratias
68 Early seafarers feared going over it
69 Not behind
70 "Eye of ___ . . ."
71 Robes of office, once
72 Breaks off
74 Like some nuts
75 Putdown
76 Has too much, briefly
78 Lift
79 Baker of song
80 Swindler, slangily
83 Some stock quotes
85 Sheet music abbr.
88 Road runner
89 Lit

by Lee Glickstein and Nancy Salomon

91 It usually has a point
93 Some farm machinery
94 Respected ones
95 Put forward
96 Goddess of peace
97 Broken
100 Range from Iowa
101 Twisted character in "Oliver Twist"
103 Bad spots for a date
104 Next
105 Unit of volume
107 Once, once
109 TV warrior
111 Initials in stone
113 Giant of old
114 Sign of a winner
115 Surrealist sculptor

ACROSS

1 Subordinate ruler
7 Former rulers of Egypt
14 Came out of sleep, old-style
20 Put on the same level
21 Treeless plain
22 It may be in a torpedo
23 Start of a verse
26 Fringe, maybe
27 "Ici on ___ français"
28 Hon
29 Take-home
30 Was bright
32 Code cracker's comment
34 Sentimental song
38 Slight manifestation
39 Maligned
44 ___ Cologne (skunk of old cartoons)
45 Climb
46 Cast off
47 Fa followers
48 Verse, part 2
54 Hoary
55 Zero population
56 Small goose
57 Spray displayers
58 Word of possibility
59 Token taker
60 One way off a ship
61 Vestibule
62 Itsy-bitsy biter
63 Record notation
64 Paradigm of happiness
66 "___ figlia dell'amore" (Verdi quartet)
69 Walks heavily
70 Festive
71 Timberjack's tool
74 Broadcasting
75 "Dred" novelist
76 Life-or-death situation
77 Manufacturing center?
78 Verse, part 3
82 Livy's "Lo!"
83 Henri's high
84 Diamond complement
85 Counseling, e.g.
86 Ice alternative: Var.
88 Scooby Doo's co-creator
90 In the habit of
92 Big mouth, slangily
93 "The Syncopated Clock" composer Anderson
94 Had something
95 Lots
99 Sicilia, e.g.
101 Bern, Geneva and Zurich
106 End of the verse
111 Kindle
112 Resembling a chanterelle mushroom in flavor
113 Mimosa family member
114 Right from the factory
115 Soul
116 Some speech sounds

DOWN

1 Shakers, e.g.
2 Cool shade
3 Mild reproofs
4 Loser's cry
5 She sprang from Zeus's head
6 Skinless
7 Grp. associated with dens
8 Record store section
9 Correct ending
10 Big game fish
11 Recent delivery
12 Sound asleep?
13 Kind of monitor
14 Hard-rock center
15 Classified
16 Gucci of fashion
17 The Green Hornet's valet
18 Discharge
19 Runs out of steam
24 W. Coast setting
25 Sweetie pie
30 Base coach's urging
31 Not say directly
33 Pilgrimage to Mecca
34 Abraham's ___ (heaven)
35 Miss Quested of "A Passage to India"
36 Jitterbug variety
37 Court call
38 Capital of East Flanders
39 Get lost in a brown study
40 Wachovia or Chase Manhattan, briefly
41 Ocean liner?
42 Big name in bonding
43 Chain component, perhaps
45 Hotfoot it
46 1953 film title hero
49 Catch
50 "Show Boat" heroine
51 "Much ___!"
52 Colliery carriers
53 Covering everything
60 Move like a puma
62 Suspended porch piece
63 Pull
64 Giant
65 Inter ___
66 Pitney's partner
67 Tennyson's Arden
68 Medieval charging need
69 Pub potable
70 Davis of Hollywood
71 Longed
72 Ready to be played, in a way
73 Herbert Marx, familiarly
75 "Tosca" villain
76 Roman encyclopedist
79 Cassowary's cousin
80 Latin word on a monument
81 Subject of "The Motorcycle Diaries"
87 Go around
88 Ancient serfs

by Frances Hansen

89 Like farmland
90 West Jordan resident
91 "Epistulae morales" writer
93 Big name in computer software
94 Take steps
95 Diego Velázquez's "Lady With ___"
96 Take on
97 Ample, poetically
98 Together, in music
100 End of a New Year's classic
102 Start of a Christmas classic
103 Ocean danger
104 Catch but good
105 Places to get steamed
107 Slick
108 A as in Austria
109 Org. that registers boxers
110 Something to drive off of

ACROSS

1 Novelist known for "locked-room" mysteries
5 Just about hopeless
10 Former first lady's name
14 Rash problem
18 Potpourri
19 Terra firma
20 Coleridge's "___ Khan"
21 "A Doll's House" heroine
22 Long-running column
25 Hostage crisis group
26 Those reversing
27 Pungent
28 What's happening
30 Major or Thatcher, e.g.
31 French department
32 Cool
33 Nook
36 "In Search Of . . ." host
37 At sixes and sevens
41 "The Wreck of the Mary ___"
42 Cafeteria
44 James Clavell best seller "___-Pan"
45 Stops up
46 Co. V.I.P.
47 Like most of Oman
48 Glossary entry
49 Dubious "gift"
50 Hammer wielder
54 Things put on houses
55 Manage
57 Leigh Hunt's "Abou Ben ___"
58 Derrières
59 Newspaper department
60 Funny Mike
61 Portobello alternative
62 Toiletry item
63 "I Believe" singer, 1953
64 Islets of Langerhans locale
67 Fugitive's creation
68 L-shaped tool
70 "I'm Real" singer's nickname
71 It's half the faun
72 Twinge
73 Modern ice cream flavor
74 Keyboard section
75 Common test subject
76 Classic doll
80 Have a cow
81 Letter wearers, e.g.
83 Find new tenants for
84 Spends pleasantly, with "away"
85 Kadett maker
86 Calls, old-style
87 Hue close to aqua
88 Video store category
91 Video store category
92 Like ocher
96 Lug
97 When some people pick up turkeys
100 Saying nothing
101 Bridge seats
102 Make beam
103 Lawn-Boy alternative
104 Pony provoker
105 Tango moves
106 Struck out
107 Crimson rivals

DOWN

1 Harry who co-founded Columbia Pictures
2 Live ___ (be someone you're not)
3 Arboreal age indicator
4 Some muscles
5 In the presence of
6 Bird making a basket
7 The libido, in psychiatry
8 Balance provider
9 Head of Iran beginning 1997
10 Shoplifter's giveaway, perhaps
11 Bidding site
12 Camera type, briefly
13 Blue
14 As originally arranged
15 Country partner?
16 Mountaineer's challenge
17 Tops
20 Popular saxophonist
23 Boiling point?
24 Captain of industry
29 Bozos
31 Belarus's capital
32 Away
33 Puff ___
34 Car dealer's offering
35 Popular negotiation location
36 Flower girl, sometimes
37 Billiards bounce
38 Worker who shouldn't have acrophobia
39 Makes
40 Makes indistinct
42 Mild oaths
43 Refreshing spots
46 Surveyors' maps
48 Microwave feature
50 Felicity
51 Entrance
52 Places of 50-Down
53 Cousin of a mole
54 Clumsy move
56 Lusitania sinker
58 Big name in infomercials
60 Poet Piercy
61 Bison features
62 Dairy treat
63 Bronchi termini
64 Candidate of 1992
65 Bufferin alternative
66 Sensitive spots
67 Pearl Mosque locale
68 Toast alternative
69 Some apples
72 Unduplicatable, in a way
74 Follow very closely
76 Defaulter's comeuppance

by Hal Turner

77 Predinner ritual
78 A long time
79 Maintained
80 Michael who won the 1989 French Open
82 Stick around

84 No longer on the bottle
86 Auto damage
87 Old hat
88 Mendicant's want
89 Great move
90 Ballet piece

91 Shocked reaction
92 Racer's path
93 Pedestal figure
94 Raipur wrap
95 Benefit package grps.

98 "Bali ___"
99 Land in l'Atlantique

ACROSS

1 One raised in church?
6 Beltmaking tool
9 Emailer's need: Abbr.
13 Hand-made percussion
18 Assembly line track
20 Word of parting
21 Ability to borrow
22 On edge
23 Something saved for a rainy day
24 Caribbean capital
25 Nog topper
26 Vessel with a spout
28 Rallying cry during the Polk administration
30 1957 film set almost entirely in one room
33 Unimportant flaw
34 Payment promise
35 Master
38 Lessen the value of, maybe
39 Changes to the bill?
42 Infiltrator
43 Hawk on the street
45 Blotto
47 Fab Four surname
48 Becomes one
49 "Young Frankenstein" assistant
50 Degrees of magnitude?
53 "Kinsey" star, 2004
55 Early manufacturer of home computers
57 Court figure Williams
60 Return date?
63 Ted with a guitar
65 Moving day need
66 0%, in a way
67 Economic org. in D.C.
69 Italian religious figure
70 Game that people rarely agree to play twice
72 Zach's old flame in "A Chorus Line"
74 First name in Objectivism
75 Historical topics
77 Make a point
78 Byproduct in petroleum refining
79 Alejandro G. Iñárritu film with the tagline "How much does life weigh?"
81 Hunts, as a house cat might
83 Glass raiser's word
84 "___ Arrives" (1967 soul album)
87 It "teaches you when to be silent," per Disraeli
88 Wee bit
89 Growing businesses
92 Lively comedies
95 Nomadic conqueror
97 Dealer's customer
98 Trust eroders
99 Kid-lit's Eloise, e.g.
102 Parts of many passwords: Abbr.
104 Imbecile
105 Ornament shape
106 "Oh wow!"
107 2004 rom-com in which a middle schooler is transformed into an adult overnight
110 Contiguous U.S. states, colloquially
114 Org. with conferences
115 At the back
119 Bee, e.g.
120 Cry of dismay
122 Routine-bound
124 Beau Brummell accessories
125 ___ Rabbit
126 Car chase sounds
127 Ability
128 Morales of "NYPD Blue"
129 Hieroglyphic symbol
130 L.P.G.A. garment

DOWN

1 "I'm ___ it!" (hick's nix)
2 Doozy
3 Use a lance
4 1960s–'70s police drama
5 Make another movie together, say
6 Roadside assistance org.
7 Harder to fool
8 "Inside ___ Davis" (Coen brothers film)
9 Adams, Monroe or Grant
10 The Company, in govt. lingo
11 1960s buddy cop sitcom, informally
12 Pop group?
13 Pottery, e.g.
14 Israelite tribe progenitor
15 Slow movements
16 Simple camera's aperture
17 Square figures
19 Pertaining to a sovereign
21 Rock or Pine
27 Broody rock genre
29 Not working, say
31 Film set assistants
32 Stocking fabric
35 Colombia's national airline
36 Re/Max competitor
37 Instantly likable
40 "The Brady Bunch" kid
41 Resource in the board game The Settlers of Catan
42 Tax-exempt bond, for short
44 Has the temerity
46 Rock band from Athens, Ga.
48 Modern rock and news/talk, for two
51 Bit of rain
52 Title IX target
54 Liven (up)
56 Visibly moved
58 Maker of candy wafers
59 Invite to dinner, say
61 Singer with the band Cult Jam
62 Figurative duration of short-lived fame
64 Mel who co-wrote "The Christmas Song"
66 Filibuster feature
68 Birdseed containers
71 Minor predecessor?
73 SeaWorld performer
76 On both sides of
80 Colorado State's team
82 Deeply offended
85 Selling well
86 First name of Dickens's Little Dorrit
89 Clues to a sunken ship's location
90 Diving helmet attachment
91 Hitchcock film with a nameless heroine

by Patrick Berry

93 Rating first used for "Red Dawn"
94 Italian gentlemen
96 Relentless faultfinder
99 Religious outfits
100 "Arabian Nights" predator

101 Serve as a go-between
103 Siesta sounds
106 Bearded ones
108 Drew in books
109 NBC sitcom set at NBC
111 Symbol of England

112 Spa wear
113 Eddie Murphy's big-screen debut
116 West End district
117 Maintain
118 For fear that
121 Sponsor of some PBS programs

123 Word often shortened to its middle letter in texts

90

TO PUT IT DIFFERENTLY

ACROSS

1 "We must go"
8 Spiral-horned grazer
12 Santa ___, Calif.
17 View with disapproval
18 Quills
20 Email folder
21 *Complete plan*
24 Brewer's supply
25 Round figures
26 Where Hecuba was queen
27 Certain monthly bill: Abbr.
28 "___ & the Women" (2000 Gere film)
29 Kind of paper
31 Many
34 *Gray fox*
39 It may help you get a grip on things
41 Skips
42 Subduer, of a sort
46 Like dams
47 Certain absentee
49 Lady of la casa
50 *Big deals*
54 What may unfold in Japanese theater?
55 Place for plates
56 Roly-poly
57 Annoy no end
59 Easter sight
61 Abbr. preceding a year
62 Grp. of women drivers
65 Whole slew
67 Sweeties
69 Like the book "Zhuangzi"
71 "No argument here"
73 "A deadline every minute" sloganeer
75 *Newspaper route*
80 Series of lows
82 Saws
83 It signals a lack of support
84 Dish name
85 Door ___
86 Says "You no-good son of a . . . ," say
88 *More united*
92 42-Across, for example
95 School boards
96 Make a selection
99 Letters in a return address?
100 Pause
103 Star trek figures?
104 Harmoniously
106 *Go figure*
112 Houses named after an old house
113 Not dead, as a football
114 One in business?
115 Malibu ___ ("The Simpsons" parody doll)
116 Top
117 Spoke impulsively

DOWN

1 Borderline
2 Heard
3 Echolocation device
4 Come down wrong, maybe
5 Part of V.M.I.: Abbr.
6 ___-jongg
7 Greek vowel
8 Joshes
9 ___ Chicago Grill
10 Skillful
11 1991 breakup newsmaker
12 A wink or a nod, maybe
13 Ford sold during Ford's presidency
14 Touches
15 Loggers' jamboree
16 1985 instrumental hit named after the main character in "Beverly Hills Cop"
18 Something an "o" lacks
19 ___ Sandoval, 2012 World Series M.V.P.
20 Words to someone who 8-Down
22 Skill sharpener
23 Pop group
29 Part of some showers
30 Sports org. whose first champ was the Pittsburgh Pipers
32 Bears witness
33 Cannon of "Heaven Can Wait"
35 Neuter
36 Certain Kindle download, for short
37 Hampers, say
38 Grammy-winning James
39 Wind or fire, maybe, but not earth
40 "Stupid me!"
43 Lightweight protective vest
44 Progressive ___
45 Led . . . or bled
46 Three-pointers: Abbr.
47 Carpentry fastener
48 A waste of good food?
49 Domain of some international law
51 Stressful work?
52 Many figures in the "Doctor Who" universe, for short
53 Something to lead with?
58 Players eligible to suit up
60 In need of coffee, maybe
62 Sprinter's assignment
63 Sci-fi vehicles
64 "Beat it!"
66 Airs from pairs
68 Item in a mechanic's back pocket
69 Nutrition bar introduced in the 1960s
70 Figures after a decimal
72 Ethnic ending
73 One speaking "out"?
74 "Al Aaraaf" writer
76 [Gross!]
77 PC menu heading
78 Confusion
79 Mall bag
81 Monopoly token replaced in 2013
85 Board
86 Recurring element
87 Sport-___
89 Dough that's been raised overseas?
90 De la Garza of "Law & Order"
91 Pestering, in a way
92 Sorts (out)

by Joe DiPietro

93 Steelhead, e.g.
94 Old F.D.A. guideline
97 Identify someone in a lineup, say
98 Conservative I.R.A. asset
101 Get worse
102 Pitch
104 Rights org.
105 Sooner city
107 Cozy footwear, informally
108 Food item dipped in ketchup
109 Largest New Deal agcy.
110 Kind of port
111 No score

PUT A LID ON IT!

ACROSS

1 Just
5 Many lines of code
8 Legitimate
13 Demolish
17 You can learn something by this
18 Portrait overlooking Tiananmen Square
19 23-Across topper
20 One getting a tax write-off, maybe
21 Filer's concern
23 Fictional archaeologist
25 28-Across topper
26 Indigo plants
27 Kramer's first name on "Seinfeld"
28 Famed frontierswoman
30 Hip-hop name modifier
31 Publishing mogul, for short
32 Toughens, as metal
33 Gain
34 40-Across topper
39 Post-boomer group
40 Subject of "Guerrillero Heroico"
42 Three-time Nobel Prize-winning organization
47 Al Bundy or Phil Dunphy
49 Nixing phrase on movie night
50 Arctic jackets
51 Shoplift, in slang
52 Site of a miracle in Daniel 3
53 They pop up in the morning
54 58-Across topper
55 ___ breve
57 Shipmate

58 Leader of the Free French
64 Quick shot?
67 Jack who ran for vice president in 1996
68 Chits
69 Modern-day hieroglyph
73 South American rodents
76 Bugs, e.g.
78 Contents of a spreadsheet
80 83-Across topper
81 Arctic masses
82 Starts of some one-twos
83 He helped move a piano in "The Music Box"
85 Violinist Leopold
86 Like Mandarin or Cantonese
87 Pinch
88 95-Across topper
91 Loan source for a mom-and-pop store: Abbr.
94 Finish on a canvas?
95 Star of "Sherlock Jr." and "Steamboat Bill Jr."
97 102-Across topper
100 Giving goose bumps, say
101 City about which Gertrude Stein said "There is no there there"
102 Italian pitchman of note
105 Something cooks put stock in
106 Catches a wave
107 More indie, say
108 Absorbed
109 Queen of Jordan

110 Ancient hieroglyph
111 Sends to oblivion
112 Co. that originated Dungeons & Dragons
113 Ballpark amts.

DOWN

1 Otto who worked on the Manhattan Project
2 Powerful bloodlines?
3 Word after in and of
4 Bit of cowboy gear
5 "Been better, been worse"
6 Quality of voices in the distance
7 Swillbelly
8 Poison compounds produced by snakes
9 Confuse
10 Mom on "Family Guy"
11 Journalist Flatow
12 Getting down, so to speak
13 Leeway
14 ___ Christi
15 Actress Kravitz of "Mad Max: Fury Road"
16 Triage locales, for short
19 Like answers on "Who Wants to Be a Millionaire"
20 Some club hires
22 West Point inits.
24 Verizon purchase of 2015
26 Title character in a Sophocles play
29 Desires
30 Perjured oneself

33 "Isn't he great!"
34 Drink that's the subject of several rules in the Code of Hammurabi
35 Still
36 Approached quickly
37 Author Jong
38 "Long ball"
40 Investment instruments, for short
41 Routine
42 Pioneering Arctic explorer John
43 Like the 13 Colonies: Abbr.
44 Barker
45 Pursuer of Capt. Hook
46 Spate
47 Twirlers
48 Invalidating
51 "Out of my way!"
52 ___ bug
54 Continental carrier
56 Velázquez's "___ Meninas"
59 Director Kurosawa
60 Like some tel. nos.
61 Eternities
62 Baltic native
63 Key with four sharps: Abbr.
64 Coors competitor
65 Billy Joel's "___ Extremes"
66 Wes of PBS's "History Detectives"
70 Spanish she-bear
71 One of the Bushes
72 Post-___
74 It parallels a radius
75 Opposite of a poker face
77 Website necessity
78 A long-established history

by Jason Mueller and Jeff Chen

79 Literature Nobelist J. M. Coetzee, by birth
81 Gusto
82 Bo's cousin on "The Dukes of Hazzard"
84 Discordant, to some
85 Museo contents
88 Mashes into a pulp
89 Basketry material
90 Cartoon cries
91 Actor John of "Full House"
92 Bit of wit
93 Angström or Celsius
94 Your, in Siena
95 Darken
96 Solo
97 Hatcher who was a Bond girl
98 Slays, informally
99 Ones going for hikes, for short?
100 As a result
102 CBS show with a 15-year run ending in 2015
103 Nucleus
104 Kerfuffle
105 Cool dude

Note: When this puzzle is completed, 12 squares will be filled with a certain keyboard symbol, which will have a different signification in the Across answers than it does in the Downs.

ACROSS

1 "I Am Not ___" (1975 show business autobiography)
6 "Shoot, shoot, shoot"
12 Cassio's jealous lover in "Othello"
18 Charge
20 Got up again
21 Comes to fruition
22 "Psst! Come hide with me!"
23 Come closer to catching
24 Takes out, as some beer bottles
25 First in a race?
26 Colt, e.g.
27 Ones doing a decent job in the Bible?
29 Magical phrase in an old tale
32 "Shoot!"
34 Takes apart
37 Drink at un café
38 Amt. often measured in ozs.
40 Drink at un café
41 Not as far from
43 LeBron James or Kevin Durant
46 One trillionth: Prefix
47 Welcome site?
48 When some tasks must be done
50 Schwarzenegger film catchphrase
52 Amazon's industry
55 Person of the hour
57 Still
58 Comment after a betrayal
61 Pen
63 Go on foot
64 Link between two names
66 Large goblet
71 Where batters eventually make their way to plates?
74 Catchphrase for one of the Avengers
77 Gap in a manuscript
81 Like some storefronts
83 Farmer, in the spring
84 Repeated bird call?
86 Is unable to
89 Bygone record co.
90 Site of the "crown of palaces"
91 Multicar accidents
93 Travel over seas?
96 N.Y.C. museum, with "the"
97 Honeymooners' site
98 GPS calculation
100 What the ruthless show
101 Author ___-René Lesage
103 What the ring in "The Lord of the Rings" is called
107 Nepalis live in them
109 Hebrew letter before samekh
110 75- and 80-Down, e.g.: Abbr.
112 Tote
113 Google browser
115 Steamy
118 Place
119 Wrinkle preventer, of sorts
120 Beezus's sister, in children's literature
121 Ones making an effort
122 Contraction with two apostrophes
123 Something matzo lacks

DOWN

1 ___ Lanka
2 "Let us spray," e.g.
3 It works for workers, in brief
4 Money, in modern slang
5 Something that may have bad keys
6 Church keys?
7 Leader of a procession
8 ___ War, "The Charge of the Light Brigade" event
9 Swanson on "Parks and Recreation"
10 Ol' red, white and blue's land
11 Material sometimes sold ripped
12 Scourge
13 Recite
14 "What ___!" (cry after some spectacular goalie play)
15 What zero bars means on a cellphone
16 Tools for people picking pockets?
17 @@@
19 Paint type
21 Soda can feature
28 Like a softball interview vis-à-vis a grilling
30 Guessed nos.
31 Assistant number cruncher
33 Art critic, stereotypically
34 Not seemly
35 More nifty
36 "Hakuna ___" ("The Lion King" song)
39 Rings on doors
42 Site of the U.S.'s only royal palace
44 Go on
45 Host
46 Course standard
49 Kettle's accuser
51 Groups that never get started
53 "Lord, is ___?"
54 Wolfish
56 Teachers' grp.
59 C equivalents
60 Royale carmaker of old
62 "Gross"
65 "So you admit it!"
67 Language in Southeast Asia
68 "Cross my heart and hope to die"
69 One seeking the philosopher's stone
70 How one person might resemble another
72 Revolutionary thinker?
73 Feeling the effects of a workout
75 L.A. institution
76 Bound
77 Wool source
78 Pasta variety
79 Conviction . . . or what's almost required for a conviction

by Tom McCoy

80 The Wahoos of the A.C.C.
82 Romanian currency
85 ___ rate (tax amount per $1,000)
87 iPod model
88 Kind of leg
92 Dictation takers
94 "Git!"
95 Be a gentleman to at the end of a date, say
97 Where many shots are taken
99 Shrewdness
102 "Things are bound to go my way soon"
104 Presidential perk until 1977
105 "That's nothing"
106 Not reacting
108 Muscles worked by pull-ups, briefly
111 Greek portico
112 1940s prez
114 Genetic stuff
116 Stand-___
117 Monopoly token that replaced the iron in 2013

ACROSS

1 Bye at Wimbledon
5 Bonnie who sang "Nick of Time"
10 Needle holder
13 Pop star with the fragrance Miami Glow
16 Scientist Pavlov
17 Move unsteadily
18 Ike's charge during W.W. II
19 What King was king of
21 *Shrink who's always changing his diagnosis?
24 Piece in early Indian chess sets
25 Grasp
26 **What ballet patrons dine on?
28 One side of a childish debate . . . or a phonetic hint to the answers to the four starred clues
30 Take care of
31 Lipton rival
32 30 Rock's location
34 Bend
37 Arias, typically
39 Aerosol sound
40 *Oregon State's mascot played by actress Arthur?
47 Festoon
50 Pick in class
51 Assuming it's even possible
53 Cross, with "off"
54 **A deal on Afro wigs?
60 Commercial lead-in to Balls or Caps
63 "Couldn't be"
64 Not so awesome
65 Court positions
66 In need of a cracker, perhaps
68 Listen to Christmas carolers?
72 Slipshod
73 Overlook
74 Multiple-choice options
75 Justice Kagan
77 Post-op locale
79 Cold War-era territory: Abbr.
80 *How actor Bill feels about houseguests?
86 Hershiser of the 1980s–'90s Dodgers
87 Cannabis ___ (marijuana)
88 Chicago suburb
92 Removes from a can?
95 **Find cake or Jell-O in the back of the fridge?
97 Hunger
98 Drawbridge locale
100 The Spartans of the N.C.A.A.
101 PBS benefactor
102 And other stuff
105 Misconstrue, as words
109 Other side of a childish debate . . . or a phonetic hint to the answers to the four double-starred clues
113 *Fall colors?
117 Talk down?
120 Yawnfest
121 **Question from El Al security?
123 Like lightning rounds
124 Tear-stained, e.g.
125 Investigate, as a cold case
126 Pianist Gilels
127 "Woo-hoo!"
128 Half of a classic Mad magazine feature
129 County of Salem, Mass.
130 High ___

DOWN

1 Small scrap
2 New Balance competitor
3 Employing strategy
4 Pyramid crosses
5 Rubbish
6 Cause of some impulsive behavior, for short
7 It might begin with a "What if . . . ?"
8 Beach walkers
9 Mere vestige
10 They may have you going the wrong way
11 Announcer's cry after a field goal
12 What knows the drill, for short?
13 It has a variety of locks and pins
14 Like buffalo meat vis-à-vis beef and pork
15 Vegas casino with the mascot Lucky the Leprechaun
17 Show piece
19 French cheese
20 Miss
22 ESPN's McEachern a.k.a. the Voice of Poker
23 Edible entry at a county fair
27 Social welfare grp. with a Peace Prize
29 Neighbor of a " ~ " key
32 30 Rock grp.
33 Pro's position
35 Check
36 Brunch spot
38 "Fire away!"
41 Dress at the altar
42 PC part of interest to audiophiles
43 Author Seton
44 Kick back
45 First name in long jumps
46 Open again, as a keg
48 Sounds of fall?
49 Odette's counterpart in "Swan Lake"
52 QB Tony
55 "Over my dead body!"
56 Prefix with realism
57 London jazz duo?
58 Sudden turns
59 Belgian river to the North Sea
60 Play for a fool
61 Restaurant chain founded by a celebrity chef
62 Febreze target
67 Goof
69 Greeting on el teléfono
70 Supercharges, with "up"
71 Get one's hands on some dough?
76 Alternative to Soave
78 Nominative, e.g.
81 Administrative worker on a ship
82 Smoke
83 Bank asset that's frozen?
84 Google ___
85 Rap shouts
89 Casino activity with numbered balls
90 Dander
91 Part of a flight plan, for short
92 Pig with pigtails

by Jeremy Newton

93 Body of science?
94 Kaplan course for H.S. students
96 Hwy. violation
97 Like bread dough and beer
99 Looney Tunes bird

103 Play the siren to
104 Chatted with, in a way
106 Emotionally distant
107 Arsenal
108 Aligns

110 Where capri pants stop
111 #2s at college
112 Inhumane types
114 Lumber mill equipment
115 Hover craft?
116 Brood

118 Film character who says "I'd just as soon kiss a Wookiee!"
119 Some pipe joints
122 King of old Rome

ACROSS

1 Get by
5 Draw ___ on
10 With 101-Across, screen icon
15 Co. that invented the floppy disk
18 Utah attraction for skiers
19 Certain graduate
20 Headquarters of Royal Dutch Shell, with "The"
21 Shellac finish?
22 Gladly, old-style
23 Tents and the like (2001–08)
26 Wraps
28 See 109-Across
29 Goes after
30 Brought (in)
31 One of two official Philippine languages, along with English
35 Flight figures, for short
36 "Case of the Ex" singer, 2000
37 1964 Charlie Chaplin book (1980–84)
41 Actress Green of "Casino Royale"
43 ___ column
45 All-inclusive, in edspeak
46 Epitome of easiness
47 Northeastern university where Carl Sagan taught
49 Egypt's Port ___
52 Soft wear, informally
54 Long stretch
55 Der ___ (Adenauer)
56 TV show since 10/11/75, eight of whose former stars appear in the circled squares in this puzzle
58 Show-off (1975–80)
62 Stockholders?
64 "Yikes!"
66 Quarter
67 Nashville inst.
68 Muff, e.g. (2005–13)
71 Dessert often topped with cream cheese (1990–93)
76 In the, in Italy
77 TV star who loved oats
79 Shirt style
80 Those girls, in French
81 Berlin standard (1990–96)
86 Spring business?
88 Ambush predators of the sea
89 Pharaoh ___
90 Padre's hermano
91 Slim and trim
93 Thing
95 Trucker's circuit: Abbr.
96 Redhead on kids' TV
99 How "You Make Me Feel" in a Van Morrison song
101 See 10-Across
102 With 120-Across, intro heard every week on 56-Across
107 First American carrier to show movies on flights
109 With 28-Across, letter opener
110 CH$_4$
111 Kitchen pad
114 Dispute
117 "___ thoughts?"
118 Ranger rival
120 See 102-Across
124 Champ's cry
125 Prefix with -centric
126 Taekwondo is its national sport
127 Makes a good impression?
128 El ___
129 Frequent target of ID thieves
130 Destructive 2012 hurricane
131 Latches, say
132 Zapper target

DOWN

1 Not so bright
2 Coat cut
3 15-time guest host of 56-Across
4 One way to get home (2000–06)
5 Cockeyed
6 1974 Best Actress for "Alice Doesn't Live Here Anymore"
7 911 respondent, for short
8 "Wheel of Fortune" buy
9 Gently sponges
10 1953 biblical movie
11 Dorm heads, briefly
12 Ottoman Empire title
13 Bird feeder fill
14 ___-skelter
15 Like the North Pole
16 English county that's home to Reading
17 Snafu
19 Animal without feet
24 Title girl in a 2002 Disney movie
25 "Cheerio"
27 Focus of urban renewal?
32 Some digital camera batteries
33 Soviet labor camp
34 Baseball's Hodges
37 John ___, greaser in "American Graffiti"
38 ___ law
39 Designer of the Florence Cathedral bell tower
40 Class
41 Digital money
42 Alessandro ___, scientist who discovered 110-Across
44 Abbr. of politeness
48 "You ___ worry"
50 Radio host Glass
51 Jeanne ___
53 Class
57 Subsidiary proposition
59 Cool
60 Does a high-wire act, e.g.
61 Centers
63 Cool
65 N.B.A. head coach Steve
69 More open to the outdoors
70 "Get ___!"
72 Find another spot, maybe
73 17-time guest host of 56-Across
74 ___ O'Hara, 2015 Tony winner for "The King and I"
75 German coal city, once
78 Bygone presidential inits.
81 Peer group member?

by David J. Kahn

82 Countermeasures
83 Democratic presidential nominee before Kennedy
84 Shirt style
85 Piece of cake in school
87 "___ we alone?"
92 11 follower
94 Colorful fish
97 "Makes me want seconds!"
98 Vitamin regimen
100 Ship's load
103 Chomps on
104 Loses it, with "out"
105 Italian mount
106 "Actually, I do"
108 Dining partner? (2005–12)
111 Counter orders
112 Lewis who sang the theme for "Avatar"
113 ". . . then again, maybe I'm mistaken"
114 Weeds
115 Old colonnade
116 Go bad
119 Does, e.g.
121 Like the border of Time magazine
122 Ultimate
123 Post-O.R. site

Big Names in E-tail

ACROSS

1 Supreme Court justice who once compared the majority's reasoning to "the mystical aphorisms of the fortune cookie"
7 Low part
12 Classify
18 A dozen for Hercules
19 Silk case
20 Words of defiance
22 Admission of a lack of familiarity with Mr. Hockey?
24 Business feature?
25 Ancient Persian
26 Like sailors' talk
27 Celebrity cook Paula
29 Curse (out)
30 Fusses
32 Kyoto concurrence
33 Less serious works by the author of "Brighton Rock"?
36 Take responsibility for
38 Makes fast
40 Roman law
41 One making a roaring start?
45 Only one person can do it
46 Fits comfortably
50 Toque
52 Reason for Brosnan fans to watch 1980s TV?
55 "Home, ___"
56 Beach fronts?
58 A title might be presented in it: Abbr.
59 Being dragged along
60 John Lennon's middle name
61 Brand name whose middle two letters are linked in its logo
62 Cameo stone
63 Some briefs
64 Round house?
65 Trying to sell one's "Au Revoir les Enfants" video?
68 Where safety goggles may be worn
71 Don Juan's mother
73 Plowmen's cries
74 "Rhyme Pays" rapper
75 "Catch-22" pilot
76 Deplete
78 Flaky stuff
79 Foam
80 Challenge for a virologist
82 Explosive side of a former tennis great?
85 Fruitcakes
87 Libation with a floral bouquet
88 Noted second-place finisher
90 Make sense of
91 "Smack!"
92 Maybe not even that
95 Rockies game
96 Comic's copy of "The Importance of Being Earnest"?
100 "Oh no!"
102 Home of Future World
106 Soil: Prefix
107 Upbeat
108 Rocky debris
110 Brazilian berry
111 Applaud
113 Assign blame to the singer of "Blurred Lines"?
117 "Lake Wobegon Days" writer
118 Writing award won multiple times by Alice Munro
119 Where Quiznos and Mapquest are headquartered
120 Erotic
121 "All I ___ Do" (Sheryl Crow hit)
122 Tavern vessels

DOWN

1 Slenderizes
2 Midshipman's counterpart
3 Residence
4 Single copy of "The Bonfire of the Vanities"?
5 N.Y.C. line
6 Questions
7 Farfalle shapes
8 Sore
9 Great Lakes' ___ Canals
10 Disperse
11 Fidgety
12 Net worth component
13 Topsiders?
14 Spain's Costa del ___
15 Go too far
16 Actress O'Connor of "Xena: Warrior Princess"
17 Saturn's largest moon
19 Rum mixers
21 "What we want most, but what, alas! we use worst," per William Penn
23 "Uh-uh"
28 Questioning interjections
31 Like Vatican guards
33 Ripsnorter
34 Pressing work
35 Fidgety
37 Japanese drama
39 Some Thanksgiving decorations
41 Dead-end position
42 Modern-day home of the ancient Ashanti empire
43 Some sites on the National Mall
44 Home of Jar Jar Binks in "Star Wars" films
46 TV's ___ Network (sports presenter)
47 Relaxes and has some fun
48 Chess's ___ ratings
49 Singers do this
51 Nutrition-related
53 Confound
54 Resident of southern Mexico
57 Llama's kin
61 Radio freq.
62 Come-___
63 Nonkosher lunch order
65 Onetime title for Obama and Clinton
66 "They got me!"
67 Preceded, with "to"
69 Former kingdom of Provence
70 Military muckety-mucks
72 Midwesterners, stereotypically
76 Modern TV feature
77 Hundred Acre Wood resident
78 Farrow or Hamm
79 Mother of Ares
80 France's ___ Polytechnique
81 Buy into "Common Sense"?
83 Post office?
84 Hardly fancy
86 "L'Amore dei Re" (Montemezzi opera)

by Dan Schoenholz

89 Sophocles tragedy
92 Sue Grafton's "___ for Innocent"
93 Come in under the radar, say
94 Artist Neiman
96 Raise, with "up"
97 Eyes
98 Poisonous snake
99 Producer of wrinkles, it's said
101 Comprehension
103 First year in Constantine's reign
104 Like some port vessels
105 Levels
108 ___ Fein
109 LAX figs.
112 Jupiter's locale: Abbr.
114 "Got it!"
115 Hankering
116 Riled (up)

ACROSS

1 Church leaders
7 Torn asunder
15 In sufficient quantity
20 Collier's transport
21 Fact addition
22 *"Truly"*
23 Halloween costume for . . . a CNN anchor?
25 Net results?
26 Three times daily, in Rx's
27 Yiddish cries
28 Scand. country
29 Bank abbr.
31 Side dish that's sometimes mashed
32 "Do we have approval?"
35 Misdeed
36 Is a buttinsky
38 7-5, e.g.
39 . . . *a former "Dateline" host?*
46 No one says his art was pointless
48 Head, for short
49 "Lord, We Ask Thee ___ We Part" (hymn)
50 Turbaned sort
51 Beehive hairstyle, e.g.
52 Brewer Coors
55 Info for an airport run
57 "Cómo ___ usted?"
58 . . . *a onetime House speaker?*
63 Fender product
64 Winter Olympics event
65 Who said "In waking a tiger, use a long stick"

66 Eastern sch. with a noted film program
67 Tuition, e.g.
68 Longtime Chicago Symphony conductor
71 One of three for J. R. R. Tolkien: Abbr.
73 "Tush!"
75 Aspects
77 ___ fault
78 Goose egg
80 Sports org. with 25-Across
82 Resembles week-old flowers, say
84 Hotel capacity: Abbr.
85 . . . *an old Notre Dame basketball coach?*
91 Doing
93 Cry of surprise
94 Like the expression "Sakes alive!"
95 Execute perfectly
96 Eponym of a hot dog chain
98 Letters before many a state's name
101 Mil. authority
102 First-aid supply
104 . . . *a silent film star?*
108 It never goes off
109 Singer Falana and others
110 ___ mission
111 Snares
113 Caviar
115 The George W. Bush years, e.g.
116 Stimpy's TV pal
117 Be unsatisfied with, say
119 Ancient Hebrew liquid measure

120 Insouciant syllables
122 . . . *a pop/folk singer with numerous 1970s hits?*
128 Gutter locales
129 Majority
130 "Time heals all wounds" and others
131 Forecast that might call for gloves and galoshes
132 Tied
133 Like a pirate's treasure

DOWN

1 One of two at a wedding
2 Wrath
3 You can't predict the weather with this
4 Do really well on a test
5 Spreadsheet input
6 Theater sign
7 Doubtful
8 Cribbage one-pointers
9 One running races for a living?
10 "True"
11 Lace
12 Con man
13 When the French toast?
14 Figure above God's throne, in Isaiah
15 How a phone may be slammed down
16 ___ juice (milk)
17 Doesn't take any chances
18 Actress Kedrova who won an Oscar for "Zorba the Greek"

19 Polite rural reply
24 Impend
30 Position of greatest importance
32 Children, in legalese
33 Like ooze
34 Scored between 90 and 100, say
37 Besides
40 Cool, as soup
41 Hard labor spot
42 Common sitcom rating
43 Equal
44 Coal extractors
45 Vistas
47 Sleep on it
53 Noted remover of locks
54 "Run to ___" (1961 hit)
56 Petty braggart
59 Summer romance, maybe
60 Carpet fuzz
61 Comment made with a handshake
62 "Be that way!"
68 Like Christmas lights
69 Tuba sound
70 Party straggler
72 Religious deg.
74 Tater Tots maker
76 "Where should ___ the check?"
79 Cell part
81 Water, e.g.: Abbr.
83 "Trick" or "treat," e.g.
86 The "V" of R.S.V.P.
87 Slimy stuff
88 Flopped
89 Maxim tear-out
90 Winter Olympics equipment
92 Too, too

by Bill Zais

97 Start of a rationalization
99 Attic function
100 Like some Roman aphorisms
103 Out of action, in baseball lingo
105 Functional
106 Really get to
107 Tic-tac-toe starters?
112 Coke, to Pepsi
113 Hwys.
114 Mouthy?
117 Sauce brand since 1937
118 Conference USA sch.
121 Actor Marvin
123 Book after Exodus: Abbr.
124 Guy whose face might get slapped
125 Mai ___
126 Gamer's prefix with pets
127 Retired boomer

FRAME JOB

ACROSS

1 "I've heard enough"
8 Consequences of downsizing
15 2014 Emmy-winning miniseries based on a 1996 film
20 Relative of a bug
21 Amu Darya outlet, once
22 Pop-up, sometimes
23 No-hunting zone
25 Mete out
26 Certifications in some college apps
27 Singular
28 Part of the neck?
30 Look shocked
31 What might result from a minor hit
32 Longtime California senator
36 Computer data acronym
40 Part of the biosphere
42 Flowed
43 Mt. Olive offerings
44 Get tough
45 Cursed
49 "Helm's ___!" (nautical cry)
50 Marsh birds
51 World Series of Poker's former Vegas home
53 Order from a sports doc
55 Info on a parking ticket
58 Something that doesn't follow the letter of the law?
60 Mars : Roman :: ___ : Norse
61 Father figures

62 Expelled politely
64 L. Frank Baum princess
65 Kind of rock
67 Bar mitzvahs, e.g.
68 City from which Vasco da Gama sailed, to locals
71 Flower girl?
72 It might be full of baloney
74 "Try ___ might . . ."
75 Taipei-to-Seoul dir.
77 It contains a lot of balloons
80 Rap sheet entry
84 Sun Devils' sch.
85 Cooperated with, e.g.
87 Indie rock band Yo La ___
88 The black ball in el juego de billar
89 Kerry's 2004 running mate
91 "Aha!"
93 Capital of Minorca
94 One-to-one, e.g.
95 Homes for Gila woodpeckers
96 Boasts
97 Weightlifting technique
103 Does in
106 What a pitching wedge provides
107 Tip of Italy, once?
108 Catchall abbr.
109 Google SafeSearch target
113 Where Rigel is
115 Brazilian tourist destination
120 Algebraic input
121 Honored academic retiree

122 First name in Disney villains
123 Apply
124 Force under Stalin
125 Spousal agreement

DOWN

1 Goodie bag filler
2 Long
3 Xeric
4 Sleep stages
5 Delta calculation, briefly
6 "Damage" director Louis
7 Big name in printers
8 Primatologist Goodall
9 Tolkien beast
10 Giant image in the sky over Gotham
11 Actor Gulager
12 Andrews or Dover: Abbr.
13 Tertius planeta from the sun
14 Leo with the 1977 #1 hit "You Make Me Feel Like Dancing"
15 Evaluator of flight risks, for short
16 Used up
17 "Chill!"
18 Search blindly
19 Furry frolicker
24 Elementary school science class item
29 Distilled coal product
31 Put-down
32 Fay Vincent's successor as baseball commissioner
33 Suffix with hex-

34 Hothead's response
35 ___ soap
36 Follow the advice "When in Rome . . ."
37 Foolish sort
38 Opaque
39 "Before ___ you go . . ."
41 Like many OPEC nations
44 Survey unit
45 Junior in the Football Hall of Fame
46 Plain to see
47 Voice-controlled device from the world's largest online retailer
48 1998 Jim Carrey comedy/drama, with "The"
50 Minor setback
52 Managed care grps.
54 Mrs. McKinley
56 Dump site monitor, for short
57 Fix, as a pool cue
59 Stick up
63 Lyme disease transmitter
66 Outdoor sports store
67 Libertine
69 Golfer Aoki
70 What Marcie calls Peppermint Patty in "Peanuts"
71 Home theater option
73 "My mistake!"
76 Some collars
78 Macy's, e.g.
79 "Stop kidding yourself"
81 Hair extension?
82 The tiniest bit
83 Crowd sound
86 88-Across + cuatro

by Zhouqin Burnikel

90 Circuit for Serena and Venus Williams, in brief
92 Derisive laugh sound
93 Ones putting on acts
97 Piece of garlic
98 Dr. Seuss environmentalist
99 Paperless I.R.S. option
100 More charming
101 Suffix with hippo-
102 Teased
104 Like black-tie affairs
105 Visible S O S
108 "Buy it. Sell it. Love it" company
109 Nut, basically
110 Like father, like son?
111 Home of the David Geffen School of Medicine, for short
112 "___ she blows!"
114 After deductions
116 Parseghian of Notre Dame
117 Street sign abbr.
118 Casino convenience
119 Staple of a rock band tour

ACROSS

1 Pushovers
8 Horn of Africa native
14 Pushed forward, as a crowd
20 Wellesley grads
21 "Same here!"
22 Paternally related
23 1982 Arnold Schwarzenegger film
25 Vintner Paul who would "sell no wine before its time"
26 Knot on a tree
27 ___ of the earth
28 Like a chestnut
29 ___ Joaquin, Calif.
30 Fell for an April fool, say
31 Verses with six stanzas
33 Bringer of peace between nations
36 ___ qué (why: Sp.)
37 NPR host Shapiro
38 Worked to the bone
39 State bordering Texas
45 Actress Pflug of "M*A*S*H"
46 Dummy
47 Wishing sites
48 Author who inspired the musical "Wicked"
50 Chiwere-speaking tribe
54 Bygone office worker
56 65 or so
57 Rose buds?
60 Spruce up
62 Op-Ed columnist Maureen
63 Spanish airline
64 Met, as a legislature
66 Jason Bourne and others
70 Big name in outdoor and fitness gear
71 2014 land-grab
73 Draft picks?
74 Tarzan's simian sidekick
76 Salad bar bowlful
79 Kung ___ chicken
80 Constellation next to Scorpius
83 Stephen of "Ben-Hur"
84 Alternative media magazine founder
85 Pep
87 Some "Fast and the Furious" maneuvers, slangily
88 Opening of a Hawaiian volcano?
91 Some auto auctions' inventory
94 Unhurriedly
98 One calling the shots, for short?
99 "Well, ___-di-dah!"
100 Land in the Caucasus
102 Deli sandwich filler
107 New ___ (official cap maker of Major League Baseball)
108 Wares: Abbr.
109 Wite-Out manufacturer
110 Caps
111 ___ me tangere (warning against meddling)
112 Costner/Russo golf flick
114 Chocolaty Southern dessert
117 Climate-affecting current
118 How some people break out on Broadway
119 Trig calculation
120 Div. for the Mets
121 It may be filled with bullets
122 Catches some Z's

DOWN

1 Fills to capacity
2 How you can't sing a duet
3 Yellowfin and bluefin
4 Cell that has multiplied?
5 Place to retire
6 Like sushi or ceviche
7 ___ knot, rug feature
8 Some bunk bed sharers, for short
9 Concubine's chamber
10 Half-baked
11 Slanting
12 Caterpillar machine
13 It comes with a charge
14 Iraqi city on the Tigris
15 Like one side of Lake Victoria
16 Ones calling the shots, for short?
17 Chatterbox
18 Ballet headliner
19 Slightly depressed
24 Workers on Times tables, briefly?
29 California wine region
32 Bread substitute?
33 Second-largest dwarf planet
34 Cuisine that includes cracklins and boudin
35 Turn a blind eye to
37 One spinning its wheels?
39 Some I.R.A.s
40 All the rage
41 Pinpoint
42 Greek sorceress
43 Nicholas Gage memoir
44 Anakin's master in "Star Wars"
49 Bridge words
51 Amateur botanists' projects
52 Yellow dog in the funnies
53 Morales of HBO's "The Brink"
55 John in the Songwriters Hall of Fame
57 Writes in C++, say
58 Utensil's end
59 "A Doll's House" playwright
61 Lawyer's clever question, say
62 Showtime crime drama, 2006–13
64 One who has crossed the line?
65 Janis's husband in the funnies
67 Rock, paper or scissors
68 Phishing lures
69 Places for links?
72 Hit AMC series that ended with a Coca-Cola ad
75 Iffy
77 Immediately preceding periods
78 Hokkaido port
79 Magician's word
81 "La ___" (Debussy opus)
82 Dunderhead
85 Intl. group headquartered in Vienna
86 One at the wheel

by Tracy Gray

89 Pellet shooters
90 Got high, in a way
92 Vinland explorer circa A.D. 1000
93 Opponents for Perry Mason, for short
94 Winning blackjack pair
95 Send
96 Romance novelist Banks
97 Going out
101 Dutch town known for tulip tourism
102 Au courant
103 Miners' entries
104 Ruy ___ (chess opening)
105 Skirt style
106 Nutritionists' prescriptions
110 Grp. of teed-off women?
113 Snoop group, in brief
114 POW/___ bracelet (popular 1970s wear)
115 Neither red nor blue?: Abbr.
116 Tres menos dos

ACROSS

1 Animals at a football game
8 Antithesis of brashness
16 One carrying a spiked club, maybe
20 Case for a lawyer
21 Lay bare
22 Worker hardly making a living wage
23 "So You Think You Can Dance," say?
25 School for James Bond
26 Plenty
27 East German secret police
28 Some letter enclosures, for short
29 A or B, but not O
30 Punk offshoot
31 Kigali native
33 A mean Amin
34 Toni Morrison novel
35 One with monthly payments
37 Shakespeare's Claudius and others
39 Added on, botanically
41 Roller coaster shout from Queen Elizabeth?
45 Geezers
46 Sprinkling on a deviled egg
49 Nuevo ___, state in Mexico
50 Klingon on "Star Trek: T.N.G."
51 It may lead to an unearned run
52 Make out
56 Sad sack
58 AOL competitor
61 Actor Hirsch of "Into the Wild"
62 Without doubt

65 Antique photo
67 ___ Ration (old dog food brand)
68 "Did you mean Doom or Dolittle?"?
70 Tools for cobblers
71 Inverse trig function
73 Succinctly
74 Battlefield cry
75 Literary inits.
76 Actress Streep
78 Coolness, in modern slang
79 Lisa, to Patty and Selma, on "The Simpsons"
80 One-___ (old ball game)
82 Is sick
85 Made an effort
87 Easily
89 Mob Boss Hall of Fame?
93 Like some jeans and apartment buildings
95 Onetime place for Saddam Hussein's image
96 Elite groups
100 Spillane's "___ Jury"
101 Camouflaged
103 Snowbird's destination
105 Wisk competitor
106 Sci-fi/historical fiction writer Stephenson
107 Decorative moldings
110 John ___, "The House of Blue Leaves" playwright
111 "Argo" setting
112 Some salad greens
113 Making a complaint at a restaurant?
116 Iowa State locale
117 Trigger autocorrect, say

118 Beat to the finish
119 Eighty-six
120 Traps in a net
121 You may want to stop reading when you see this

DOWN

1 Hot Wheels maker
2 In
3 "Mad Men" extras
4 Crows' cries
5 "Gee," in Glasgow
6 "Meet the Press" competitor
7 Company that encourages people to lie?
8 Mardi Gras time
9 Locale of the Battle of Tippecanoe
10 Runs the show, briefly
11 Dots in la mer
12 ___ Maar (Picasso's muse)
13 Formal identification
14 Bono bandmate
15 Answer with a salute
16 Precedes at a concert
17 "That milky liquid belongs to me!"?
18 Cousin of a tendril
19 Baseball or Supreme Court lineups
24 Calrissian of "Star Wars" films
31 Put back on the payroll
32 Dudley Do-Right's love
36 Moseys along
38 E.U. member not in NATO: Abbr.
40 Part of a winter stash
42 One with brand loyalty?

43 "Oh . . . my . . . God!"
44 Brian who wrote the score for "Me and Earl and the Dying Girl"
46 Glimpse on the sly
47 Munitions suppliers
48 One in line to rule the ocean?
50 Peter who directed "Picnic at Hanging Rock"
53 Man's name that's Hebrew for "my God"
54 1970 hit with the lyric "I'm down on my knees, / I'm begging you please to come home"
55 Roger who wrote "The Boys of Summer"
57 Stick-in-the-mud types
59 Edit some film
60 Like measuring cups, often
63 Nutritional fig.
64 Cattle calls
66 ___ Trail (Everglades highway)
68 PBS station in the Big Apple
69 Chorus line leader?
72 Japanese porcelain
74 Dis but not dat?
77 "Fargo" assent
81 Negligent
83 Screen abbr.
84 Things found between the poles?
86 Closed tight
87 Show some dumbfoundedness about
88 Declaration on Día de San Valentín

by Alan Arbesfeld

89 Add one's two cents
90 Get cozy
91 Books often not read
92 Built-up
94 "Prove it!"
97 Kind of number
98 Cataleptic state
99 Margaret who founded Planned Parenthood
102 Jefferson's religious belief
104 Mathematician who was the subject of the book "The Man Who Loved Only Numbers"
108 Start of the Bay State's motto
109 Nurses at a bar
111 Calvary inscription
114 Book before Esth.
115 Skater Midori

ACROSS

1 Big gasbag?
6 Sex therapy subject
12 Rap
18 Cat and mouse
20 First name among celebrity chefs
21 Achieve widespread recognition
22 Warrior who follows "the way of the warrior"
23 Charged (with)
24 Part of a mob
25 *Threshold of major change*
27 Heroic deeds
28 Eritrea's capital
29 Small body of medical research
31 Jack in the box, once?
33 Attempt to debug?
34 Soundly defeat, informally
38 Arthur Conan Doyle title
39 *Catchphrase from "Jerry Maguire"*
42 Actress Larter of "Heroes"
43 A little light
45 Homer's neighbor on "The Simpsons"
47 ___ facto
48 Winnie-the-Pooh greeting
50 Jet black
51 Like Nahuatl speakers
54 Puffs
56 "31 Days of Oscar" channel
57 Hail or farewell
58 Crocodile tail?
61 Latin lover's word
62 Dance class
63 They sit for six yrs.
65 *Was a victim of price gouging*
70 ___ Lilly and Company
71 Struggles (through)
73 Dweller along the Wasatch Range
74 "That's lovely!"
75 *Rush to beat a deadline*
80 Not aweather
81 Penultimate countdown word
82 Messenger ___
83 One of the Golden Girls of 1980s–'90s TV
85 Nonexpert
86 Cubs' home
87 Surrounded by
90 Danced to Xavier Cugat, say
92 "Supposing that's true . . ."
93 Modern spelling?
94 Madame's "mine"
97 Sites for R.N.s and M.D.s
98 Skedaddles
100 Prince's inits.
101 *Mark that's hard to hit*
104 Red Cross work
106 Where to find some ham
107 "___ in Calico" (jazz classic)
109 It makes flakes
110 Biceps exercise
113 Steamed dish that may be prepared in an olla
115 Rapper né Andre Young
117 *British pool stick*
122 Fort ___ National Monument
123 They'll make you blush
125 Reindeer relative
126 "That makes sense now"
127 Early Mexicans
128 Up
129 Businesswoman/ philantropist ___ Heinz Kerry
130 Auto identifiers
131 Launch dates

DOWN

1 Sons of, in Hebrew
2 Drooping
3 Exasperated cry in the morning
4 "A Few Good Men" men
5 First option
6 Rented
7 Last stage of metamorphosis
8 Dogs
9 Rankles
10 Coke Zero, for one
11 "Every dog has his day" and others
12 Zimbabwe's capital
13 It's in the eye of the beholder
14 Formal occasions
15 Be unable to make further progress
16 Part of a Mario Brothers costume
17 Equity valuation stat
18 Prince Edward Isl. setting
19 Talks with one's hands
26 Exact
30 Newfoundland or Labrador
32 Singer Tori
34 Weight room figure
35 Board game popular throughout Africa
36 ___ Games
37 Puffed-grain cereal
40 Language that gave us "bungalow" and "guru"
41 Exact
44 Really enjoy oneself
46 Intimate apparel size bigger than C
49 Jesus on a diamond
52 Site of King Rudolf's imprisonment, in fiction
53 Santa ___
55 Sour candy brand
57 Nile River spanner
59 Typical end of a professor's address?
60 ___ Place (Butch and Sundance companion)
64 Six, in Seville
66 Berry of "Monster's Ball"
67 Beneficial to
68 The best policy, supposedly
69 Exact
72 Winter-related commercial prefix
76 Hoffer or Holder
77 Green garnish
78 Two past Tue.
79 Exact
84 President Garfield's middle name
87 Tire pressure indicator
88 "Let's Get It Started" rapper
89 "Rikki-Tikki-___"
91 Reebok competitor
92 "Positively Entertaining" network

by Samuel A. Donaldson and Jeff Chen

93 Thingamajig
95 It might follow a showstopping performance, in modern lingo
96 Hot
99 Not black-and-white

102 Code of silence
103 Exact
105 Conehead
108 Caffè __
111 Sports star-turned-model Gabrielle
112 Author Dahl

114 They go around heads around Diamond Head
116 Russian legislature
118 Big name in microloans

119 Subject of the 2002 book "The Perfect Store"
120 Turns bad
121 Exact
124 Draft org.

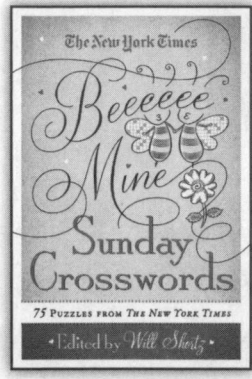

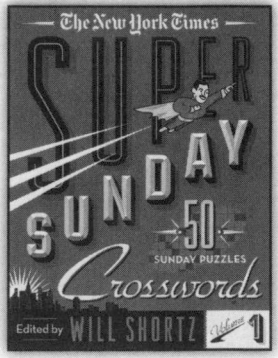

1

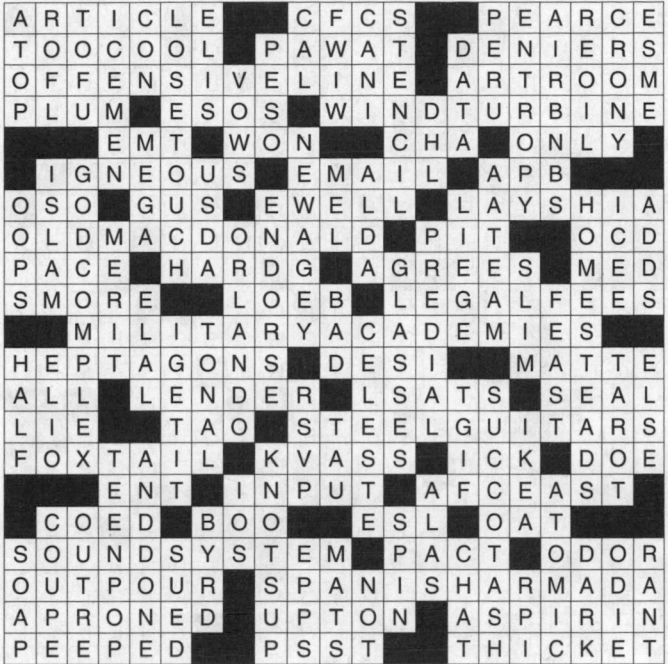

```
A R T I C L E . . C F C S . . P E A R C E
T O O C O O L . P A W A T . D E N I E R S
O F F E N S I V E L I N E . A R T R O O M
P L U M . E S O S . W I N D T U R B I N E
. . E M T . W O N . . C H A . O N L Y . .
. I G N E O U S . E M A I L . A P B . . .
O S O . G U S . E W E L L . L A Y S H I A
O L D M A C D O N A L D . P I T . . O C D
P A C E . H A R D G . A G R E E S . M E D
S M O R E . L O E B . L E G A L F E E S .
. M I L I T A R Y A C A D E M I E S . .
H E P T A G O N S . D E S I . . M A T T E
A L L . L E N D E R . L S A T S . S E A L
L I E . T A O . S T E E L G U I T A R S .
F O X T A I L . K V A S S . I C K . D O E
. E N T . I N P U T . A F C E A S T . .
. C O E D . B O O . E S L . O A T . . .
S O U N D S Y S T E M . P A C T . O D O R
O U T P O U R . S P A N I S H A R M A D A
A P R O N E D . U P T O N . A S P I R I N
P E E P E D . P S S T . . T H I C K E T
```

2

```
C R U S T . P E R M . J A N E . G O O F S
T U S H Y . A S I A . O D O R . A D M E N
R E C A P . N A P S . S O T S . M I S D O
. P I C K U P T H E P I E C E S . .
A R L E N E . L E A P T . O T T A W A
T E A . G O O V E R T H E E D G E . R E C
O P I E . K I D S . S E G O . B A T H
N O R M A R A E . O L D B E T S Y
. P L A Y W I T H M A T C H E S .
P I G E O N S . R A I T T . E L A T I O N
A D O R E . S E E D I E R . U P D O S
Y O L O . H O T . B E D . I R A . A L F A
. F R E E D O M O F A S S E M B L Y .
. S E R E N E . P O S I E S .
B A M . G E T I T T O G E T H E R . P A R
A R I A S . T E A R S I N T O . G N O M E
L E N D . P A R T I E S D O W N . E P I C
S W E R V E . . . . A L L P R O
A E R I E S . P I C T U R E . N O S E I N
M O V E I T . P E R F E C T . A B O R T S
. N A N N Y . M O M E N T S . S E N S E
```

3

Puzzle 3

A	D	D	L	E			L	O	L	Z		A	D	S		T	E	S	T	
T	R	A	I	T	S		A	P	I	A		F	R	O		U	N	C	U	T
W	I	R	E	T	A	P	P	I	N	G		L	O	U	D	M	O	U	T	H
O	N	E	F	A	C	E	D		E	A	R		P	R	O	M		L	E	A
O	K	D		S	S	R		U	T	E	R	I		N	I	B	L	E	T	
D	I	N	A		K	P	O	P		N	O	T	A	T	E	D				
	N	O	T	I	F	I	E	S		W	E	B		D	A	S	A	N	I	
	T	W	O	L	E	T	T	E	R	W	O	R	D	S		Y	O	G	A	
	O	N	O	R		T	I	S		O	A	K		I	N	N				
E	V	E	R	S	O		S	P	A	T		B	L	M		I	S	I	T	
S	A	N	S		D	O	U	B	L	E	C	R	O	S	S		P	E	T	E
S	L	I	T		R	R	S		O	A	R	S		T	E	A	S	E	D	
A	I	G		I	C	E		B	F	F		J	I	N	N					
Y	U	M	A		T	H	R	E	E	F	E	E	T	U	N	D	E	R		
	M	A	L	A	W	I		M	D	S		C	U	S	T	O	M	E	R	
	B	I	O	D	O	M	E		M	O	T	T		A	P	E	S			
L	A	M	A	R	R		N	A	C	H	O		W	H	A		E	A	P	
A	L	A		I	K	E	A		K	I	T		F	O	U	R	B	A	L	L
S	T	O	N	E	S	O	U	P		P	O	P	A	W	H	E	E	L	I	E
H	A	R	E	S		N	T	H		T	W	I	T		S	N	E	E	Z	E
	R	I	O	T		S	O	D		O	N	C	E		A	R	D	E	N	

4

M	O	A	T		I	F	S	O		R	A	D	A	R		E	N	A	C	T
O	N	M	E		M	A	I	D		I	R	U	L	E		X	E	N	O	N
M	E	A	N	G	I	R	L	S		G	R	E	A	S	E	P	A	I	N	T
S	U	N	D	A	N	C	E		S	H	A		N	H	L	E	R			
	P	A	R	S		E	N	T	I	T	Y		B	O	I	L		C	A	T
		I	K	E		T	O	R	O	S		E	O	S		S	H	I	A	
M	A	G	L	E	V	T	R	A	I	N		C	A	T	E	C	H	I	S	M
A	L	L	S	T	A	R		T	U	C	S	O	N		L	I	L	L	E	
N	E	O		S	N	U	G		S	U	L	A		O	L	I	V	I	E	R
E	X	A	M		I	L	S		E	A	C	H	T	I	M	E				
D	A	T	I	N	G	S	I	T	E		W	H	I	T	E	B	R	E	A	D
	B	Z	O	O	M	B	O	M	B		K	E	A		S	E	T	I		
A	M	A	Z	O	N	S		K	I	L	O		S	W	A	Y		N	W	A
L	A	D	E	N		M	E	R	E	L	Y		A	S	O	C	I	A	L	
L	I	O	N	E	S	S	E	S		A	D	V	E	N	T	U	R	E	R	S
O	N	U	S		T	N	N		B	R	I	E	F		O	W	E			
W	E	T		D	I	E	U		A	Y	E	S	I	R		I	A	T	E	
	B	L	E	E	P		N	E	S		L	E	S	S	T	H	A	N		
C	A	L	L	I	G	R	A	P	H	Y		G	I	F	T	H	O	R	S	E
O	N	I	O	N		A	G	A	M	E		E	N	I	D		R	E	E	L
S	A	U	T	E		T	E	P	I	D		S	G	T	S		S	E	L	L

5

Puzzle 5:

```
T A D . . O B A M A . E P I C . . P E N .
A W E S . P A R E D . C E N A . A L T E R
F A N T A S Y S U P P O R T S . S U S H I
F R I E D . . O P A H . S E A O T T E R S
Y E S W E C A N . G O F O R B A R O Q U E
. . S N O B . L E N I N . A R I . . . .
I D S . N A P A . E T N A . . D E E T .
F A L C O N C A R E S S E D . P E P S I S
S N E A K . I L Y A . . L E E R . I C K Y
O O P S I E . A N T E S . . D I S D A I N
. T H E R O U X I N T H E T O W E L .
P I L E S O N . . N O R A D . R A M A P O
E T A S . D E E D . . A R G O . M I T E R
R E T I R E . D E R I D E A P R I C O T S
. M E N U . . S P I T . M R E D . . R E O
. . . B I N . A P R E S . R A I N . .
G R A V Y T E R R A I N . C A S T A N E T
R E C O R D S E T . E G G O . . A D E L E
A C U T E . T H U N D E R C O L L A P S E
F A R E D . E A R N . L O O F A . L A I N
. P A R . A B E E . S W A T S . . L E S
```

6

Puzzle 6:

```
A C T A S . G N A R L . S T R I P . A D E S
H A I T I . M O N E Y . A R E N A . S E R A
S P E L L C A S T E R . D I S C I . L D R S
. . . A E R . R I C A R D O . U N L E A S H
J O H N N Y C A S H . E L D E R L A W .
C L A T T E R . . O S T E E N . E T O I L E
R I V A L R I E S . A N D . R I S E F R O M
E V E . . E X H A L E . N O M S G . A N E
W E N T . A R E A R . C H I N A . R E I G N
. . W E S . S G S . B U C . G U E S S E D
A S S I S T S . R E H A S H . E R A S E R S
L A W S U I T . U N E . H O N . G T I .
L I E T O . A U G E R . E L I S E . E T S Y
O D D . H T T P S . M I D A C T . . H I E
T H E A S H E S . B I C . S E A T A N G L E
S I N G T O . E L R O Y S . . R E C O I L S
. . E R U P T I O N . T A L K S T R A S H
H O G W A S H . S C E N E R Y . T R E . .
O R E O . A I M T O . A T O N E S E L B O W
S C A R . N A M E D . G H A N A . S C O N E
E A R N . D L I N E . S O R E R . S O W E D
```

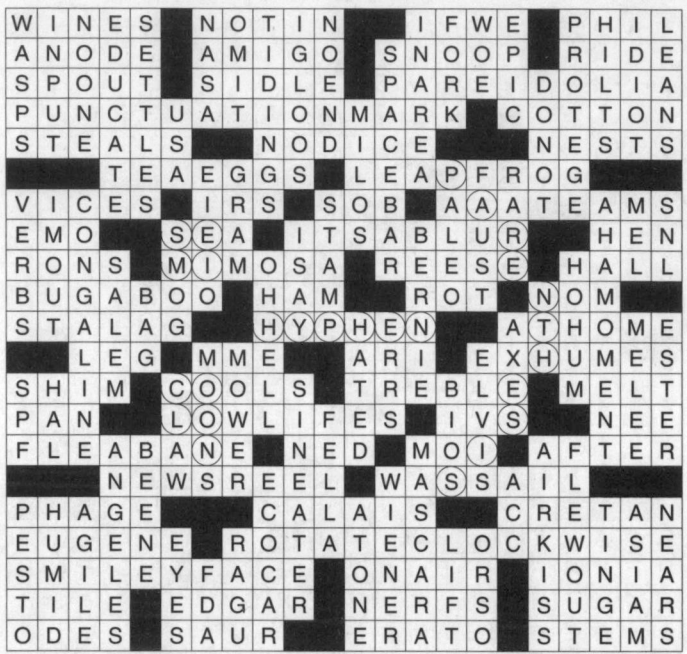

| W | I | N | E | S | | N | O | T | I | N | | | I | F | W | E | | P | H | I | L |

Grid 7:

```
WINES  NOTIN    IFWE  PHIL
ANODE  AMIGO   SNOOP  RIDE
SPOUT  SIDLE  PAREIDOLIA
PUNCTUATIONMARK  COTTON
STEALS  NODICE     NESTS
    TEAEGGS  LEAP(F)ROG
VICES  IRS  SOB  AAATEAMS
EMO  (SEA)  ITSABLUR   HEN
RONS (MIMOSA)  REESE  HALL
BUGABOO  HAM   ROT   (NOM)
STALAG  (HYPHEN)   ATHOME
  LEG  MME   ARI  EXHUMES
SHIM (COOLS)  TREBLE  MELT
PAN (LOWLIFES)  IVS    NEE
FLEABANE  NED  MOI  AFTER
  NEWSREEL   WAS(S)AIL
PHAGE    CALAIS   CRETAN
EUGENE  ROTATECLOCKWISE
SMILEYFACE  ONAIR  IONIA
TILE  EDGAR  NERFS  SUGAR
ODES  SAUR   ERATO  STEMS
```

Grid 8:

```
BEEFIER  LAPDOGS   HAREM
ECLIPSE  OHHENRY   AMARE
THOROUGHFAIRIES   HADES
HONE  RIOTS  MON  PANICS
   BRASS    PANAMAHAITI
ALTOON  ESAU    DANA
DORMICE  WILDCARD  UTNE
DOUBLEDIARIES  CARPOOL
EST   SHY   FIDO  AROMA
REHUNG  AZURE  ONETOTEN
  SHOULDERHAIRINESS
SWEATSIT  GOTTI  OREIDA
TORUS  BONE   ITE    EER
YOULOSE  BOOKSONTAIPEI
ELMS  CLEANUPS  GETSORE
   PREP   THOR  LOUPES
POLKAIDIOTS   ITEMS
EMINEM  GPA  ADREP  PAPA
CAMEL  FRESHPAIROFEYES
KNOLL  DARKISH  PROCESS
SISTA  AMASSES  STETSON
```

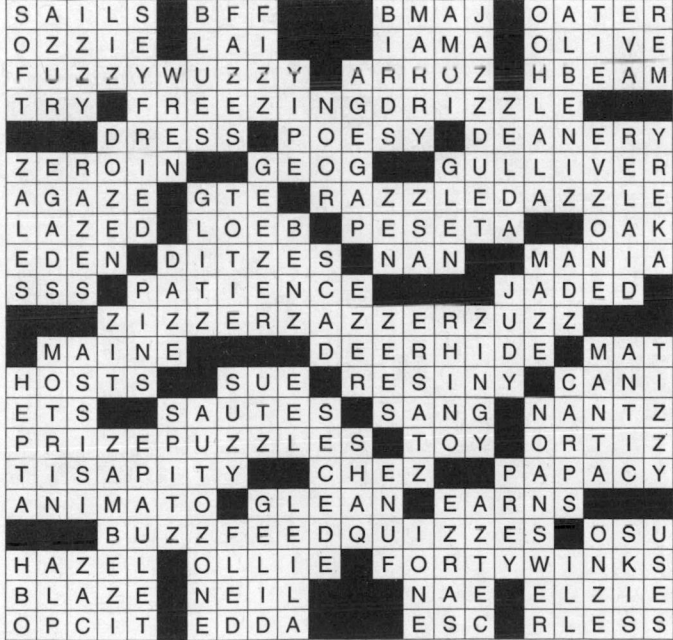

11

```
L A S   A T O M S   E E K   L A D I E S
A S A   S A R A H   E L L E   O R O N Y M
P S Y C H O A N A L Y S I S   G I J O E S
C U S H Y   O R E O   M O N S O O N S
A C M E   I S W E A R I T   S I S   E H S
T H E R E D C A R P E T   P A N E L S A W
      P I E R S   C P A   E D D A
P E L O T O N   T S H I R T C A N N O N
A L O U   M E A N I E   G L U E D   A W K
C L A I M S   N O N E   T A B O O S
K A N J I   S I M O N S A Y S   B O R O N
      A T H O M E   O K I E   M O R A L E
A M A   R A D A R   T O L D T O   E N D S
B I N G E W A T C H E R   O R E S T E S
U N T O   O Y E   I D I O T
J O B O F F E R   C H A N E L N O F I V E
A R E   A L S   U K U L E L E S   O N E D
   R E S T U P O N   M O R T   B A S T E
G O T H A M   F L Y M E T O T H E M O O N
A L L E L E   T I M E   I R A I L   L E I
R E E S E S   T A D   A O R T A   E S C
```

12

```
O M I T S   S C H W A B   O N S P E C
H A D I T   T R A I N O R   P R E H E A T
S L I D E   R O G E T S T H E S A U R U S
N A D I R   O P S   N E U R O T I C
A L I E N S   W W I   S U N   H E M
P A T R O N O F T H E A R T S   I M A G E
      L L B E A N   O L E   G O N G S
S T O I C   G I S T   B A E   D E U C E S
T O C C A T A   S A T A N   H A T R E D
A T H E N A   W I N E S   L E N I N
G O O   T H E R E I N S P I R I T   U F O
      M O O N Y   G S P O T   E N U R E D
   S T O N E D   S H E L L   B L O G G E D
E C H O E S   N E T   A L O E   W H E T S
T R E S S   A O L   H Y E N A S
T U T E E   C H A R T E R E D P L A N E S
A B E   M R I   I S R   F O M E N T
   A S S O O N A S   S O U   W O O D Y
B O A C O N S T R I C T O R S   C E C I L
A R C A D E S   I N P E A C E   A B O V E
A S T R A Y   G A S P A R   L A N E S
```

13

```
A L L A H ■ ■ D E B I T ■ C D C ■ S P A T
M O I R A ■ T E X A C O ■ L A O ■ H U L A
O F F E N S I V E R E B O U N D ■ I T E M
S T E W ■ A M I S S ■ I B E T ■ C E A S E
■ ■ ■ E D G E S ■ R A I S E H E L L ■
F L O O R E X E R C I S E ■ ■ O L D I S H
R I L K E ■ S U I T ■ D U N E ■ D E E
A P A ■ W E S ■ S T A R T I N G B L O C K
Y O Y O T R I C K ■ Y O G I ■ S A N T A
■ ■ H O N D A ■ M A D I S O N ■ R I O T
S H A W ■ S E R V I C E L I N E ■ E T R E
C O D E ■ T R A I L E R ■ T R I A D ■ ■
O R A L B ■ O M A N ■ ■ T E E N M O V I E
U N P L A Y A B L E L I E ■ P S I ■ I N A
T I T ■ T A D A ■ O K R A ■ D O O R S
S N A P O N ■ S E V E N T E N S P L I T
■ T A N G E R I N E ■ ■ E L A T E ■
R O I L S ■ Y U R I ■ D E L I S ■ N E W T
A W O L ■ D E S I G N A T E D H I T T E R
Z I N E ■ J U T ■ M O U S S E ■ M O N A E
Z E S T ■ S P Y ■ A R B Y S ■ P E A R S
```

14

```
P A T ■ R A S C A L S ■ ■ P E N ■ S E P
E C O ■ E M M Y L O U ■ W A G E ■ A P E
T H E W [HIT/MISS] A L B U M ■ H I T O R M I S S
F E T A ■ S R O ■ D E P O R T ■ D I D I T
O D O R S ■ T N T ■ R E M E E T ■ A B L E
O F T ■ A S I S A Y ■ P E T R I ■ M O O R
D O O R D I E ■ L I V E R A N [DO/DIE] N I O N S
■ R E A D S ■ M U N I ■ P S S T ■ ■
■ M E T R E S ■ L O L ■ T H R I L L
I M P O S E O N ■ B E H E A D ■ ■ O D E A
M O U N T R U S H [MORE/LESS] ■ M O R E O R L E S S
P O P E ■ E A S E L S ■ S U R E L E T S
S T A S I S ■ N S A ■ N O S I D E ■ ■
■ S H A H ■ T H O N ■ A D D T O
M A R C H [IN/OUT] G O R D E R S ■ I N O R O U T
A V E R ■ A R T I E ■ H E P C A T ■ U T E
D A Z E ■ T O N N E S ■ S H E ■ S A C H S
E R O D E ■ N E S T E A ■ A B C ■ S H O T
W I N O R L O S E ■ W H I R L [WIN/LOSE] D T O U R
A C E ■ A I M S ■ U S R O U T E ■ F S U
Y E S ■ S P Y ■ P O S S E S S ■ F E N
```

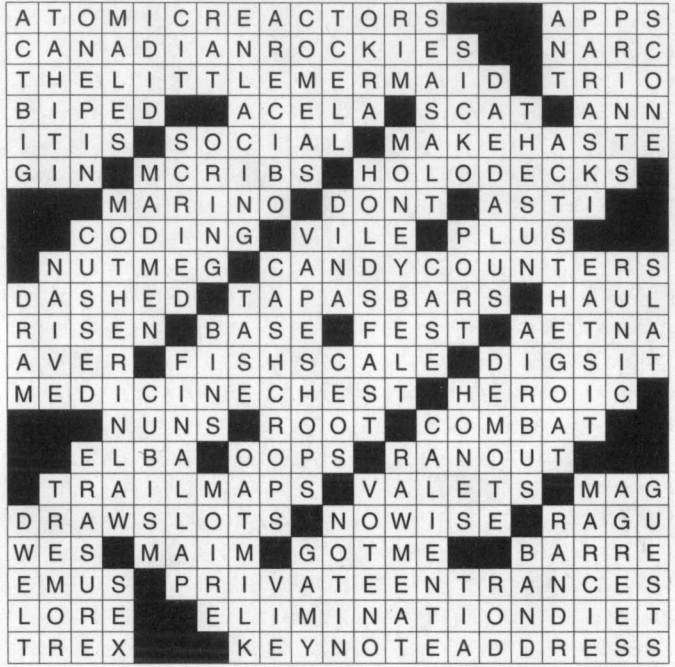

15

Grid 15:

A	T	O	M	I	C	R	E	A	C	T	O	R	S			A	P	P	S
C	A	N	A	D	I	A	N	R	O	C	K	I	E	S		N	A	R	C
T	H	E	L	I	T	T	L	E	M	E	R	M	A	I	D	T	R	I	O
B	I	P	E	D		A	C	E	L	A		S	C	A	T	A	N	N	
I	T	I	S		S	O	C	I	A	L		M	A	K	E	H	A	S	T	E
G	I	N		M	C	R	I	B	S		H	O	L	O	D	E	C	K	S
	M	A	R	I	N	O		D	O	N	T		A	S	T	I	
C	O	D	I	N	G		V	I	L	E		P	L	U	S	
N	U	T	M	E	G		C	A	N	D	Y	C	O	U	N	T	E	R	S
D	A	S	H	E	D		T	A	P	A	S	B	A	R	S		H	A	U	L
R	I	S	E	N		B	A	S	E		F	E	S	T		A	E	T	N	A
A	V	E	R		F	I	S	H	S	C	A	L	E		D	I	G	S	I	T
M	E	D	I	C	I	N	E	C	H	E	S	T		H	E	R	O	I	C
	N	U	N	S		R	O	O	T		C	O	M	B	A	T	
	E	L	B	A		O	O	P	S		R	A	N	O	U	T	
	T	R	A	I	L	M	A	P	S		V	A	L	E	T	S		M	A	G
D	R	A	W	S	L	O	T	S		N	O	W	I	S	E		R	A	G	U
W	E	S		M	A	I	M		G	O	T	M	E			B	A	R	R	E
E	M	U	S		P	R	I	V	A	T	E	E	N	T	R	A	N	C	E	S
L	O	R	E		E	L	I	M	I	N	A	T	I	O	N	D	I	E	T
T	R	E	X		K	E	Y	N	O	T	E	A	D	D	R	E	S	S

Grid 16:

L	A	S	S		O	G	R	E		B	O	A	R		I	T	S	O	U	T
A	U	T	O		R	O	A	D		A	R	L	O		G	R	U	N	G	E
P	R	E	G	N	A	N	C	Y	B	R	A	I	N		N	I	N	T	H	S
P	A	T	O	O	T	I	E		S	O	L	I	D	F	O	O	D	
	O	N	E	G		E	I	N		O	U	R		A	N	I	N
G	L	A	D	E		H	O	W	D	E	D	O		N	A	M	E	O	N	E
L	O	L		S	T	R	E	E	T	S	M	A	R	T	S		M	F	A
E	V	I	C	T	I	N	G		L	I	Q	U	I	D	D	I	E	T
N	E	G	R	O	N	I		A	D	T		T	I	N		O	U	N	C	E
S	Y	N	O	D		G	O	F	A	R		A	S	S	E	T	S
	M	O	T	H	E	R	W	I	T		A	M	Y		T	E	S	T
D	R	E	W		I	T	D		G	A	S	G	I	A	N	T	S	
R	E	S	E	T	S		G	A	U	D	Y		R	O	S	I	E
A	M	P	L	E		L	I	E		E	R	Y		T	H	E	F	E	D	S
P	O	O	L	N	O	O	D	L	E		S	H	U	F	F	L	E	S
E	D	U		P	L	A	S	M	A	S	C	R	E	E	N		M	A	I
R	E	S	U	M	E	D		O	N	T	O	P	O	F		S	T	A	L	E
Y	L	E	M		A	E	R		A	N	G		O	A	H	U	
	P	A	N	D	E	R	I	N	G		F	U	R	I	K	A	K	E
R	E	W	I	N	D		M	I	N	D	O	V	E	R	M	A	T	T	E	R
H	E	A	R	Y	E		I	C	E	T		O	T	T	O		U	R	N	S
O	K	D	E	A	R		T	A	Z	O		L	A	H	R		K	A	T	E

Grid 17:

```
D I L A T E S ■ P O G O ■ A L T ■ F E M A
E C O C I D E ■ A W A Y ■ T O E ■ A X I S
F R O M D U S K T I L L D A W N ■ B O N K
T Y P E A ■ A E O N ■ ■ E L L S ■ I T E M
■ ■ S L U M D O G M I L L I O N A I R E
A S S ■ ■ R E S T ■ O W L ■ F R A N C ■
H A T F U L ■ ■ C R O S S E ■ G O F O R
O C E A N S E L E V E N ■ A S H ■ I M O
O H A R A ■ G E M S ■ D S L ■ I T I S N T
T A K E L E A V E ■ P E W ■ T R Y T H I S
■ ■ W E D D I N G C R A S H E R S ■ ■
C A N A R D S ■ D O S ■ N E E D A L I F T
S H O R T I ■ Y S L ■ P E E R ■ N O R A H
I O S ■ ■ E R E ■ I N H E R E N T V I C E
S K I P S ■ E S S A Y S ■ ■ U S E N E T
■ ■ R E R A N ■ E T S ■ A C T I ■ A D A
T H E G O D F A T H E R P A R T I I ■
A B E L ■ S A R A ■ ■ E R I E ■ T O P A Z
T O B E ■ P I C T U R E I N P I C T U R E
A G O G ■ O R E ■ G U L L ■ I N H A L E D
R O B S ■ T E D ■ H E S S ■ D A Y S P A S
```

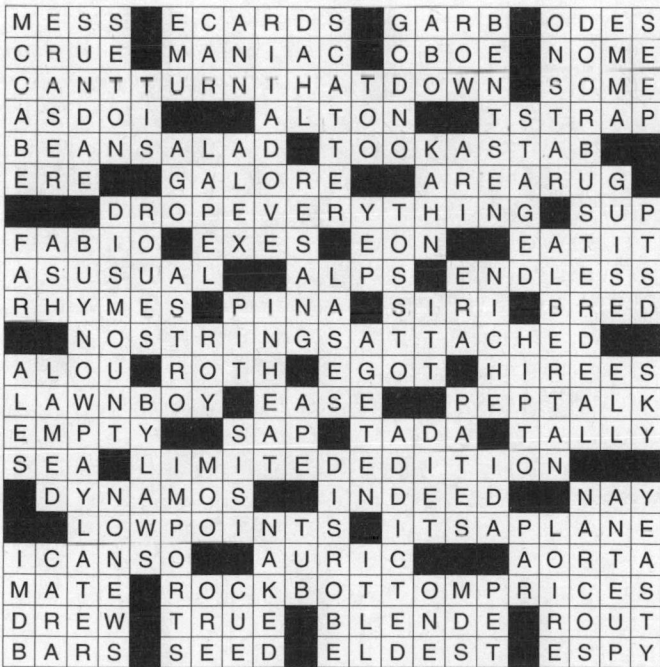

Grid 18:

```
M E S S ■ E C A R D S ■ G A R B ■ O D E S
C R U E ■ M A N I A C ■ O B O E ■ N O M E
C A N T T U R N I H A T D O W N ■ S O M E
A S D O I ■ ■ A L T O N ■ T S T R A P
B E A N S A L A D ■ T O O K A S T A B ■
E R E ■ G A L O R E ■ A R E A R U G
■ ■ D R O P E V E R Y T H I N G ■ S U P
F A B I O ■ E X E S ■ E O N ■ E A T I T
A S U S U A L ■ A L P S ■ E N D L E S S
R H Y M E S ■ P I N A ■ S I R I ■ B R E D
■ N O S T R I N G S A T T A C H E D ■
A L O U ■ R O T H ■ E G O T ■ H I R E E S
L A W N B O Y ■ E A S E ■ P E P T A L K
E M P T Y ■ S A P ■ T A D A ■ T A L L Y
S E A ■ L I M I T E D E D I T I O N ■
■ D Y N A M O S ■ I N D E E D ■ N A Y
■ L O W P O I N T S ■ I T S A P L A N E
I C A N S O ■ A U R I C ■ A O R T A
M A T E ■ R O C K B O T T O M P R I C E S
D R E W ■ T R U E ■ B L E N D E ■ R O U T
B A R S ■ S E E D ■ E L D E S T ■ E S P Y
```

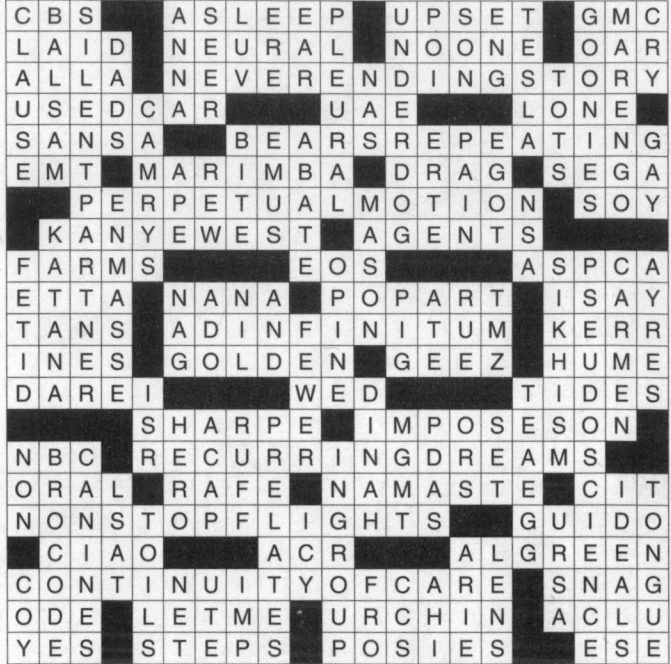

21

```
A C T S   A R I   P J S     H A I T I A N
T H R U   B U S R O U T E   U N N E R V E
P E A N U T[BELL]B U T T E R   D E G R E E S
  F I N N   A N I     A R P   N O R A
  S L I T S   S N I C K E R[HEART]D O O D L E
  I N I T S     M O S D E F   D R Y A D
G I N G E R[TREE]S N A P     L E T S   O R G
E N G   A T A N Y   T O L L[ANGEL]H O U S E
A N A T   D A N E   R E M   T O A D
R A W R   A R C   K E R N S   P E T S
S T A U B   T H I N[STAR]M I N T   E T H E R
  E Y E R   O T O E S   O R B   T E L E
  S A G S   T W A   F R A U   A B E S
F I G[ELF]N E W T O N   O L E I C   E N O
I L E   C L E O     S H O R T[CANE]B R E A D
D I N A H   L O G J A M   S E L E S
O A T M E A L[MAN]R A I S I N   R A C K S
  R A D S   Y E S   M E A   S I N E
C O I N O P S   C O O K I E C U T T E R S
D R F A U C I   O N I O N D I P   A E R O
C R Y S T A L   S L O   Y D S   L S A T
```

22

```
O R D A I N   A P A C H E   I M I G H T
C O U L D A   U S O T O U R   M O T H E R
H O R S E B A C K R I D E R   O P P O S E
O M A H A   P L S   T I V O S   R U S E
  A T S E A   N O R T H P O L E
R E G R E T   T W I G   Y E A S
P R E P   A T R A I N   G E R M   G E O
M I T T   P U B L I C H O U S E   S O A P
S C H O O L T I E S   E W E   B O O Z E
  I N S E T   B R I S K   O B G Y N
A R T   T R U E F A L S E T E S T   L E S
B O C C E   T R A C T   N I C H E
A B H O R   I V E   M A I N T H E M E S
C O E D   S P E A R H E A D E D   D A T A
I T D   T E E S   E N H A L O   G P A S
  A N N A   S P A S   W R E S T S
  S O F T D R I N K   N A N A S
P A I R   L O O I E   T O P   C A N A L
I C L O U D   W O R K O U T T H E B U G S
C H E E S E   A N T E N N A   A M E N R A
S A D D E N   N E S S I E   G E T S A T
```

23

24

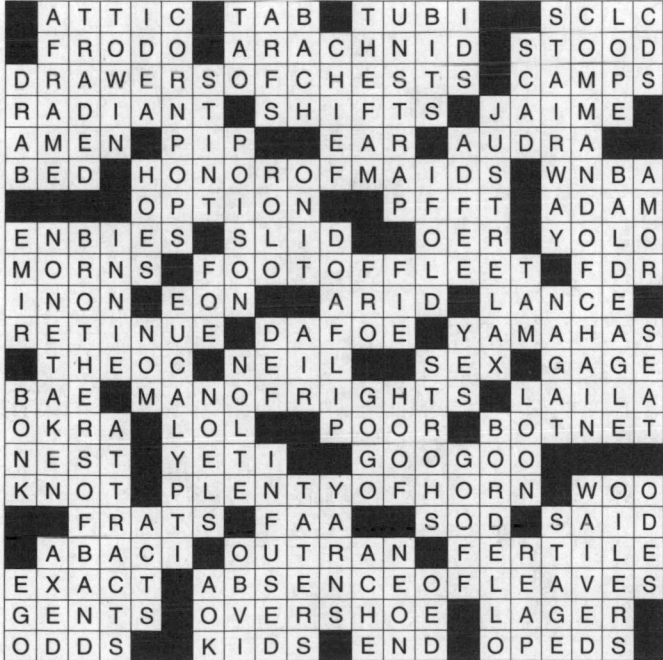

27

Grid 27:

S	C	R	E	A	M	O	■	■	F	O	L	D	U	P	■	F	R	O	S
I	N	E	X	P	E	R	T	■	A	V	E	R	S	E	■	L	E	I	A
B	E	S	TRAP	A	L	B	U	M	■	C	E	A	S	E	S	■	Y	A	N	K
S	T	U	■	■	O	S	M	O	S	I	N	G	■	■	T	R	I	C	K	S
■	■	R	O	A	N	■	■	O	I	L	S	U	P	■	■	A	N	T	S	■
F	O	R	I	N	S	T	A	N	C	E	■	E	A	R	W	I	G	■	■
O	N	E	N	D	■	E	S	L	■	■	O	R	C	H	E	S	TRAP	I	T	S
S	E	C	T	■	TRAP	P	I	S	T	S	■	K	O	B	E	■	T	I	E
S	I	T	S	O	N	■	T	W	O	B	I	T	■	S	H	E	H	E	R
E	L	S	■	R	O	O	K	■	I	R	O	N	E	D	■	A	Z	E	R	A
■	■	B	A	D	D	E	S	T	■	U	N	N	E	R	V	E	■	■
A	C	O	R	N	■	S	P	I	C	E	R	■	T	A	C	O	■	P	M	S
D	O	R	A	G	S	■	T	A	H	I	N	I	■	■	A	C	C	R	U	E
D	N	A	■	E	X	E	C	■	O	N	E	C	U	P	■	■	H	E	R	A
S	TRAP	L	E	S	S	G	O	W	N	■	■	A	L	E	■	M	A	D	A	M
■	■	M	O	W	G	L	I	■	V	O	N	TRAP	P	F	A	M	I	L	Y
■	T	O	A	D	■	D	I	S	O	W	N	■	■	R	I	P	S	■
S	I	M	I	A	N	■	M	I	S	S	O	U	L	A	■	P	O	P
N	O	E	L	■	O	N	T	I	L	T	■	T	R	A	P	D	O	O	R	S
I	N	G	E	■	L	E	A	N	T	O	■	■	E	S	P	O	U	S	E	S
T	S	A	R	■	A	T	R	I	S	K	■	■	S	E	X	I	E	S	T

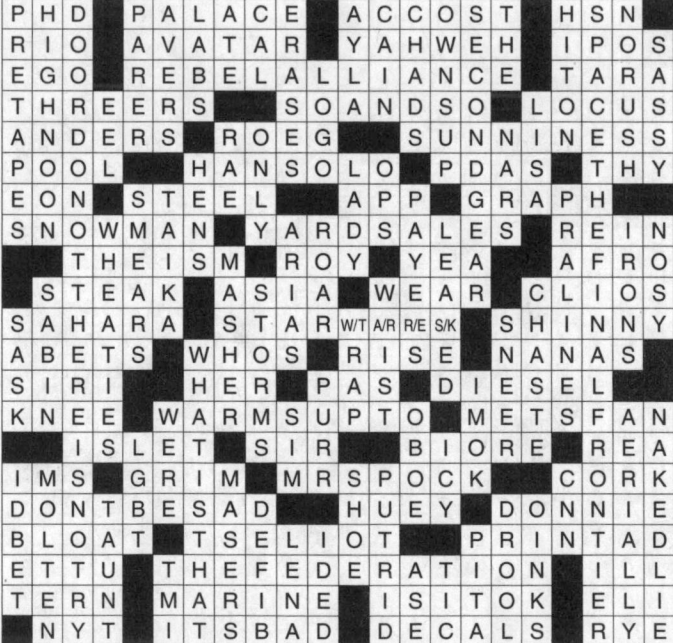

28

Grid 28:

P	H	D	■	P	A	L	A	C	E	■	A	C	C	O	S	T	■	H	S	N	■
R	I	O	■	A	V	A	T	A	R	■	Y	A	H	W	E	H	■	I	P	O	S
E	G	O	■	R	E	B	E	L	A	L	L	I	A	N	C	E	■	T	A	R	A
T	H	R	E	E	R	S	■	■	S	O	A	N	D	S	O	■	L	O	C	U	S
A	N	D	E	R	S	■	R	O	E	G	■	■	S	U	N	N	I	N	E	S	S
P	O	O	L	■	H	A	N	S	O	L	O	■	P	D	A	S	■	T	H	Y
E	O	N	■	S	T	E	E	L	■	■	A	P	P	■	G	R	A	P	H	■
S	N	O	W	M	A	N	■	Y	A	R	D	S	A	L	E	S	■	R	E	I	N
■	T	H	E	I	S	M	■	R	O	Y	■	Y	E	A	■	A	F	R	O
■	S	T	E	A	K	■	A	S	I	A	■	W	E	A	R	■	C	L	I	O	S
S	A	H	A	R	A	■	S	T	A	R	W/T	A/R	R/E	S/K	■	S	H	I	N	N	Y
A	B	E	T	S	■	W	H	O	S	■	R	I	S	E	■	N	A	N	A	S	■
S	I	R	I	■	H	E	R	■	P	A	S	■	D	I	E	S	E	L	■
K	N	E	E	■	W	A	R	M	S	U	P	T	O	■	M	E	T	S	F	A	N
■	I	S	L	E	T	■	S	I	R	■	B	I	O	R	E	■	R	E	A
I	M	S	■	G	R	I	M	■	M	R	S	P	O	C	K	■	C	O	R	K
D	O	N	T	B	E	S	A	D	■	H	U	E	Y	■	D	O	N	N	I	E
B	L	O	A	T	■	T	S	E	L	I	O	T	■	P	R	I	N	T	A	D
E	T	T	U	■	T	H	E	F	E	D	E	R	A	T	I	O	N	■	I	L	L
T	E	R	N	■	M	A	R	I	N	E	■	I	S	I	T	O	K	■	E	L	I
■	N	Y	T	■	I	T	S	B	A	D	■	D	E	C	A	L	S	■	R	Y	E

29

The circled letters can be replaced, in order, by the letters of VALENTINE to make new words Across and Down.

30

31

Puzzle 31 (across rows):
- ATMCARDS · BUREAU · ATIT
- POOHPOOH · EASESIN · LIME
- PIRATESOFTHECARIBBEAN
- SLR · TOOHARD · SCOURGE
- IPAS · ERE · CHESSSET
- ITSAWONDERFULLIFE
- LOOSELY · ONEUP · PEGS
- LENS · VEG · PUTON · GARRET
- THETOWERINGINFERNO
- YAHOO · NORSE · CARPARK
- ESE · OLSEN · AKITA · TEE
- STRIKER · SPADE · IPASS
- THEDEVILWEARSPRADA
- EMBODY · EARLS · TAB · YVES
- RAYS · PASTE · KENDALL
- WHENHARRYMETSALLY
- GLACIERS · HAI · SAYS
- RECITAL · GORILLA · PCS
- ANIGHTMAREONELMSTREET
- PINA · HAYRIDE · EMPANADA
- ENGR · SNARLS · TOYMAKER

32

Puzzle 32 (across rows):
- APPETIT · IMOUT · PACIFIC
- SHALALA · NAOMI · ATACAMA
- SATIRES · SCONE · UPSELLS
- ISH · P · TIPS · OPTS · A · LIT
- SET · ESE · ORE · IKE
- IROC · TRACY · GLOSS · ONES
- VITA · ATEALOT · WART
- ISITON · C · ADO · H · ELWOOD
- SACRED · HOW · ALEPPO
- OCTOBER · BONUS · TRILLED
- PHONEME · OKAPI · HAALAND
- OER · ASFOR · I · LSATS · CEE
- DRY · N · OBE · LAT · K · ERR
- RODS · SINS
- SOD · NAMEOFTHEGAME · CHO
- THEHELP · MOWER · BARGAIN
- ALVEOLAR · O · DISGORGE
- FOIA · ORAL · SEGO · OSHA
- FOLLOWTHEBOUNCINGBALL
- KEELEY · GOPRO · FINELY
- DRED · SWING · CURE

33

34

35

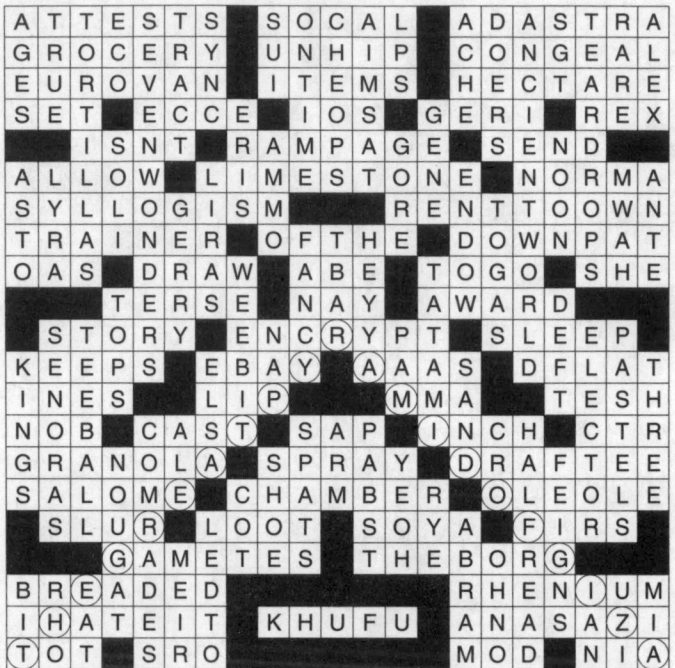

```
ATTESTS  SOCAL  ADASTRA
GROCERY  UNHIP  CONGEAL
EUROVAN  ITEMS  HECTARE
SET ECCE IOS GERI REX
    ISNT RAMPAGE SEND
ALLOW LIMESTONE NORMA
SYLLOGISM  RENTTOOWN
TRAINER OFTHE DOWNPAT
OAS DRAW ABE TOGO SHE
  TERSE NAY AWARD
 STORY ENCRYPT SLEEP
KEEPS EBAY AAAS DFLAT
INES LIP MMA TESH
NOB CAST SAP INCH CTR
GRANOLA SPRAY DRAFTEE
SALOME CHAMBER OLEOLE
 SLUR LOOT SOYA FIRS
  GAMETES THEBORG
BREADED  RHENIUM
IHATEIT KHUFU ANASAZI
TOT SRO   MOD NIA
```

36

```
LIFTUP PFFT PELT SWAN
ACROSS REARWIPER CECE
SEAOFTRANQUILITY HEIR
TBILL AIDS ROCS SOUND
ILLS APSE SETSOFTONGS
NUT SUPERVHS NEAL
GEYSERED ERASE BROCHE
 TEAR BROWED REFLEX
UNLADE JESUSLIKE TEAT
NEARS RUNED TAZ HAVE
DOCS SANDSOFTIME ONIN
ESTO ORK FAUNA MUSED
ROOF BADRATING TIGERS
GUSTAF NODULE SETH
OLEOLE ANDRE FASTTALK
  MOST WIDEOUTS DEE
SONOFTARZAN ARRS PANE
AVERT PEET ARCO GAMIN
LIAR STATEOFTENNESSEE
ENTO RADARTRAP ANTONY
MEOW SPYS COGS EXANTE
```

37

```
W I S P   T R A S H Y   S C A R F   E W E
A S T A   V I R T U E   K O R E A   V O L
I T I C   S P O K E S P E R S O N   E O S
F O L K   P E A     O W N   B O N D I
    L A B O R R E P R E S E N T A T I V E
G R A B A T   M A A M   R I P S O N E
I O T A S   M A O R I     T S E   G N P
F L I G H T A T T E N D A N T   A S E A
S E T   R U L E D   A M O Y   C U T E R
    S L I D     O D O R   B O G A R T
  W H I T E C O L L A R W O R K E R
I M H O M E   A G E D     P I E R
S U A V E   U S E D   N A F T A   I N T
A L T E   T H E A T E R D I R E C T O R
W E D   C H I     H O G A N   R O S I E
  T O E H O L D   X E N O   P A L T R Y
P R I V A T E I N V E S T I G A T O R
O A K E N   S E I     N I T   R I D E
K I N   C I R C U I T J U D G E   S C A N
E N O   E R R O R   N A T I O N   I K I D
S S W   L A S S O   T R E A T S   N Y S E
```

38

```
S A H L   S C R I P   J O L L A   G T O S
A L O E   E L I D E   U N I O N   R A N T
A P P T   R A T I N C R E A S E   E P E E
R E D S H I R T   O R O N O   M I A M I S
    I L O N A   T B I R D   P I S T E
S T A I R S   F U S E   M A C A D A M S
T A M P A   H A T C R I M E S   N A S A L
A B O   S E E N T O   N A R C   N U K E
M O N A   S A N I T A R Y C O D   R I P
P O D I A T R Y   R E B S   A B S E N T
    D U H S   A B I D E   G M A N
P O M A D E   A R I E   H E A D A C H E
O C A   R U B G O L D B E R G   P R A M
L A D D   R I O T   O I L M E N   Y U M
I L I U M   I N N A M O N L Y   A M I T Y
S A N D A L E D   A M E S   A M I N E S
  C R U E L   A L I S T   S T U N G
R E H A S H   F R O N D   S T O R E S U P
I T I N   I C E C R E A M C O N   O H S O
B A N C   G O R E N   Y O U V E   L A N E
S H A H   H O N D A   S I D E D   A M A T
```

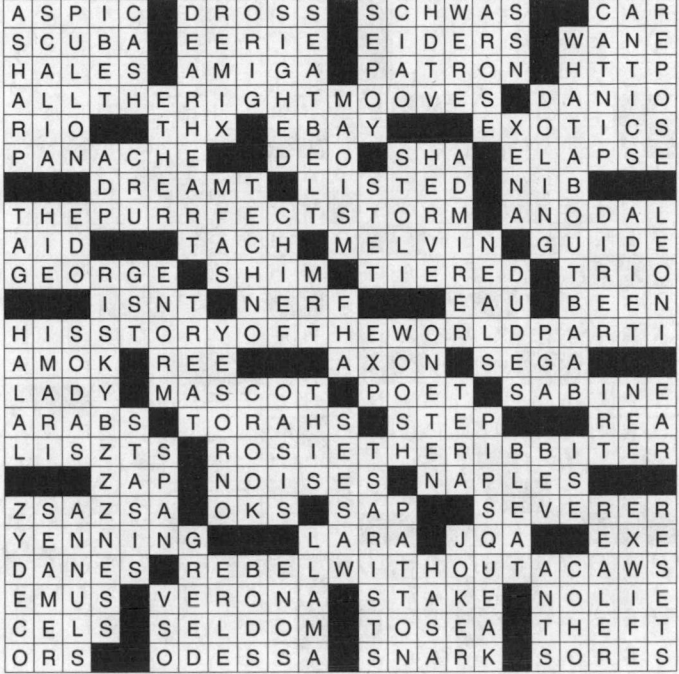

41

A	S	P	I	C		D	R	O	S	S		S	C	H	W	A	S			C	A	R
S	C	U	B	A		E	E	R	I	E		E	I	D	E	R	S		W	A	N	E
H	A	L	E	S		A	M	I	G	A		P	A	T	R	O	N		H	T	T	P
A	L	L	T	H	E	R	I	G	H	T	M	O	O	V	E	S		D	A	N	I	O
R	I	O			T	H	X		E	B	A	Y			E	X	O	T	I	C	S
P	A	N	A	C	H	E		D	E	O		S	H	A		E	L	A	P	S	E
	D	R	E	A	M	T		L	I	S	T	E	D		N	I	B				
T	H	E	P	U	R	R	F	E	C	T	S	T	O	R	M		A	N	O	D	A	L
A	I	D		T	A	C	H		M	E	L	V	I	N		G	U	I	D	E
G	E	O	R	G	E		S	H	I	M		T	I	E	R	E	D		T	R	I	O
	I	S	N	T		N	E	R	F			E	A	U		B	E	E	N
H	I	S	S	T	O	R	Y	O	F	T	H	E	W	O	R	L	D	P	A	R	T	I
A	M	O	K		R	E	E			A	X	O	N		S	E	G	A
L	A	D	Y		M	A	S	C	O	T		P	O	E	T		S	A	B	I	N	E
A	R	A	B	S		T	O	R	A	H	S		S	T	E	P			R	E	A
L	I	S	Z	T	S		R	O	S	I	E	T	H	E	R	I	B	B	I	T	E	R
			Z	A	P		N	O	I	S	E	S		N	A	P	L	E	S
Z	S	A	Z	S	A		O	K	S		S	A	P			S	E	V	E	R	E	R
Y	E	N	N	I	N	G				L	A	R	A		J	Q	A			E	X	E
D	A	N	E	S		R	E	B	E	L	W	I	T	H	O	U	T	A	C	A	W	S
E	M	U	S		V	E	R	O	N	A		S	T	A	K	E		N	O	L	I	E
C	E	L	S		S	E	L	D	O	M		T	O	S	E	A		T	H	E	F	T
O	R	S			O	D	E	S	S	A		S	N	A	R	K		S	O	R	E	S

42

S	T	A	R	T	O	F	F		T	I	M	P	A	N	I		H	I	Y	A
P	O	R	E	O	V	E	R		A	N	D	I	R	O	N		O	L	A	V
I	H	O	P	E	I	W	I	N	I	H	I	S	P	O	T		M	L	L	E
T	O	M					S	E	T	A			S	N	O	W	E	D	I	N
S	E	A	N	S		A	B	S	O	L	V	E		E	T	A		R	E	G
				I	H	A	V	E	T	O	F	O	L	D		O	N	B	A	S	E
S	P	I	K	E	L	E	E			L	I	A	M		D	O	W
H	E	R	O	E	S			G	A	P		H	B	O			S	T	D	S
I	W	A	N	T	A	F	U	L	L	H	O	U	S	E		H	O	W	I	E
I	T	I		T	U	N	E	D	I	N			S	A	M	O	S	A
T	E	S		F	I	N	D	E	R		F	E	I	N	T	S		C	C	S
A	R	E	O	L	A			I	N	O	R	D	E	R			A	R	I
K	E	A	N	U		I	M	I	N	F	O	R	A	H	U	N	D	R	E	D
E	R	L	E		P	A	T		C	T	S			D	E	E	D	E	E
	L	A	S		O	X	E	N			M	A	E	W	E	S	T	S
S	T	I	L	T	S		I	M	T	H	E	D	E	A	L	E	R
I	R	V		U	H	S		S	H	A	R	O	N	S		L	E	A	P	T
G	O	E	S	D	E	A	F		B	R	I	T					M	A	I
N	O	G	O		I	D	L	I	K	E	A	N	O	T	H	E	R	A	C	E
A	P	O	P		L	A	O	T	I	A	N		R	E	A	S	O	N	E	R
L	S	T	S		A	T	W	O	R	S	T		S	A	W	S	T	A	R	S

43

T	H	R	E	E	P	A	R	T		B	A	R	K		I	M	P	A	L	E
B	I	E	N	V	E	N	U	E		A	L	I	E		M	A	R	I	A	N
A	S	P	H	A	L	T	E	D		N	O	T	E		P	R	O	N	T	O
	L	A	D	L	E			E	Q	U	A	L	L	E	N	G	T	H	S	
	M	A	N	N			D	I	E	U				O	L	E	O			
J	O	Y	C	E	C	A	R	O	L	O	A	T	E	S			L	I	C	S
I	D	E	E		E	B	O	N	Y		M	E	R		I	F	N	O	T	
F	E	D		S	L	E	W			P	A	S	S		A	D	E	S	T	E
			H	E	L	E	N	A	B	O	N	H	A	M	C	A	R	T	E	R
S	A	P	O	R			M	I	A			T	A	T			O	R	E	
A	R	A	N	T	X	A	S	A	N	C	H	E	Z	V	I	C	A	R	I	O
N	I	N		M	D	C		H	U	E				U	L	E	E	S		
J	A	C	K	I	E	J	O	Y	N	E	R	K	E	R	S	E	E			
U	N	H	E	W	N		T	O	A	D		A	U	K	S		P	B	S	
A	N	O	N	O		C	U	Z		S	U	S	H	I		C	R	A	T	
N	A	S	D		C	H	R	I	S	E	V	E	R	T	L	L	O	Y	D	
			R	A	T	A			O	P	A	L			O	A	R	S		
M	A	R	Y	B	E	T	H	H	U	R	T			S	I	G	M	A		
G	L	A	D	Y	S		Y	A	L	E		E	L	O	N	G	A	T	E	S
M	E	R	E	S	T		P	I	L	L		D	O	W	D	I	N	E	S	S
T	E	E	N	S	Y		O	L	A	Y		S	U	N	Y	A	T	S	E	N

44

A	C	C	E	D	E		C	H	A	C	H	A		M	A	L	A	G	A	S
B	U	R	R	O	S		P	O	S	H	E	R		A	L	A	B	A	M	A
I	T	E	N	D	S	H	A	P	P	I	L	Y		N	A	T	U	R	E	L
D	E	A		G	O	O		H	E	L	L		S	I	C			B	L	T
E	S	S	A	Y		P	I	E	C	E	O	F	C	A	K	E		L	I	E
D	Y	E	S			S	W	A	T	S		A	R	C		S	T	E	A	D
			H	A	M		A	D	S		P	T	A	S		P	E	D		
M	A	S		C	A	W	S			S	O	A	P			A	P	B		
A	T	H		C	R	E	A	M	F	I	L	L	E	D		A	S	H	E	N
O	T	O		E	L	I		D	I	L	L			I	N	T	E	R	N	E
R	E	P	A	P	E	R		S	N	E	A	D		V	O	L	T	A	G	E
I	M	P	U	T	E	D		I	N	C	A		E	D	A			S	A	D
S	P	I	N	S		O	N	B	A	C	K	W	A	R	D	S		E	L	L
	T	N	T			A	O	N	E			I	S	E	E		S	S	E	
	G	I	A		S	I	N	S		C	T	S		D	S	C			
R	A	C	E	R		A	L	E		S	A	U	L	T			A	B	C	S
A	G	E		F	I	R	E	S	T	A	R	T	E	R		A	L	O	H	A
D	E	N			R	A	D		A	R	N	O		O	U	R		L	E	S
I	N	T	O	T	A	L		A	L	T	E	R	E	D	S	T	A	T	E	S
A	D	E	L	I	N	E		S	O	R	R	E	L		M	O	R	O	S	E
L	A	R	A	M	I	E		K	N	E	A	D	S		C	O	R	N	E	D

45

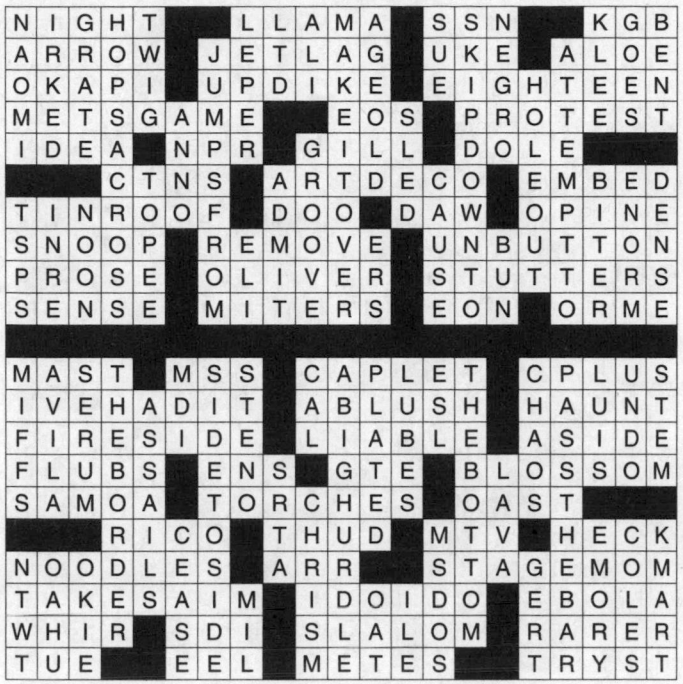

N	I	G	H	T		L	L	A	M	A		S	S	N			K	G	B
A	R	R	O	W		J	E	T	L	A	G		U	K	E		A	L	O	E
O	K	A	P	I		U	P	D	I	K	E		E	I	G	H	T	E	E	N
M	E	T	S	G	A	M	E			E	O	S		P	R	O	T	E	S	T
I	D	E	A		N	P	R		G	I	L	L		D	O	L	E			
		C	T	N	S		A	R	T	D	E	C	O		E	M	B	E	D	
T	I	N	R	O	O	F		D	O	O		D	A	W		O	P	I	N	E
S	N	O	O	P		R	E	M	O	V	E		U	N	B	U	T	T	O	N
P	R	O	S	E		O	L	I	V	E	R		S	T	U	T	T	E	R	S
S	E	N	S	E		M	I	T	E	R	S		E	O	N		O	R	M	E

M	A	S	T		M	S	S		C	A	P	L	E	T		C	P	L	U	S
I	V	E	H	A	D	I	T		A	B	L	U	S	H		H	A	U	N	T
F	I	R	E	S	I	D	E		L	I	A	B	L	E		A	S	I	D	E
F	L	U	B	S		E	N	S		G	T	E		B	L	O	S	S	O	M
S	A	M	O	A		T	O	R	C	H	E	S		O	A	S	T			
		R	I	C	O		T	H	U	D		M	T	V		H	E	C	K	
N	O	O	D	L	E	S		A	R	R		S	T	A	G	E	M	O	M	
T	A	K	E	S	A	I	M		I	D	O	I	D	O		E	B	O	L	A
W	H	I	R		S	D	I		S	L	A	L	O	M		R	A	R	E	R
T	U	E		E	E	L		M	E	T	E	S			T	R	Y	S	T	

46

A	S	A	P			N	A	S	H		A	F	T	E	R	L	I	F	E
C	A	R	O	M		L	A	N	C	E		G	L	A	D	I	A	T	O	R
E	B	O	L	I		O	C	T	A	L		N	E	W	E	S	T	E	G	G
S	E	W	I	N	G	T	H	E	B	L	U	E	S		N	E	T			
			T	I	E	T	O			W	A	S	H			R	I	F	F	
B	I	S	E	C	T		S	T	E	E	R			L	A	S	C	A	L	A
I	T	E	R	A	T	E		O	N	E		B	A	A	L		E	L	A	L
S	A	W		B	E	W	A	R	E	K	N	U	C	K	L	E		S	I	P
O	L	A	V		R	E	F	S			O	R	D	E	R	S		E	L	S
N	I	G	E	R		S	T	O	O	P	S		C	R	E	S	T	S		
S	C	E	N	E	S			S	L	E	E	P		D	E	N	T	A	L	
		A	D	L	I	B	S		S	A	D	I	S	M		S	U	E	D	E
A	D	D		I	L	O	I	L	O			U	K	E	S		T	W	O	S
L	U	V		C	A	R	D	I	N	A	L	S	I	N	E	W		A	R	S
T	R	I	M		G	E	E	S		C	O	X		U	P	A	T	R	E	E
E	S	C	A	P	E	D		E	T	U	I	S			T	S	E	T	S	E
		T	E	R	I			S	N	E	E			P	O	I	S	E		
			S	E	T		C	O	L	D	H	A	R	D	C	A	S	H	E	W
I	L	L	B	R	E	W	E	D		O	I	L	E	D		I	H	A	T	E
R	E	T	A	R	D	A	N	T		U	R	G	E	S		L	O	T	T	E
A	D	D	R	E	S	S	T	O		T	E	A	S				T	H	U	D

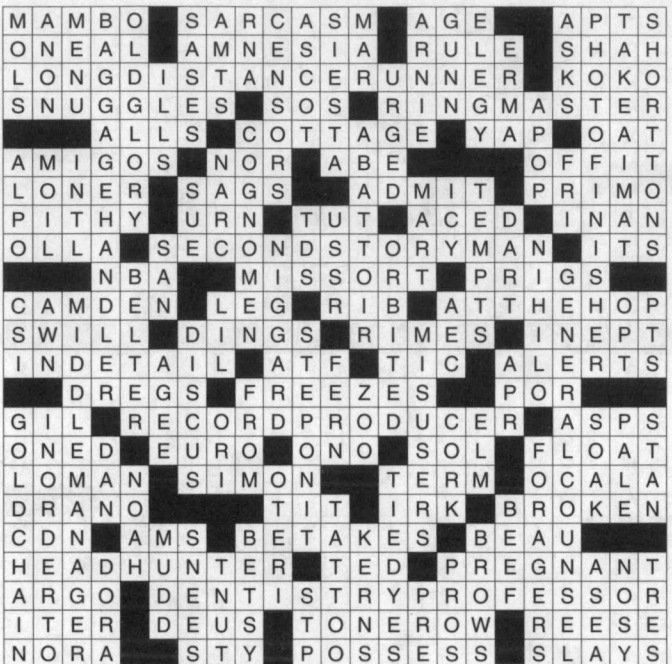

```
H A S T   J U D I     R I P O F F   A T T
O L I O   A G I N   S E C U L A R   T H O
T H E T A B L E H O P P I N G W A I T E R
T I R E S   I T A L I A     A N Y T I M E
E R R   F O E   S E E I N G     E L A N
A T A F O U R S T A R R E S T A U R A N T
    I R T   H E T     E A R T H A
  T H E   V I E   E P A   E A S T E R S
W H O S E O N L Y   E L A T E D   I C E T
H E S   S T D   O P P O S E D   Y O U D O
A S T U T E   P U R P O S E   C A N A R D
R H I N O   H E R O I N E   S O W   D O G
F O L D   H A S S L E   S E E M S T O B E
S W E E T O N   E R A   M A A   H R E
    R E L O A D   R O I   K E A
T O A S K D I N E R S I F T H E Y W A N T
A T R I   D E A C O N   O R D   L E I
R O A D I E S   G A S O I L   I S E R E
S O M E F R E S H G R O U N D P E P P E R
A L I   S I L L I E S   S T E P   O P I E
L E S   O K A Y E D   E O N S   T O D D
```

```
S A V E M E   T G I F   A C M E   S P A N
P R I M A L   R I C A   T H A D   W E D O
A G L A R E   A D A M   V A N G U A R D S
M O L L Y C O D D L E S   I N A M B U S H
S T A L L   R E A L   P A N A R A B
      A E S O P   S A T S   S Y B I L
O F F A N D O N   J A Y W A L K S   O S O
A L A D D I N   F O G   T W I N   A B E S
S A N E S T   C O D E   B E S T B E T
I N N S   C A R I B   T H E A R M Y
S K Y   C H E S T E R F I E L D S   S D S
    P A R I A H S   U R G E S   P O R T
B R A Z I L S   S E E D   C H I C L E
L O C O   D E A L   H E R   S H A N K A R
A S K   T A D P O L E S   S E I Z E S O N
B A S S I   I D E S   M A T T E
    O T A L G I A   S I T U   L A T K E
A V O C A D O S   P E N N Y P I N C H E S
N I C K N A M E S   T A U R   T U R R E T
A C H E   R A Y E   T I T I   S T E E L E
T E S T   K N E W   A L E C   A S S E S S
```

51

```
ADAPTOR  APPLIERS  USAF
RELIEVE  CRABTREE  FIFE
YANKEEDEREKJETER   OLGA
ALIENRACES     ELEV VHS
NIC    ANO  SPA   SNIPEAT
SNO  AWS  SMASH  ACORNS
      IVE  HEARKENS  ELM
MISDID  AMNESIAC  PIERS
ABELS  SRI    NTH  RODIN
RECYCLED  EXGI  OWE  APO
SRO  ABA  DIODE  LAS  LOO
AIN  ROB  INXS  BASILISK
LADER  AGA    MAR  DESTE
ANGLE  SUPERMAN  PEWTER
    OMN  STENCILS  IND
OWLETS    ROAST  TNT  ALP
REFRACT    SSN  TAO  EER
ACH  LOAF    OVERCHARGE
TAOS  THEELEMENTHELIUM
ORLY  COLLAGEN  ALLOFME
REED  HELIPORT  REDEYED
```

52

```
BAND   HEB  ANCHOR  TOGO
ALOOF  OLA  COHERE  IBID
LORDOFTHESTRINGS   GOLD
DEMORALIZE    RATCHETS
    TRY    ADS  INERT
ATWAR    PATRICKSTEWING
SHIVA  DEE  ASA  HEANEY
SEVENYEARSTITCH    DEAR
ARE  ESSIE    SOOT  PLO
MEDIGAP  AXES  PRIMATE
    STROLLERCOASTER
DETENTE  SEAN  ELLIOTT
CAR  SINS    BLAME  HRE
EVAC  CATCHSOMESTRAYS
LITHOS    BUM  AIN  ERROL
STOUTWARDBOUND  ARENA
    TRACE  EST  OMB
ENDZONES    APOSTASIES
GOOP  STALLTHEKINGSMEN
ORCA  EILEEN  LIE  STILE
SASH  ACESIT  EER  STYE
```

53

F	U	J	I		O	F	A	L	L		D	U	M	P	S		M	A	S	H
I	P	O	D		A	U	T	I	S	M	E	N	C	A	M	P	E	R	T	E
E	L	H	I		F	R	E	Q	U	E	N	T	F	L	I	E	R	O	B	E	Y
S	O	N	G	BIRD				N	E	E	R		G	L	O	W	W	O	R	M
T	A	J		M	A	G	BIRD	H	O	U	S	E		E	T	T	A		R	N	A
A	D	A	Y	A	G	O		E	U	R		T	E	T		E	D	I	S	O	N
	M	O	N	E	T		R	A	C	E		A	S	S	A	I	L
P	I	E	D		I	R	A		C	A	T	BIRD	S	E	A	T		N	E	W	S	Y
A	N	S	A		S	E	N	T		R	S	T		Y	E	G	G		I	T	S
G	P	A		A	M	A	N	A		G	E	N	A		S	E	A	BIRD	L	O	L
E	R	U	P	T		L	A	C	T	O		E	S	C	O	R	T		F	D	R
R	O	D	M	A	N		K	E	N		S	E	R		E	A	R	L	Y	BIRD
	B	U	S		O	K	A	Y	E	D		T	S	A	R	S		B	A	I	L	S
G	A	B		W	A	R	N		P	O	P	S		S	U	N	BIRD	S		F	I	E
I	T	O		A	M	A	D		E	L	O		S	N	O	B		R	E	N	E
S	E	N	A	T		F	R	E	E	A	S	A	BIRD	G	R	R		A	P	E	D
		V	E	R	T	E	X		E	R	I	N		E	A	R	N	A
F	I	G	A	R	O		T	BIRD	S		T	E	A		R	I	O	T	I	N	G
I	N	O	BIRD	D	O	G		B	A	N	I	S	H		S	N	O		N	E	E
A	V	E	R	S	E	T	O		A	S	E	C			M	A	T	E	Y
S	E	S	E		O	R	N	I	T	H	O	L	O	G	I	S	T		L	I	D	S
C	R	A	M		S	O	O	T	H	E		E	L	I	N	O	R		A	N	T	E
O	T	T	O		S	W	I	S	S		A	G	A	N	A		I	G	O	R

54

L	I	L	A	C		C	H	I	C	O	S		O	P	S		P	U	L	I
U	R	I	C	H		S	O	N	O	R	A		N	E	U	R	O	T	I	C
C	O	N	T	A	M	I	N	A	T	E	S		T	E	M	E	R	I	T	Y
E	N	D	O	R	A		O	B	O	L	S		O	P	A	R	T
N	O	R	R	I	S		R	I	P		M	A	S	C	U	L	I	N	E
C	R	O	S	S		D	A	T	A		N	A	S	H		N	Y	N	E	X
Y	E	S		M	O	A	B		X	F	A	C	T	O	R		H	A	P
		B	A	S	I	L		I	A	N		W	H	E	R	E	T	O
P	A	C	E		I	M	E	T		L	E	G	O		O	W	E	R
S	T	O	S	S	E	L		R	E	S	T	O	C	K		I	W	I	S	H
A	T	M		P	R	E	C	I	P	I	T	A	T	I	O	N		T	O	E
T	Y	P	E	E		R	E	C	I	T	E	D		L	O	G	S	O	F	F
	A	L	A	D		Y	E	T	I		S	E	L	Z		E	R	A	T
B	O	D	Y	R	U	B		H	E	S		N	I	E	C	E
A	P	R		C	U	R	T	E	S	T		C	A	S	H		S	E	T
K	E	E	P	A		S	E	A	T		I	T	O	N		A	D	A	M	S
U	N	S	I	G	H	T	L	Y		P	R	U		G	R	A	N	P	A
	L	E	I	L	A		S	M	E	A	R		L	I	E	F	O	R
U	N	I	O	N	R	E	P		K	A	N	G	A	R	O	O	W	O	R	D
F	E	A	S	T	E	R	S		I	N	D	I	G	O		T	O	R	I	O
O	N	M	E		S	S	E		P	I	S	C	E	S		S	O	D	O	M

55

```
R A M A D A   ■   D E B I T   ■   S A G   ■   G A M
E N A M E L   ■   P O M A D E   ■   T V A   ■   E R A
S A R A N F E R G U S O N   ■   P A R S O N S
T P K   ■   O I L Y   ■   ■   S N A K E   ■   D O R I A
■   ■   S O M E L I K E I T N O T   ■   E D G E D
A P O D   ■   ■   A N O X   ■   T O E I N   ■   E S A
L A U D E S   ■   G R A M P   ■   P R O N O M   ■
I N T E R N S   ■   M A I S   ■   C O N C U R
■   ■   S N O W B U S I N E S S   ■   S C O N E
W I N T E R E R S   ■   D O N O T   ■   E E N I E
O L A   ■   ■   E D I T S   ■   T A R A S   ■   A T L
O L S O N   ■   E D E M A   ■   T E N T O N N E S
L E T G O   ■   N E R O S W E L C O M E   ■
F R Y E R S   ■   ■   R O T O   ■   E R N E S T O
■   ■   P E S T E R   ■   T I E R S   ■   M I D E A R
F E U   ■   E L V I S   ■   ■   T E E S   ■   B L U R
O L D E R   ■   A S I G N O F R E L I E F   ■
M E D I A   ■   N E G R O   ■   ■   I R A N   ■   S A W
E V I N C E D   ■   N E R D O F B U F F A L O
N E N   ■   E N E   ■   A C T O R S   ■   R E A M E R
T N G   ■   S S R   ■   L O E W E   ■   A R R E S T
```

56

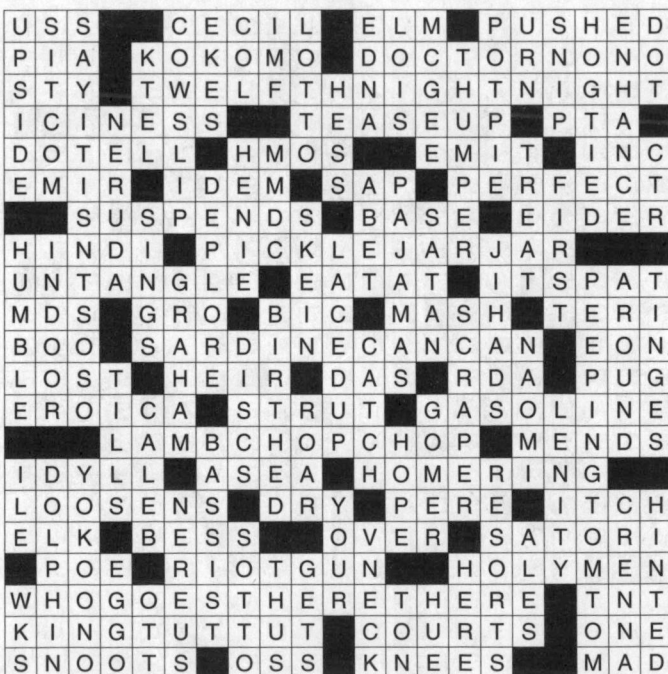

```
U S S   ■   C E C I L   ■   E L M   ■   P U S H E D
P I A   ■   K O K O M O   ■   D O C T O R N O N O
S T Y   ■   T W E L F T H N I G H T N I G H T
I C I N E S S   ■   T E A S E U P   ■   P T A   ■
D O T E L L   ■   H M O S   ■   E M I T   ■   I N C
E M I R   ■   I D E M   ■   S A P   ■   P E R F E C T
■   ■   S U S P E N D S   ■   B A S E   ■   E I D E R
H I N D I   ■   P I C K L E J A R J A R   ■
U N T A N G L E   ■   E A T A T   ■   I T S P A T
M D S   ■   G R O   ■   B I C   ■   M A S H   ■   T E R I
B O O   ■   S A R D I N E C A N C A N   ■   E O N
L O S T   ■   H E I R   ■   D A S   ■   R D A   ■   P U G
E R O I C A   ■   S T R U T   ■   G A S O L I N E
■   ■   L A M B C H O P C H O P   ■   M E N D S
I D Y L L   ■   A S E A   ■   H O M E R I N G   ■
L O O S E N S   ■   D R Y   ■   P E R E   ■   I T C H
E L K   ■   B E S S   ■   ■   O V E R   ■   S A T O R I
■   ■   P O E   ■   R I O T G U N   ■   H O L Y M E N
W H O G O E S T H E R E T H E R E   ■   T N T
K I N G T U T T U T   ■   C O U R T S   ■   O N E
S N O O T S   ■   O S S   ■   K N E E S   ■   M A D
```

```
DESI IZOD  FINAL  APSOS
ETAS RENE  ALERO  STENT
BATHMANANDROBIN  PATER
 TITAN PIA   RANGE SHE
 SEAT MAMBOS NOOR  BOA
 RAZORSOFTHELOSTARK
IRS DOT    FAA  DEVISE
DANNON SAW RHETT SLED
THEBREAKFASTSCRUB
AREA  MYRRH  GORILLA
GAZETTE ODETS UNPLUGS
 HEROINE AHEAP  AGEE
 PERMSOFENDEARMENT
PAST SAFER MDS ROARAT
OBLADI  ABA   AMY SSS
SHAVINGPRIVATERYAN
TOV STAR TSTRAP LIBS
DRE COLAS  CAR  AWGEE
ARRAU WISHYOUWEREHAIR
TEENS ASTER MALT TUNA
EDDYS YESES AXIS STEW
```

```
JAL PUTT SONANCE   RDS
ADA ESAI ALIBABA  PEEL
MOSTROCK TENONER  OMNI
ENTO FOIST JOURNALISM
SALIVA HIYA   XAXES
VIALS AGOGO GAITER
ISPEOPLEWHOCANTWRITE
 PALEST LOGIA  THAT
AGES RASH JELLS MYRRH
RESHOE ODER ESSO ETE
INTERVIEWINGPEOPLEWHO
SER LEND ENYO  EELIER
ETAPE SEPOY PARD INDY
NIDI SERIF MUCOUS
CANTTALKFORPEOPLEWHO
 MAUMEE SPARK ASHEN
AARON  COED  ATTICA
FRANKZAPPA ASNER ATTN
TUNE ATEATON CANTREAD
EBAY PARVENU ARIA SRO
RAT SNEERAT ALEX TEN
```

```
. S H U T A W A Y . A P R O N . G R E S .
A T O M I C A G E . R A I S E . L A Y U P
B E T W E E N T H E L I N E S . A N E R A
A A A . U S S . X I N G . T O D D L E R
B L I M P . A S P S . A E R I . I B E
. R E S . I M P O S E A G A G O R D E R
. M B A . O B E Y S . L G E . L U S T S
B I A N N U A L . P I A N O B A R .
E S L . S T R I P S E A R C H E S . S B A
R E L I E D . A I R E . Y O S . S T A S
B R O N C O . G I R L S . T O T A L S
E L O I . O L D . A G O G . O D E N S E
R Y N . D R A W I N G A C R O W D . D A S
. Y E S S I R E E . O P O S S U M S
A B O U T . G M A . A S P E N . O P S
L A C K O F C H A R A C T E R . T L C .
I N A . N E A T . P H Y S . R O O S T
C A N C A N S . S H O E . I C I . M M E
E N A C T . P A N E L D I S C U S S I O N
S A D I E . A X I A L . T H E S T I C K S
. S A I D . R E T R O . S U S P E N S E
```

```
C C C . G O R . D E G A S . C H A L E T
A L A M O D E . O R A T E . S H A R O N A
R E S A L E S . G R E E T . P A R E N T S
F A S T F L E E T . L E A V E S P A G E S
U R I S . L A M A S . P O E M . U R E
L E N . L I G H T F A I R . B L E S S
. D O S S I E R . A W A R D . S R I .
. P O N D . S P I L T . F E A S T E D
D E P O R T . W H E T S . W A X . T O N I
E L A T E . P I E D . E D U C E . S W I T
T O R T . R A Z E . A R E S . H A S H
O I S E . O P E R A . J U S T . B E R L E
U S E D . Y E N . S L A N T . S E E D E R
R E D S T A R . S H O U T . T A L L .
. A I L . S T E R N . P I C A S S O
C R A W L . S O U N D T O L L . A P E
E E N . C A R D . S N E E R . A L A S
R A G S T A T T E R S . S A F E V A U L T
I S O L A T E . N A O M I . I N E R T I A
S O L A C E D . T R U S T . S E R P E N T
E N A M O R . S E R G E . H E Y . D E E
```

C	O	P	A		B	E	O	F		S	T	A	L	K		G	C	L	E	F
E	R	A	T		A	T	N	O		W	I	D	E	N		L	A	I	N	E
D	A	N	R	A	T	H	E	R		A	N	J	O	U		A	R	B	Y	S
E	T	A	I	L		I	S	A		M	O	U	N	T	A	R	A	R	A	T
D	E	M		L	U	C	I	T	E		R	N	A		F	E	T	A		
			T	E	N		D	I	X	I	E	C	R	A	T	S		T	W	A
	F	O	G	G		E	M	I	L		T	D	S			C	H	E	R	
P	U	R	R	E	R		D	E	L	L	A			E	S	T	R	E	E	T
S	T	A	Y	S	A	T		E	I	G	E	R		C	R	A	B	B	Y	
S	A	T		T	A	I	L		T	A	X	I		R	A	T	A			
T	H	E	P	I	E	D	P	I	P	E	R	O	F	H	A	M	E	L	I	N
	R	I	F	F		S	P	A	R		D	E	B	T			A	D	E	
J	U	N	E	A	U		A	S	S	A	M			O	C	T	A	N	E	S
A	L	I	T	T	L	E		A	T	O	W	N		H	E	P	C	A	T	
M	A	T	A		U	Z	I		E	T	R	E		P	A	T	E			
A	N	Y		P	I	R	A	T	E	S	H	I	P		A	R	S			
		H	O	A	R		M	E	N		S	T	E	A	D	S		H	A	D
S	P	O	I	L	E	D	B	R	A	T		E	N	A		A	W	A	R	E
P	R	U	N	E		R	O	A	M	S		S	T	R	A	T	A	G	E	M
C	A	S	K	S		O	N	T	O	P		U	H	O	H		R	A	N	I
A	T	E	S	T		P	I	E	R	S		P	E	N	H		D	R	A	T

M	E	A	D	O	W		M	U	S	E	S		S	S	H	A	P	E	D
A	D	D	U	C	E	D		A	S	O	N	E		L	E	E	T	I	D	E
C	H	A	N	T	S	O	F	R	E	I	G	N		O	N	T	O	P	I	C
			G	E	T	A	L	I	F	E		D	E	U	S			E	N	O
C	A	R	E	T	S		U	N	U		L	O	N	G	E	S	T	D	A	Y
O	L	I	O			B	O	L	L	O	F	C	H	I	L	E			
C	A	T	N	I	P	S		O	A	F	S		R	A	B	B	I	
O	R	E		N	E	O		S	P	O	T		I	N	S	T	A	L	L
A	M	O		F	E	I	N	T	O	F	H	A	R	T	E		A	W	O	L
	F	L	O	P		E	R	M	A		L	O	E	W		B	L	O	B
J	A	W	E	R		P	L	O	P		G	L	U	M		S	L	O	P	E
A	T	E	A		M	A	L	L		B	I	O	G		A	L	E	F
I	B	I	D		A	I	S	L	E	O	F	W	H	I	T	E		W	P	A
M	A	G	P	I	E	S		D	I	T	S		O	R	D		A	R	T
E	T	H	I	C		S	P	I	N		C	A	S	H	C	O	W	
	P	E	A	C	E	O	F	G	N	U	S			O	K	L	A
U	N	D	E	R	B	E	L	L	Y		O	N	O		A	B	U	S	E	R
R	E	O		B	A	L	I		O	R	P	H	A	N	E	D	
G	A	Z	E	B	O	S		T	H	Y	M	E	O	F	K	N	I	G	H	T
E	L	E	V	A	T	E		I	M	E	A	N		T	H	I	N	A	I	R
D	E	S	E	R	T	S		C	O	R	N	S		S	N	I	P	P	Y

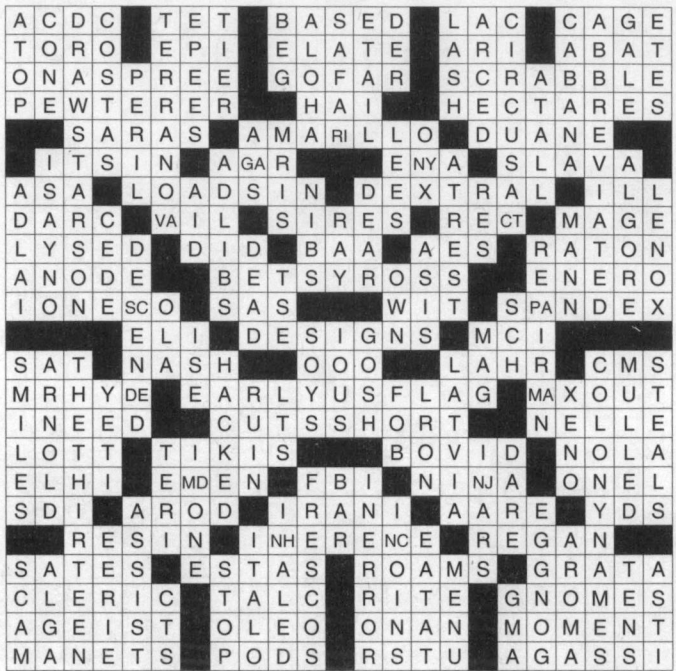

63

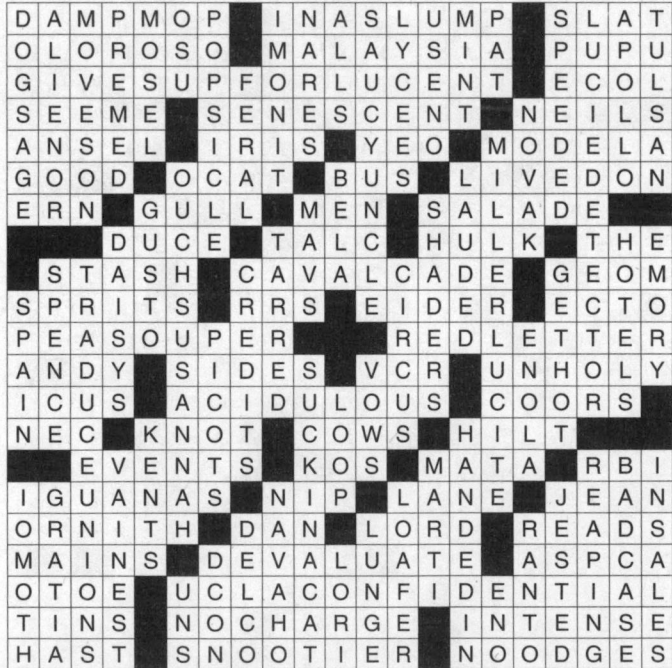

64

65

```
T A C T I C   B A D H A I R   C E M E N T
I D O I D O   A L I E N E E   A S I T I S
F I N D I N G H I M W A S P U R E L U C K
F A K E   J E T T A     E N L   D I E S
        A O L     G O I T A L O N E
H E S U N B E L I E V A B L E A T W O R K
E L A N D   E E O   U G O   T D S   D I I
A L I C I A   A N E M O N E     L O G S
T I N     N O S I R     D E F T   O R E S
H E T O O K C H A N G E S E R I O U S L Y
      B E L T     S O X     E L M S
W E W E R E A L L T O U C H E D B Y H I M
E N O S   S L O E     D O U S E     U N O
I N R E     U N C L E A N   S T E R N O
G U M   O F A   T A O   T A B   E L S I E
H I S S K I L L I S B E I N G W A S T E D
      A S S A U L T E D     I R K
S P U R   H M S     U M B R A   M O M A
W A S T E N O T I M E C A L L I N G H I M
A V E R S E   E L E M E N T   T Y R O N E
M E R E S T   R E S I D E S   H U S H E S
```

66

```
F A Q   A P P A L L   E D I T   C R U D
E C U   O C E A N I C   E U R O   R A R E
I T I   W H E R E T H E R E S A Q U I L L
N I C K N O L T E   A R I D     A X L
T O K E   O E I L   I M E A N I T   B B L
S N E E   S R A   S M A R T A S A Q U I P
    R N S   S L I T     E N T R U S T S
E B B E T S   S N O R E D   H I E
P E A N U T S   S W E D I S H   E R I
E R S   P O I N T   Q U A K E F O R E S T
E E K   I N S E R T   C R E W E L   L E E
S T E A D Y Q U I R K   I G E T A   E E S
  S T S   O R D A I N S   R A T T A I L
    T A N   E X M A T E   S H A S T A
I R R I T A T E     I S N T   E V E
Q U A R T Z A N D A L L   D H L   E Q U I
S E C   A I R R A G E   S O R E   R U P P
    E X C   O R E S   P R O M E N A D E
H O W T H E Q U E S T W A S W O N   V A C
A J A R   L E T T   A N T E I N G   E T A
G O Y A   I D E O   T W E E N S   R E C
```

71

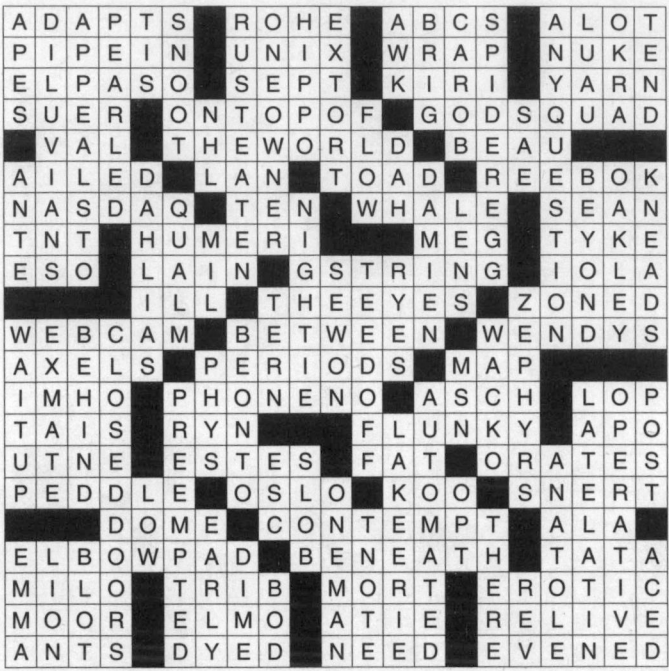

A	D	A	P	T	S		R	O	H	E		A	B	C	S		A	L	O	T
P	I	P	E	I	N		U	N	I	X		W	R	A	P		N	U	K	E
E	L	P	A	S	O		S	E	P	T		K	I	R	I		Y	A	R	N
S	U	E	R			O	N	T	O	P	O	F		G	O	D	S	Q	U	A	D
	V	A	L		T	H	E	W	O	R	L	D			B	E	A	U		
A	I	L	E	D		L	A	N		T	O	A	D		R	E	E	B	O	K
N	A	S	D	A	Q		T	E	N		W	H	A	L	E		S	E	A	N
T	N	T		H	U	M	E	R	I			M	E	G		T	Y	K	E
E	S	O		L	A	I	N		G	S	T	R	I	N	G		I	O	L	A
			I	L	L		T	H	E	E	Y	E	S		Z	O	N	E	D
W	E	B	C	A	M		B	E	T	W	E	E	N		W	E	N	D	Y	S
A	X	E	L	S		P	E	R	I	O	D	S		M	A	P			
I	M	H	O		P	H	O	N	E	N	O		A	S	C	H		L	O	P
T	A	I	S		R	Y	N			F	L	U	N	K	Y		A	P	O
U	T	N	E		E	S	T	E	S		F	A	T		O	R	A	T	E	S
P	E	D	D	L	E		O	S	L	O		K	O	O		S	N	E	R	T
			D	O	M	E		C	O	N	T	E	M	P	T		A	L	A	
E	L	B	O	W	P	A	D		B	E	N	E	A	T	H		T	A	T	A
M	I	L	O		T	R	I	B		M	O	R	T		E	R	O	T	I	C
M	O	O	R		E	L	M	O		A	T	I	E		R	E	L	I	V	E
A	N	T	S		D	Y	E	D		N	E	E	D		E	V	E	N	E	D

72

N	A	T	O		I	T	H	A	C	A		E	N	S		R	E	N	T
O	L	I	N		M	A	R	C	O	S		H	O	T	E	L	M	A	I	D
M	E	M	O	R	Y	C	H	I	P	S		S	T	E	P	S	O	V	E	R
S	T	E	R	E	O		D	E	A	D		R	A	E			A	B	A
G	A	D		B	U	S	H		D	O	C	U	M	E	N	T	J	A	M
		S	U	R	R	E	A	L		T	O	M	S		A	H	O	R	A
S	T	O	C	K	M	A	R	K	E	T	D	I	P		L	G	A	
L	A	B	R	E	A		B	A	T	A	A	N		R	A	G	T	I	M	E
A	R	I	A	D	N	E		A	L	S		R	E	C	E	S	S	E	D
W	A	S	P			S	C	O	T	C	H	T	A	P	E	R	O	L	L	S
			D	I	T	T	O			O	K	A	Y	S			
C	O	M	P	U	T	E	R	F	R	E	E	Z	E	S		G	A	T	E
B	R	O	O	D	E	R	S		E	R	A		T	I	R	A	D	E	S
S	I	M	M	E	R	S		T	W	I	S	T	S		C	O	M	E	A	T
		P	D	S		T	H	R	E	E	H	O	L	E	P	U	N	C	H
A	T	Y	O	U		H	E	R	O		S	U	R	E	B	E	T	
F	O	A	M	P	E	A	N	U	T	S		T	A	U	T		G	A	P
L	O	C		T	B	A		E	A	S	T		C	O	U	R	S	E
A	B	H	O	R	R	E	N	T		S	H	R	I	N	K	W	R	A	P	S
C	A	T	T	R	E	A	T	S		H	E	A	R	S	E		N	I	C	K
	D	S	C	S		S	S	E		A	S	P	E	C	T		S	L	A	Y

B	A	T		A	R	R	A	N	T		E	S	T	E	R		A	T	R	A
E	P	A		G	U	I	N	E	A		C	O	R	G	I		T	H	E	N
R	O	C	K	E	T	L	A	W	N	C	H	A	I	R	S		M	E	L	T
E	L	K	E		T	E	L		A	D	O	P	T	E	E		O	D	I	E
F	L	O	P	P	Y	D	E	S	K	S		S	O	T	S			I	N	C
T	O	N	T	O			C	P	A		N	U	N	S		M	C	V	I	E
			L	O	F	T	Y		S	O	D	S		G	A	R	A	N	D	
	A	F	F	I	X	E	S		A	C	T	S		A	R	R	A	N	G	E
S	L	U	I	C	E	D		S	P	A	T		B	I	O	T	I	C		
C	O	T	T	E	N		C	U	P	B	O	A	R	D	W	A	G	O	N	S
O	H	O			C	A	L	L	B	O	X	E	S			M	I	A		
W	A	N	T	T	O	M	A	K	E	A	B	E	D		F	R	I	E	N	D
		T	O	O	K	O	N		G	R	A	D		G	U	A	R	D	E	D
S	T	O	R	M	I	N		L	A	D	D		S	A	S	H	A	Y	S	
P	A	R	S	E	E		G	A	T	S		R	U	L	E	R				
E	X	P	O	S		C	O	N	E		L	A	M		A	N	S	E	L	
A	T	E		C	L	O	D		S	O	F	A	S	C	H	O	I	C	E	
K	I	D	S		R	E	D	F	L	A	G		T	A	O		E	E	K	S
S	T	O	P		E	N	J	O	Y	Y	O	U	R	S	H	E	L	V	E	S
O	L	E	O		S	C	O	R	N		U	T	A	H	A	N		E	R	E
F	E	S	T		T	H	E	M	E		T	E	N	A	N	T		S	T	E

R	A	S	T	A	S		B	A	S	H	E	D		B	R	E	A	K	U	P
A	L	L	O	U	T		I	L	L	I	N	I		R	E	D	T	A	P	E
G	L	I	N	D	A		G	M	I	N	O	R		I	M	E	A	N	I	T
G	E	N	E	I	N	A	B	O	T	T	L	E		B	I	N	D	S		
E	L	K	S		L	E	N			S	E	X			A	D	D			
D	E	Y		S	O	U	N	D	B	A	R	R	E	R		C	A	S	I	O
		F	I	R	M		A	W	A	R	E		P	A	S	C	A	L		
B	A	D	E	G	G	S		S	C	A	N	S		I	L	L	W	I	L	L
A	L	I	E	N	S		S	T	O	I	C		A	R	A	F	A	T		
T	O	N	T	O		P	E	I	N	T	H	E	S	K	Y		N	Y	P	D
C	N	N		R	E	R	U	N			A	H	E	A	D		C	H	E	
H	E	E	L		J	U	S	T	M	A	R	R	E	D		E	T	H	A	N
		R	A	V	E	N	S		O	P	A	L	S		B	A	R	E	S	T
S	E	A	R	A	C	E		C	R	A	Z	Y		C	A	R	A	F	E	S
W	I	N	G	I	T		B	R	A	C	E		R	U	M	P				
A	R	D	E	N		S	O	I	L	E	D	S	U	E	M	E		T	S	E
P	E	A		L	I	P				T	N	T			D	A	T	A		
	M	A	D	A	M		B	E	D	T	I	M	E	S	T	O	R	E	S	
I	H	O	P	E	S	O		A	R	E	O	L	A		H	U	N	G	R	Y
C	A	V	E	M	E	N		L	O	C	A	L	S		A	T	H	E	N	A
E	Y	E	S	O	R	E		T	S	K	T	S	K		Q	U	O	T	A	S

75

Grid 75:

```
A J A R ■ I L S A ■ T W I G ■ A L A S K A
S A G A ■ N O T I ■ H O N E ■ L A P E L S
T R O T ■ F O U R T E E N T H S T R E E T
A G R E E O N ■ P E R ■ W O O S ■ H E R ■
R O A D S ■ ■ L O S E S B I G ■ ■ R E N O
■ N E X T S T O P T I M E S S Q U A R E ■
■ ■ ■ R I O T S ■ S U R E ■ A N N E X ■ ■
■ I M E A N I T ■ I N R E ■ K N I T ■ ■ ■
S T A N D C L E A R O F T H E D O O R S ■
L A R V A E ■ L I L ■ B E A N ■ O I L ■ ■
A L L Y ■ G O E S O F F O N ■ T O R O ■ ■
B I O ■ S C A R ■ C O E ■ A C U M E N ■ ■
■ A N O T H E R T R A I N I S C O M I N G
■ ■ P E A L ■ W I L L ■ L O T U S E S ■ ■
■ A C R I D ■ F I G S ■ T E N O R ■ ■ ■ ■
■ T R A N S F E R H E R E F O R T H E A ■
B A Y H ■ I L L T R E A T ■ ■ T E L L Y ■
I T O ■ P E R T ■ V I M ■ O F V A L U E ■
K I N D L Y S T E P I N S I D E ■ D I M S
E M I N O R ■ I M A C ■ U V E A ■ T O N E
D E C A D E ■ P U R E ■ P E S T ■ O T I S
```

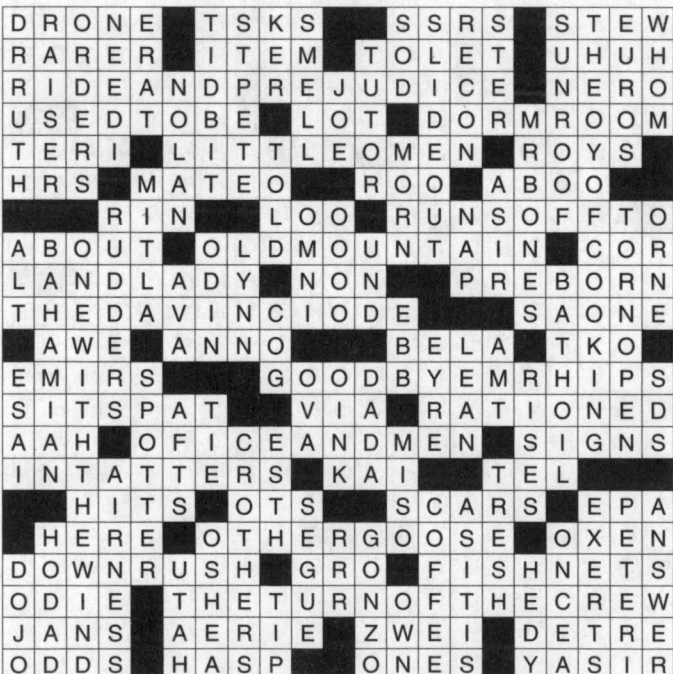

76

Grid 76:

```
D R O N E ■ T S K S ■ ■ S S R S ■ S T E W
R A R E R ■ I T E M ■ T O L E T ■ U H U H
R I D E A N D P R E J U D I C E ■ N E R O
U S E D T O B E ■ L O T ■ D O R M R O O M
T E R I ■ L I T T L E O M E N ■ R O Y S ■
H R S ■ M A T E O ■ R O O ■ A B O O ■ ■ ■
■ ■ ■ R I N ■ L O O ■ R U N S O F F T O
A B O U T ■ O L D M O U N T A I N ■ C O R
L A N D L A D Y ■ N O N ■ P R E B O R N ■
T H E D A V I N C I O D E ■ ■ S A O N E ■
■ A W E ■ A N N O ■ B E L A ■ T K O ■ ■ ■
E M I R S ■ ■ G O O D B Y E M R H I P S
S I T S P A T ■ V I A ■ R A T I O N E D
A A H ■ O F I C E A N D M E N ■ S I G N S
I N T A T T E R S ■ K A I ■ T E L ■ ■ ■
■ ■ H I T S ■ O T S ■ S C A R S ■ E P A
■ H E R E ■ O T H E R G O O S E ■ O X E N
D O W N R U S H ■ G R O ■ F I S H N E T S
O D I E ■ T H E T U R N O F T H E C R E W
J A N S ■ A E R I E ■ Z W E I ■ D E T R E
O D D S ■ H A S P ■ O N E S ■ Y A S I R
```

```
N E W S   M T A   A D O   H O M E S A L E
A L O T   B U C K L E S   E V A P E R O N
H E R O S A N D W I C H   F O R E N O O N
S A L O N   A C A C I A     L E A N N E
    D D E     N I M   M A R I S T
S A S   E E R O S A A R I N E N   E R O S
A L F   R E A P     L I L T S   E R I C H
L E A   S T I E S   S K I T   D O N E E
E R I K A   E N R A G E S   A C T S S A D
M O R A S S   I A G O   H U R L   T E N S
      T H E R O S E T T A S T O N E
B L A H   L A N E   B A K U   D R R U T H
Y O G A M A T   R H Y M E R S   A S S A Y
A W A R E   A W H O   A S P E R   D I P
G E T I N   T I E R S   E K E D   I N O
E D E N   J A P A N E S E R O S E   P T S
        E M O T E D   C O P     B I L
C H E R U B     T R I C I A   U B O L T
A E R O L O G Y   Z E R O S U M G A M E S
P I L S E N E R   A C E T A T E   R A N K
P R E S S E R S   R Y E   W O W   S T A S
```

```
M A N I C   L E A F   O L G A   S E R F S
A R E N A   E R G O   B O O N   A S O R T
S C O T M A S T E R   L A N D R Y S O A P
H O N   E L S E   E Z I N E   A N O M I E
      S L O E   S T A G   O H N O   M D T
J E W E L E R S L O P E   N E G   L A N E
O T I T I S   O Y L       R O T A T O R
T E S S A   C O L D W A T E R F A C E T S
D R E   M A N Y   O L E G   F I T
O N O   M A P   T R I A G E   W I C C A
W A N D E R E D L O N E L Y A S A C L O D
N L E R S   K E E N O N   T I N   E L M
      I S O   C O I F   A P E X   A L I
A F T E R N O O N O F A F A N   D I N E R
T R E S S E D       S I N   R E N E G E
T E N T   L I Z   A H O S E D I V I D E D
E D S   L I N E   D E N T   E D I T
M E T E O R   P H O N E   G A G A   K E Y
P R O D F A T H E R   M A I D E N A N T S
T I N E A   E Y R E   A R A L   C H O R E
S C E N T   T R O D   N Y N Y   E S T E R
```

79

81

```
S A D   N I P S     I M A R I     F L O P S
A N A L O G U E     I R O N E D     A U D I O
M A N I T O B A     S A L T L I C K C I T Y
B I C K E R S T R E E T     O R I E N T S
A L E E       T E E     T A T E R S
      A K E L A     B O O K I E S     W A D
M R S     G I V E M E A B R I C K     J I M I
C E N S U R E     U S E I N     S O C I O
C N O T E S     C P R     S T R E A K E R
L E W I S     C H E E R U P     O M A N I
    W F L     Q U I C K E R O A T S     M S S
      L E T U S     S A S S E R S     P I L E D
B L I T H E S T       U M A     P I R A T E
L A C T O     U S U A L     L A C O N I C
E L K O     B I R T H D A Y K I C K     D N A
D O S     A I R B A S E     A I D E S
      B U N I O N     E L L     A P E S
B O A R D E D     S I R L O I N S T I C K
U N D E R T I C K I N G     T O E T O T O E
S C O N E     U P E N D S     O N E O N O N E
T E S T Y     M A N G O     N A D A     N O T
```

82

```
A L L * S     T R I B     S C R A M     L O A D
V I O L A     O O N A     T H E R E     U N D O
A P R I L     B Y F I T S & * T S     T & E M
S P E N T     E A R T H     L E I S     H O P E
T I N G E D     L O S E     E A S E M E N T S
      D I G I N     S I R     T S A R
    C W T     M I S T     E R S     R A N T O
P L E A S A N T     T V A     P A G I N @ E D
H & L I N G       I R E     B I T E S     I L E
D E L L A     A D M E N     R E E L     N O E S
    S T O P T H E # @ %  *  & C U S S I N G
S T I R     W O K E     S T E E P     H E W E D
T I M     A I L E D     O L D     P A C I N O
U N E A R N E D     O L E     S H A R E D I N
B E D I M       S T U     C H A N     S E C
      R O A D     I T T     R E M I T
# S T E R L I N G     I C E D     C E N S E S
C & I D     C A I N     O R @ E D     N A O M I
A I D A     A L T E R N @ I V E     % I L E S
K E E L     P E R R Y     E V I L     E V E N S
E R S E     P R O S E     S E L L     R E D D Y
```

83

```
R I F T S   E L M S   F L A R E   H A V E
A L L A H   T O O T   L A V E R   O M E N
Y O U R E G H A N A B U Y A F A T B I R D
      R O O F   K R I S     H O R S E
S O F F I T S   R E A D   C A R E S S E D
U P L I F T   A E O N   S H O A T
S T U F F A N D P U T I T I N J A P A N
H I K E S   E M I T   D I C E   E P O S
I C E S   T W I N   T I T O   S A T I R E
    B E E R   K R O C   C A L I S T A
T A I W A N L E G W I T H T H E O T H E R
A L M O N D S   R A T S   R A N T
L O A V E S   C O N E   F I N S   G R I T
L U G E   C R U Z   S L U G   P E E V E
  D O N O T L E T A N Y O N E R U S S I A
    D R O P S   I R A E   U N T I E S
B A C K D A T E   S K I T   L I C E N S E
E N R O L     S O O N   P A N T
F E E D Y O U R H U N G A R Y G U E S T S
I A M A   U N I O N   E V I L   A L O H A
T R E K   R O P E D   S E G A   L I N E D
```

84

```
P G S   F E B   I A M     P O M A D E
D O E S   O L E S T R A   P E R C A L E S
Q U A K E R F L O A T S   A G I T A T E S
B A S A L T   F L Y C H R O M O S O M E
A C C   K E E P T O   O I S E
C H A S E   S H Y   T S P S   S I T T E R
H E L P   E T A   S K I P I T   S H U L A
    L E T T E R S T O D E A R F L A B B Y
T W O C A R   A I R   E R N I E   T E A S
R E P I N E   O N U S     P U B S
E S S A Y   P H O T O F L O P   I N F E R
    L A M E   L I A R   O T O O L E
E A S T   I A M B I   L I I   R E J O I N
F L A I R T R A F F I C C O N T R O L
T O S E A   L I L I T H   L E S   K I R K
S E E S T O   N A T E   B E T   M E S O N
    W A L T   T O S S E R   H B O
F L O R A L H I S T O R Y   L I A N E S
L I M A B E A N   H E A D F L U S H E R S
A N I S E T T E   A D D S A L T   A S T O
W A T E R S   I S E   A B E   S A S
```

85

L	O	O	N			A	L	A			I	B	I	Z	A			S	T	O	L	E
E	T	N	A		M	A	R	K	T	W	A	I	N			B	O	R	E	A	L
W	I	T	H	O	U	T	S	A	Y	I	N	G	T	H	E	W	O	R	D	I
D	O	H		F	S	T	O	P				S	E	A	B	E	D			
E	S	E		T	E	E	N		A	S	P		S	L	O	T		T	L	C
R	E	F	E	E	D	S		W	I	L	L	I		E	P	O	C	H	A	L
		O	V	A			J	A	M	A	I	C	A	N			R	E	B	A
A	D	U	E		C	H	E	R		T	E	E	M		S	H	I	M	O	N
T	U	R	N		R	A	F	F	L	E	S		E	Q	U	A	T	O	R	
E	M	T	S		U	N	F	A	I	R		D	R	U	B	S		N	U	S
A	B	H	O	R		S	E	R	T		D	I	I	I		H	O	R	N	E
T	W	O		A	D	O	R	E		M	U	S	C	L	Y		G	O	I	N
	A	F	F	I	R	M	S		C	A	N	T	A	T	A		L	E	O	N
G	I	J	A	N	E		O	O	H	S		O	N	S	O		E	D	N	A
E	T	U	I		A	N	T	I	H	E	R	O			P	R	O			
S	E	L	L	E	R	S		C	L	I	N	T		F	R	E	S	C	O	S
T	R	Y		M	I	T	T		L	E	D		F	L	E	A		T	U	M
		S	E	C	R	E	T				P	R	E	S	S		R	T	E	
W	R	O	T	E	A	O	N	E	S	E	N	T	E	N	C	E	W	I	L	L
V	A	N	E	R	N		S	A	M	M	Y	S	O	S	A		A	N	E	T
A	D	A	M	S		E	R	A	S	E		N	E	N		G	E	T	S	

86

W	H	I	R	R		D	M	I	T	R	I		O	P	E	R	A	H	A	T
O	O	Z	E	D		I	A	M	B	I	C		R	E	D	I	V	I	D	E
W	H	A	T	A	M	E	S	S	A	G	E		E	L	I	C	I	T	O	R
S	O	A	S		A	S	S		A	T	H	L	E	T	E		C	B	S	
	S	K	I	E	R		E	S	C		E	A	S	E		G	H	E	E	
		N	A	V	Y	Y	A	R	D	A	G	E		P	E	R	I			
	D	C	A	R	E	A		W	E	I	S	S		A	I	R	I	N	G	S
H	O	H		F	L	O	U	T	E	D		E	G	G	I	N	G	O	N	
A	R	E	O	L	A		P	O	P	U	P	A	D	A	G	E		P	R	O
L	A	C	T	A	T	E	D		P	A	R	I	T	Y		L	O	E	B	
	K	O	P		A	R	I	D		L	I	F	E		T	I	S			
A	N	T	S		T	R	A	D	E	S		I	S	T	H	A	T	S	O	
N	E	H		H	O	T	F	O	O	T	A	G	E		H	E	R	A	L	D
T	W	I	L	I	G	H	T		O	N	A	D	A	R	E		G	U	S	
I	T	S	O	K	A	Y		A	S	P	I	N		R	E	D	D	E	R	
	O	W	E	S		B	U	M	S	T	E	E	R	A	G	E				
P	I	U	S		T	A	T	A		A	F	L	D	E	C	A	F			
O	R	T		A	T	A	L	O	S	S		D	E	E		I	M	A	X	
S	E	A	R	C	H	M	E		H	O	O	V	E	R	D	A	M	A	G	E
E	N	G	I	N	E	E	R		E	N	T	E	R	S		R	A	N	I	N
D	E	E	P	E	N	D	S		D	E	T	E	S	T		P	L	A	N	A

87

S	A	T	R	A	P		B	R	I	T	I	S	H		A	W	A	K	E	D
E	Q	U	A	T	E		S	A	V	A	N	N	A		S	A	L	A	M	I
C	U	T	T	H	E	P	A	P	E	R	F	O	L	D	A	N	D	T	I	E
T	A	S	S	E	L	S			P	A	R	L	E		T	O	O	T	S	
			N	E	T		S	H	O	N	E		A	H	A					
B	A	L	L	A	D		G	L	I	N	T		T	R	A	D	U	C	E	D
O	D	I	E		S	H	I	N		S	H	E	D		S	O	L	A		
S	E	N	T	E	N	C	E	D	T	O	T	H	I	S	J	O	B	A	M	I
O	L	D		N	O	O	N	E		B	R	A	N	T		V	A	S	E	S
M	A	Y		S	L	O	T		P	L	A	N	K		E	N	T	R	Y	
		G	N	A	T		C	R	I	M	E		L	A	R	K				
B	E	L	L	A		S	L	O	G	S		G	A	L	A		A	D	Z	
O	N	A	I	R		S	T	O	W	E		P	E	R	I	L		C	E	E
W	O	N	D	E	R	C	O	U	L	D	A	L	E	G	A	L	C	H	A	P
E	C	C	E		H	A	U	T		N	I	N	E			H	E	L	P	
S	H	E	R	B	E	R	T		H	A	N	N	A		U	S	E	D	T	O
		Y	A	P		L	E	R	O	Y		A	T	E						
A	H	E	A	P		I	S	O	L	A			C	A	N	T	O	N	S	
F	I	N	D	A	W	A	Y	T	O	B	E	A	T	T	H	E	W	R	A	P
A	R	O	U	S	E		N	U	T	L	I	K	E		A	C	A	C	I	A
N	E	W	E	S	T		E	S	S	E	N	C	E		N	A	S	A	L	S

88

C	A	R	R		B	L	E	A	K		B	E	S	S		I	T	C	H
O	L	I	O		E	A	R	T	H		K	U	B	L	A		N	O	R	A
H	I	N	T	S	F	R	O	M	A	B	E	L	A	R	D		S	W	A	T
N	E	G	A	T	O	R	S		T	A	N	G	Y		D	O	I	N	G	S
			T	O	R	Y		M	A	R	N	E		N	E	A	T			
A	L	C	O	V	E		N	I	M	O	Y		C	O	N	F	U	S	E	D
D	E	A	R	E		D	I	N	I	N	G	O	A	T	E	S		T	A	I
D	A	M	S		P	R	E	S			A	R	I	D		T	E	R	M	
E	S	P		B	L	A	C	K	W	E	S	S	O	N		L	I	E	N	S
R	E	G	U	L	A	T	E		A	D	H	E	M		R	U	M	P	S	
		O	B	I	T	S		M	Y	E	R	S		M	O	R	E	L		
	F	L	O	S	S		L	A	I	N	E		P	A	N	C	R	E	A	S
A	L	I	A	S		B	U	R	N	S	W	R	E	N	C	H		J	L	O
G	O	A	T		P	A	N	G			O	R	E	O		T	I	E	R	
R	A	T		R	A	G	G	E	D	Y	A	M	O	S		C	A	L	V	E
A	T	H	L	E	T	E	S		R	E	L	E	T		W	H	I	L	E	S
		O	P	E	L		D	I	A	L	S		T	E	A	L				
A	C	T	I	O	N		G	E	N	R	E		O	R	A	N	G	I	S	H
L	O	U	T		T	H	A	N	K	S	G	I	V	I	N	G	A	D	A	M
M	U	T	E		E	A	S	T	S		E	L	A	T	E		T	O	R	O
S	P	U	R		D	I	P	S		D	E	L	E	D		E	L	I	S	

89

A	L	T	A	R		A	W	L		A	C	C	T			C	L	A	P	S
G	U	I	D	E	R	A	I	L		C	I	A	O		C	R	E	D	I	T
I	L	L	A	T	E	A	S	E		T	A	R	P		H	A	V	A	N	A
N	U	T	M	E	G		E	W	E	R		54	40	O	R	F	I	G	H	T
		12	A	N	G	R	Y	M	E	N			N	I	T		I	O	U	
A	C	E		M	A	R		N	O	S	E	J	O	B	S		M	O	L	E
V	E	N	D		L	I	T		S	T	A	R	R		F	U	S	E	S	
I	N	G	A		P	H	D	S		N	E	E	S	O	N					
A	T	A	R	I		S	E	R	E	N	A		A	P	R	I	L	15		
N	U	G	E	N	T		B	O	X	E	S		S	K	I	M		I	M	F
C	R	I	S	T	O	52	P	I	C	K	U	P		C	A	S	S	I	E	
A	Y	N		E	R	A	S		S	C	O	R	E		E	T	H	A	N	E
	21	G	R	A	M	S		M	O	U	S	E	S		S	A	L	U	D	
	A	R	E	T	H	A		T	A	C	T		M	I	T	E				
F	A	R	M	S		R	O	M	P	S		H	U	N		U	S	E	R	
L	I	E	S		C	I	T	Y	G	I	R	L		N	O	S		A	S	S
O	R	B		G	O	D		13	G	O	I	N	G	O	N	30				
T	H	E	L	O	W	E	R	48	N	C	A	A		D	O	R	S	A	L	
S	O	C	I	A	L		O	H	N	O		I	N	A	G	R	O	O	V	E
A	S	C	O	T	S		B	R	E	R		S	C	R	E	E	C	H	E	S
M	E	A	N	S		E	S	A	I		E	Y	E		S	K	O	R	T	

90

I	T	S	T	I	M	E			K	U	D	U			C	L	A	R	A	
F	R	O	W	N	A	T		S	P	I	N	E	S		O	U	T	B	O	X
F	I	N	I	S	H	A	H	E	A	D	O	F	S	C	H	E	D	U	L	E
Y	E	A	S	T		O	R	B	S		T	R	O	Y			T	E	L	
	D	R	T		M	A	N	I	L	A		L	O	A	D	S	O	F		
	A	G	E	B	E	F	O	R	E	B	E	A	U	T	Y					
	P	I	N	E	T	A	R		O	M	I	T	S		T	A	S	E	R	
F	E	M	A	L	E		T	R	U	A	N	T		S	E	N	O	R	A	
G	R	A	N	D	O	P	E	N	I	N	G	S	A	L	E	S		F	A	N
S	I	N	K		R	O	T	U	N	D			E	A	T	A	T			
	L	I	L	Y		E	S	T	D		L	P	G	A		S	C	A	D	
	D	E	A	R	S			T	A	O	I	S	T		T	R	U	E		
U	P	I		W	A	Y	B	E	H	I	N	D	T	H	E	T	I	M	E	S
M	O	O	I	N	G		A	D	A	G	E	S			N	O	V	O	T	E
P	E	T	R	I		P	R	I	Z	E		M	U	T	T	E	R	S		
		O	N	E	A	F	T	E	R	A	N	O	T	H	E	R				
S	T	U	N	G	U	N			S	L	A	T	E	S		O	P	T		
I	R	S		R	E	S	T		M	A	G	I			A	S	O	N	E	
F	O	R	M	F	O	L	L	O	W	I	N	G	F	U	N	C	T	I	O	N
T	U	D	O	R	S		I	N	P	L	A	Y		S	I	L	E	N	T	I
S	T	A	C	Y		P	E	A	K			B	L	U	R	T	E	D		

91

F	A	I	R			I	F	S			V	A	L	I	D			R	A	Z	E
R	O	T	E		M	A	O		F	E	D	O	R	A		D	O	N	O	R
I	R	S	A	U	D	I	T		I	N	D	I	A	N	A	J	O	N	E	S
S	T	E	T	S	O	N		A	N	I	L	S		C	O	S	M	O		
C	A	L	A	M	I	T	Y	J	A	N	E		L	I	L					
H	E	F		A	N	N	E	A	L	S		W	I	N		B	E	R	E	T
			G	E	N	X			C	H	E	G	U	E	V	A	R	A		
R	E	D	C	R	O	S	S		T	V	D	A	D		S	E	E	N	I	T
A	N	O	R	A	K	S		B	O	O	S	T		F	U	R	N	A	C	E
E	G	G	O	S			K	E	P	I		A	L	L	A			T	A	R
		C	H	A	R	L	E	S	D	E	G	A	U	L	L	E				
P	I	C			K	E	M	P		I	O	U	S			E	M	O	J	I
A	G	O	U	T	I	S		B	U	N	N	Y		D	A	T	A	S	E	T
B	O	W	L	E	R		B	E	R	G	S		L	E	F	T	J	A	B	S
S	T	A	N	L	A	U	R	E	L			A	U	E	R					
T	O	N	A	L		N	I	P		P	O	R	K	P	I	E		S	B	A
			T	K	O		B	U	S	T	E	R	K	E	A	T	O	N		
		T	O	Q	U	E		E	E	R	I	E		O	A	K	L	A	N	D
C	H	E	F	B	O	Y	A	R	D	E	E		C	O	N	S	O	M	M	E
S	U	R	F	S		E	D	G	I	E	R		A	T	E		N	O	O	R
I	B	I	S		D	O	O	M	S		T	S	R		E	S	T	S		

92

S	P	O	C	K			O	H	C	R	U	D		B	I	A	N	C	A
R	U	S	H	A	T		R	E	R	O	S	E		P	A	N	S	O	U	T
I	N	H	E	R	E		G	A	I	N	O	N		U	N	C	A	S	E	S
		A	D	A	M		A	R	M		F	I	G	L	E	A	V	E	S	
			O	P	E	N	S	E	S	A	M	E			N	E	R	T	S
U	N	M	A	K	E	S		E	A	U		N	T	W	T		V	I	N
N	E	A	R	E	R	T	O		N	B	A	S	T	A	R		P	I	C	O
M	A	T		A	S	A	P			I	L	L	B	E	B	A	C	K	
E	T	A	I	L		H	O	N	O	R	E	E		A	T	R	E	S	T
E	T	T	U	B	R	U	T	E		W	R	I	T	E					
T	R	A	I	P	S	E		A	K	A		C	H	A	L	I	C	E	
		I	H	O	P	S		H	U	L	K	S	M	A	S	H			
L	A	C	U	N	A		T	O	L	E	A	S	E		S	O	W	E	R
N	E	V	E	R	M	O	R	E		C	A	N	T			E	M	I
A	G	R	A		P	I	L	E	U	P	S		P	A	R	A	S	A	I	L
M	E	T		I	S	L	E		E	T	A		N	O	M	E	R	C	Y
A	L	A	I	N		M	Y	P	R	E	C	I	O	U	S				
	H	I	M	A	L	A	Y	A	S		N	U	N		S	C	H	S	.
H	A	N	D	B	A	G		C	H	R	O	M	E		E	R	O	T	I	C
S	I	T	U	A	T	E		H	A	N	G	E	R		R	A	M	O	N	A
T	R	Y	E	R	S			T	W	A	S	N	T		Y	E	A	S	T

93

```
T A T A   R A I T T   F I R     J L O
I V A N   D O D D E R   E T O   B L U E S
F I C K L E T H E R A P I S T   R A J A H
F A T H O M   D A N C I N G C U I S I N E
    I S N O T     S E E T O   N E S T E A
N Y C     A R C     S O L I     S S S
B E A A S A B E A V E R   D E C K O U T
C A L L O N   I F E V E R   T E E D
    B U Y O N E G E T O N E F R I Z Z Y
S N O   N A H     L A M E R   P L E A S
C O D E D   H A R K   P O O R   L E D G E
A B O R C   E L E N A     I C U   S S R
M U R R A Y L O V E S C O M P A N Y
    O R E L   S A T I V A   S K O K I E
  P A R D O N S   D I G U P D E S S E R T
Y E N   M O A T     M S U     N E A
E T A L I A   T W I S T   I S T O O
A U T U M N S P E C T R U M   H A G G L E
S N O R E   A R E Y O U F O R I S R A E L
T I M E D   W E T   R E O P E N   E M I L
Y A Y     S P Y   E S S E X   S E A S
```

94

```
P A S S   A B E A D   T R A S H   I B M
A L T A   A L U M N A   H A G U E   C E E
L I E F   P O R T A B L E S H E L T E R S
E N V E L O P S     S I R   A T T A C K S
R E E L E D   T A G A L O G   E T A S
    M Y A   M Y A U T O B I O G R A P H Y
E V A   S P I N A L     E L H I     P I E
C O R N E L L   S A I D   M O C   E R A
A L T E   S N L   G R A N D S T A N D E R
S T I E S   E E K   A R E A   T S U
H A N D W A R M E R   C A R R O T C A K E
    N E I   M R E D   T E E   E L L E S
E A S T E R P A R A D E   S P A   E E L S
A N T   T I O   L E A N   A R T I C L E
R T E   E L M O   S O F R E E   B I N
L I V E F R O M N E W Y O R K   T W A
  D E A R   M E T H A N E   B R I L L O
C O N T E S T   A N Y   I S L A N D E R
I T S S A T U R D A Y N I G H T   I W O N
G E O   K O R E A   E T C H E S   N I N O
S S N   S A N D Y   S H U T S   G N A T
```

95

Puzzle 95

S	C	A	L	I	A		B	A	S	S	O		A	S	S	O	R	T
L	A	B	O	R	S		C	O	C	O	O	N		S	H	O	V	E	I	T
I	D	O	N	T	K	N	O	W	H	O	W	E		S	I	L	E	N	T	I
M	E	D	E		S	A	L	T	Y			D	E	E	N		R	E	A	M
S	T	E	W	S		H	A	I		L	I	G	H	T	G	R	E	E	N	E
			O	W	N		S	E	C	U	R	E	S		L	E	X
M	G	M	L	I	O	N		S	O	L	O			N	E	S	T	L	E	S
C	H	E	F	S	H	A	T		B	U	N	S	O	F	S	T	E	E	L	E
J	A	M	E	S		B	R	A	S		I	T	A	L		I	N	T	O	W
O	N	O		K	O	O	L		O	N	Y	X		B	V	D	S
B	A	R		S	H	O	P	P	I	N	G	M	A	L	L	E		L	A	B
		I	N	E	Z		H	A	W	S		I	C	E	T		O	R	R
D	R	A	I	N		M	I	C	A		H	E	A	D		E	B	O	L	A
V	O	L	C	A	N	I	C	A	S	H	E		N	U	T	C	A	S	E	S
R	O	S	E	T	E	A		H	A	R	E		P	R	O	C	E	S	S
			P	O	W		I	F	A	T	A	L	L		E	L	K
J	O	K	E	R	S	W	I	L	D	E		E	E	K		E	P	C	O	T
A	G	R	O		R	O	S	Y		S	C	R	E	E		A	C	A	I
C	L	A	P	F	O	R		L	A	Y	I	T	O	N	T	H	I	C	K	E
K	E	I	L	L	O	R		O	H	E	N	R	Y		D	E	N	V	E	R
	S	T	E	A	M	Y		W	A	N	N	A		S	T	E	I	N	S

96

Puzzle 96

V	I	C	A	R	S		I	N	P	I	E	C	E	S		A	M	P	L	Y
O	R	E	C	A	R		F	O	O	T	N	O	T	E		N	O	L	I	E
W	E	R	E	W	O	L	F	B	L	I	T	Z	E	R		G	O	A	L	S
	T	I	D		O	Y	S		S	W	E		A	P	R		Y	A	M
I	S	I	T	A	G	O			S	I	N		P	R	I	E	S
S	E	T		T	O	M	B	S	T	O	N	E	P	H	I	L	L	I	P	S
S	E	U	R	A	T		L	A	V		E	R	E		M	Y	S	T	I	C
U	P	D	O		A	D	O	L	P	H		E	T	A		E	S	T	A
E	Y	E	O	F	N	E	W	T	G	I	N	G	R	I	C	H		A	M	P
		S	L	A	L	O	M		M	A	O		N	Y	U		F	E	E
S	O	L	T	I		I	N	I	T		P	O	O	H		M	I	E	N	S
T	O	A		N	I	L		N	H	L		D	R	O	O	P	S
R	M	S		G	R	A	V	E	D	I	G	G	E	R	P	H	E	L	P	S
U	P	T	O		O	H	O		Q	U	A	I	N	T		N	A	I	L
N	A	T	H	A	N		U	S	S		C	M	D		I	O	D	I	N	E
G	H	O	S	T	B	U	S	T	E	R	K	E	A	T	O	N		D	U	D
	L	O	L	A	S		O	N	A			E	N	T	R	A	P	S
R	O	E		E	R	A		R	E	N		R	U	E		H	I	N
T	R	A	L	A		B	L	A	C	K	C	A	T	S	T	E	V	E	N	S
E	A	V	E	S		L	E	G	A	L	A	G	E		A	D	A	G	E	S
S	L	E	E	T		E	V	E	N	E	D	U	P		I	L	L	G	O	T

```
S P A R E M E ■ J O B C U T S ■ F A R G O
W I R E T A P ■ A R A L S E A ■ A L E R T
A N I M A L S A N C T U A R Y ■ A L L O T
G E D S ■ L O N E ■ ■ F R E T ■ G A P E
■ ■ ■ D E N T ■ B A R B A R A B O X E R
A S C I I ■ F A U N A ■ ■ R A N ■ ■ ■
D I L L S ■ H A R D E N ■ S W O R E A T ■
A L E E ■ S O R A S ■ T H E R I O ■ M R I
P L A T E N U M B E R ■ M A I L F R A U D
T Y R ■ P A S ■ L E D O U T ■ O Z M A
■ G A R A G E ■ R I T E S ■ L I S B O A
R O S E ■ H O A G I E ■ A S I ■ N N E
C O M I C B O O K ■ P R I O R A R R E S T
A S U ■ H E L P E D ■ T E N G O ■ O C H O
■ E D W A R D S ■ O H I S E E ■ M A H O N
■ T I E ■ ■ C A C T I ■ C R O W S
C L E A N A N D J E R K ■ O F F S ■ ■ ■
L O F T ■ L I R A ■ ■ E T A L ■ S M U T
O R I O N ■ C O P A C A B A N A B E A C H
V A L U E ■ E M E R I T A ■ C R U E L L A
E X E R T ■ R E D A R M Y ■ Y E S D E A R
```

```
P A T S I E S ■ S O M A L I ■ S U R G E D
A L U M N A E ■ I D O T O O ■ A G N A T E
C O N A N T H E B A R I A N ■ M A S S O N
K N A R ■ E N D S ■ O L D ■ S A N ■ B I T
S E S T I N A S ■ E N T E C O R D I A L E
■ ■ P O R ■ A R I ■ R A N R A G G E D
C H I H U A M E X I C O ■ J O A N N ■ ■
D O D O ■ W E L L S ■ B A U M ■ O T O E
S T E N O ■ D E E ■ C I N N A T I R E D S
■ N E A T E N ■ D O W D ■ I B E R I A
S A T ■ T R A I N E D A S S I N S ■ R E I
C R I M E A ■ O X E N ■ C H E E T A ■
A L F A S P R O U T S ■ P A O ■ N O R M A
B O Y D ■ U T N E ■ O O M P H ■ U I E S
■ M A U N A ■ R E P O S S E D C A R S
A T L E I S U R E ■ R E F ■ L A H ■
C H E N R E P U B L I C ■ H A M S A L A D
E R A ■ G D S ■ B I C ■ L I D S ■ N O L I
T I N C U P ■ M I S S I P P I M U D P I E
E L N I N O ■ I N S O N G ■ T A N G E N T
N L E A S T ■ A G E N D A ■ S N O O Z E S
```

99

M	A	S	C	O	T	S		T	I	M	I	D	I	T	Y		O	G	R	E
A	T	T	A	C	H	E		U	N	C	L	O	T	H	E		P	E	O	N
T	H	E	W	H	I	R	L	E	D	S	E	R	I	E	S		E	T	O	N
T	O	N	S		S	T	A	S	I		S	A	S	E	S		N	O	T	E
E	M	O		R	W	A	N	D	A	N		I	D	I		S	U	L	A	
L	E	S	S	E	E		D	A	N	E	S		G	R	A	F	T	E	D	
			T	H	E	R	O	Y	A	L	W	H	E	E		C	O	O	T	S
P	A	P	R	I	K	A			L	E	O	N		W	O	R	F			
E	R	R	O	R		N	E	C	K		L	O	S	E	R		M	S	N	
E	M	I	L	E		C	L	E	A	R	L	Y		T	I	N	T	Y	P	E
K	E	N	L		W	H	I	C	H	D	O	C	T	O	R		A	W	L	S
A	R	C	S	I	N	E		I	N	A	W	O	R	D		I	M	H	I	T
T	S	E		M	E	R	Y	L		S	W	A	G		N	I	E	C	E	
	O	C	A	T		A	I	L	S			E	S	S	A	Y	E	D		
B	Y	F	A	R		W	H	A	C	K	S	M	U	S	E	U	M			
L	O	W	R	I	S	E		D	I	N	A	R		A	L	I	S	T	S	
I	T	H	E		H	I	D		S	U	N	B	E	L	T		E	R	A	
N	E	A	L		O	G	E	E	S		G	U	A	R	E		I	R	A	N
K	A	L	E		W	H	I	N	I	N	G	A	N	D	D	I	N	I	N	G
A	M	E	S		M	I	S	S	P	E	L	L		O	U	T	R	A	C	E
T	O	S	S		E	N	M	E	S	H	E	S		S	P	O	I	L	E	R

100

	B	L	I	M	P		L	I	B	I	D	O		H	I	P	H	O	P
A	N	I	M	A	L	S		E	M	E	R	I	L		A	R	R	I	V	E
S	A	M	U	R	A	I		T	A	S	K	E	D		R	I	O	T	E	R
T	I	P	P	I	N	G	P		G	E	S	T	S		A	S	M	A	R	A
			N	A	N	O	B	O	T		P	A	A	R		S	W	A	T	
S	M	O	K	E		S	I	R		S	H	O	W	M	E	T		A	L	I
P	A	L	I	S	H		N	E	D		I	P	S	O		H	A	L	L	O
O	N	Y	X		A	Z	T	E	C	A	N			S	W	E	L	L	S	
T	C	M		A	V	E		D	U	N	D	E	E		A	M	O			
T	A	P		S	E	N	S		P	A	I	D	T	H	R	O	U	G	H	T
E	L	I		W	A	D	E	S		U	T	A	H	N		O	O	H		
R	A	C	E	A	G	A	I	N	S	T	T		A	L	E	E		O	N	E
			R	N	A		S	O	P	H	I	A		L	A	Y		D	E	N
	A	M	I	D	S	T		R	U	M	B	A	E	D		I	F	S	O	
W	I	C	C	A		A	M	O	I		E	R	S		S	C	O	O	T	S
H	R	H		M	O	V	I	N	G	T		A	I	D		O	N	R	Y	E
A	G	A	L		M	I	C	A		A	R	M	C	U	R	L				
T	A	M	A	L	E		D	R	D	R	E		S	N	O	O	K	E	R	C
S	U	M	T	E	R		R	O	U	G	E	S		C	A	R	I	B	O	U
I	G	E	T	I	T		O	L	M	E	C	S		E	L	E	V	A	T	E
T	E	R	E	S	A		P	L	A	T	E	S		D	D	A	Y	S		

The New York Times

SMART PUZZLES

Presented with Style

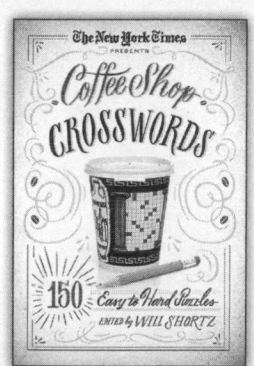

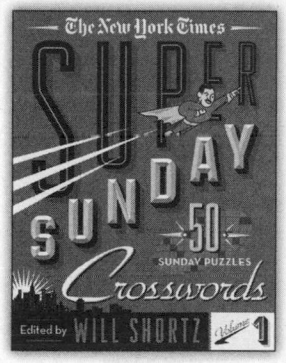

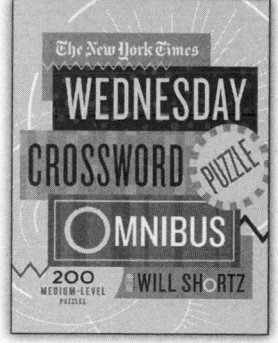

Available at your local bookstore or online at
us.macmillan.com/author/thenewyorktimes

 ST. MARTIN'S GRIFFIN